Y0-ASI-067

COMPLETE GUIDE TO PASTEUP

Walter B. Graham

Second Edition

This book is dedicated to the
hometown printers of the world.

Second Edition...
Second Printing, 1981
Third Printing, 1982
Fourth Printing, 1984

Copyright 1975, 1980
Walter B. Graham

All rights reserved. Except for brief quotations in critical
reviews, no part of this book may be reproduced or utilized in
any form or by any means, electronic or mechanical, including
photocopying, recording or by an information storage and
retrieval system, without permission in writing from the
author. Inquiries should be addressed to Walter B. Graham,
P. O. Box 369, Omaha, Nebraska 68101.

Library of Congress Catalog Number 75-8161
ISBN number 0-912920-40-8
Order number 117

Printed in the United States of America

Table of Contents

Foreword

As I wrote this book I imagined that I was instructing a beginner in pasteup who was starting to work in my own company. It's information that I want people to know, and remember if they are to be effective in camera-ready preparation.

I cannot emphasize too strongly the need for a dedicated interest in the field. Those who truly enjoy the work, who have a feeling of accomplishment, and can't wait to start work on the next job, are those who find a real place in this work. While this criterion is true in many fields of endeavor, I think it is more so in the field of pasteup—mechanical art—typesetting—layout.

The problem in trying to teach pasteup is that there are several hundred ideas that a person needs to know all at once. One problem begets another and by the same token one solution begets another. The experience on one kind of a job may be helpful on another, but on the other hand the same rule may not apply. For example, you may have instructed on a particular two-color job that overlays must be prepared over the base pasteup. On a following job, the graphic artist may apply the same rule, but actually the overlays are not required because the color separation is simple, and it's better to have all the elements on one base sheet so the camera operator can shoot two negatives and block off the desired areas on each negative using orange paper and opaque.

For those new to pasteup, this book is to be studied, not just read. By properly studying the ideas and techniques, you must then put the ideas into practice. All of the ideas presented are sound and practical and have proved themselves time and again as efficient techniques for a variety of pasteup preparation.

The ideas are intended to keep pasteup as simple as possible, as exemplified by the board system, as described in this text.

Many schools will welcome the ideas in this book, because instructors can teach pasteup with a system in mind. The more widely the system is adopted, the better our industry will be as more and more learn and use it.

I may refer to various product brands from time to time in this book. I have worked with a variety of items and have found some to fit a particular job rather well, but I do recognize that there are other products on the market which can accomplish comparable results. Many brand names in our field become generic terms.

Walter B. Graham
P. O. Box 369, Omaha, Nebraska 68101

Foreword to the Second Edition

The first edition of this book, Complete Guide to Pasteup, went through seven printings from 1975 to 1980. It was a best seller in the graphic arts industry and was highly accepted by those working the graphic arts marketplace and by the educational field.

This second edition is now updated to reflect new ideas in regard to methods and techniques. New products and tools have come on the market to further enhance the Graham Pasteup System.

For Graphic Artists . . .
IMPORTANT POINTS TO REMEMBER

After your pasteup is complete . . . look at it . . . realize . . .

A MISTAKE CAN BE VERY COSTLY.

Paper and plates are EXPENSIVE and a mistake will . . . COST MONEY.

After a job is printed it is no good for anybody else. Prevent errors by catching them on the pasteup.

CHECK IT OVER

1. Are there any misspelled words?
2. Is alignment correct and accurate?
3. Will the pasteup photograph in the camera and result in a quality negative? Is some copy light or characters broken?
4. Read the original instructions to check and double check.
5. Are all instructions on a tissue overlay, so the camera personnel will not need to ask questions?
6. Does the pasteup have trim marks on it to aid in platemaking?

BE CRITICAL . . . BE CAREFUL . . . AND DOUBLE CHECK,
and learn to take responsibility in the preparation of camera-ready pasteup.

1

Introduction

KEEP IN MIND

Anyone preparing pasteups must keep in mind that what they put down on the base sheet will be photographed.

It is what the camera will see that is important. A red patch on a pasteup will pick up on photographic film exactly the same as if it were black. Any blemish, broken-type letters, dirt specks will pick up on a film negative and result in poor quality printing or additional work opaquing and touching up the negative. There is no substitute for a good clean pasteup.

When the negative is made from your pasteup, remember that the lines, type output, art, etc. will come up *clear* on the film negative. This negative is then positioned on a sensitized offset plate in an exposure unit so the light will expose through the clear parts of the negative to produce the image on the plate.

Those blemishes that may appear on your pasteup will pick up on the negative and, if they are not opaqued out by the stripper, they would show up on the plate. A clean pasteup should require very little opaquing to save time in plate preparation.

Who qualifies as a GRAPHIC ARTIST?

Generally, businesses have had to train their own personnel to perform pasteup work for printing. Most of the time the basic qualification has been for someone with an artistic background and the ability to type.

We can set forth some guidelines when seeking individuals for the pasteup field. These guidelines are meant to be guides only, and as in any set of guides there are exceptions.

Men and women work in the pasteup field and may enter the craft as a result of art or secretarial training.

Helpful qualifications for pasteup work:

1. An artistic talent involving a sense of good design.

2. Common sense and the ability to apply the learning on one kind of job to that of another.

3. Typing—error-free along with reasonable speed.

4. Manual dexterity to handle tools of the trade. This may develop from sewing, hobby/craft work and model construction.

5. Knowledge of the rules of grammar and the ability to learn to spell or look up words not known.

6. Good retention . . . to remember what is verbally discussed regarding the desires of a customer who wants something set up. Everything cannot be written out in detail, and one must be able to remember what is required.

7. To visualize what is desired on a printed page is necessary to have some idea of what the finished product will look like before going ahead and using trial and error methods which can be costly.

8. Form good habits quickly and break bad habits. Be willing to accept the direct proved methods of procedure particularly in practicing with the tools of trade.

Pasteup, litho negative and offset plate.

9. Be interested and curious to see the output of the job. Have enough interest to analyze and evaluate a job after it has been printed. This self-analysis should point out how the job could have been improved.

The Graphic Artist—a modern day compositor

Graphic Artists today are modern day "compositors" taking the place of those who made up pages with hot type metal slugs and hand-set foundry type.

The pasteup method offers far more opportunity to express creativity than the compositor who assembled metal elements. Today pasteup is prepared in an office atmosphere, and we have the opportunity to freely use illustrations, border tapes, rules along with type output because we can print anything written, printed or drawn with the offset process. There is no need to purchase cuts. Illustrations might be taken from a file of clip art and placed on a pasteup to be photographed along with the type output and get printed at no extra charge.

The ease of producing photographs and line illustrations at lower cost is what prompted offset printing to grow and expand into the dynamic field that it is today.

What is a Pasteup?

We are not talking about art work, even though an artist will often perform the pasteup task as an adjunct to the art work he has prepared. Pasteup is often referred to as mechanical art.

A simple definition of pasteup is:

Affixing pieces of photographable material on a surface to render the assemblage camera-ready.

The definition may sound simple, but there is a great deal of know-how, procedure, and technique to produce the most direct, easiest and logical camera-ready pasteup.

If a reproduction calls for a tint or shaded area within it, what is the best way to prepare the pasteup? The words camera-ready encompass a lot of meaning because true camera-ready pasteup does not allow for unneccessary labor and material usage in the camera and stripping departments.

Lack of knowledge in attaining true camera-ready pasteups can result in higher cost negatives and stripping.

A SYSTEMATIC APPROACH TO CAMERA-READY PREPARATION

1. Pasteup Preparation System

If the preparation of printing can be systematized, the work flow will be simpler and faster. Better communication will result among those who are involved

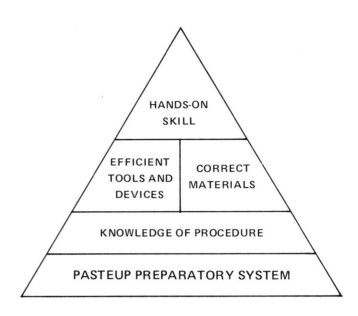

in the camera-ready creation. It therefore behooves a printing prep department to set up a systematic approach as the basis for an efficient operation.

2. Knowledge of Procedure

For those working in preparation services, it becomes necessary to understand how to prepare printing so it is truly camera-ready.

3. Efficient Tools and Devices

An assortment of tools and devices can greatly aid efficient pasteup preparation. Knives, boards, t-squares, burnishers, and mechanical drawing instruments are but a few of the tools necessary to prepare camera-ready art.

4. Correct Materials

Certain materials must be available to put to use as needed for specific pasteups. Masking films, overlay materials, base sheets for specific uses are a few of the supply items we must have on hand.

5. Hands-on Skill

A skilled and experienced Graphic Artist will develop the skills of using the tools of the trade with finesse and swiftness, yet with accuracy.

A SIMPLE PASTEUP— LETTER WITH LETTERHEAD

Perhaps the most basic simple camera-ready preparation is to type a letter on a letterhead to use as an original in a copyboard or copier.

MOVING & STORAGE COMPANY
TELEPHONE PL 0303 • 3034 SPRAGUE STREET • OMAHA, NEBRASKA

Dear Customer:

I want to thank you on behalf of our company for the contract to handle the moving requirements of your company employees. It is indeed a pleasure to begin business with a new customer.

The signing of the contract is an expression of confidence, and I want you to know that we recognize the responsibility we have for maintaining that confidence.

The most important thing to the customer of any product or service is the character of the supplying organization; its resources; its facilities; its reputation; and its standards of service.

You have at your beck and call every facility of our company. We would like to be useful to you beyond the mere necessities of business transaction.

The experience and services of our firm are available to you in any problem you every may have. We would like to have you use them.

In any emergency when the representative assigned to your account may not be available, do not hesitate to write, wire or phone us here at headquarters.

We appreciate your business. We want to continue to deserve it.

Sincerely,

Wendell P. Clark

Wendell P. Clark
President

While this simple direct preparation seems trouble-free, it may not be without problems.

The Blue Ink Signature

One soon discovers that signatures on letters written in blue ink can present difficulty in reproduction of a quality signature reproduction. A pen with black ink is therefore handed to an author for use in writing a quality camera-ready signature. Or the signature may be requested written on a separate slip of paper to position in the signature area on the letter.

Misspelled Words

A misspelled word must be corrected. How? Retype an entire paragraph? A paragraph may be retyped and errors created on that portion which was correct in the first place; therefore, thoughtful, careful proofreading of all new typing is a must. The correct word may be pasted on top of the incorrect word if the alignment of this small paste-in is accurate. Sometimes a misaligned word appears aligned when pasted in position, but shows up crooked on the final printing. The use of the light table becomes a useful aid when overmounting words and lines because this light source provides illumination for visibly viewing the correct placement.

Removal of Blemishes or Extra Words

Because the letter is not to be used for correspondence, a product called graphic white may be used to cover up any deletions, spots or blemishes. Our concern now becomes oriented toward "what the camera will see" rather than creation of a page to use as correspondence.

Adding or Deleting Lines of Copy

When an author adds or deletes copy, adjustments are necessary. The letter is cut apart and the copy inserted. Generally this procedure is handled by affixing the entire letter on a base sheet and adjusting for the additional or deleted copy. Or, a light table and grid may be used to splice insertions using tape on the face down original.

How Many Learned Pasteup

By preparing these simple letter pasteups, many learn the art of getting work camera-ready. What often starts out as a very simple preparation, may get more complicated. One soon learns the importance of careful attention to detail so the final printed product will reproduce properly without embarrassing imperfections.

<table>
<tr><td colspan="2">HOURS WORKED IN ONE YEAR</td></tr>
<tr><td>52 Weeks X 40 hours</td><td>= 2080 HOURS</td></tr>
<tr><td>2 weeks vacation and 6 holidays</td><td>= -128 HOURS</td></tr>
<tr><td>Total <u>Net</u> Hours</td><td>= 1952 HOURS</td></tr>
</table>

HOURLY COST RATE FOR PASTEUP

		AMOUNT EMPLOYEE EARNS PER HOUR			
		2.00/HR.	3.00/HR.	4.00/HR.	5.00/HR.
1.	No. of Productive Hours	1952	1952	1952	1952
2.	Investment	1000 00	1000 00	1000 00	1000 00
3.	Rate of Depreciation	10%	10%	10%	10%
	FIXED CHARGES				
4.	Depreciation	100 00	100 00	100 00	100 00
5.	Rent and Heat	60 00	60 00	60 00	60 00
6.	Fire Insurance.	35 00	35 00	35 00	35 00
	VARIABLE CHARGES				
7.	Direct Labor, 2080 Hours	4160 00	6240 00	8320 00	10400 00
8.	Indirect Labor, 20%	832 00	1248 00	1664 00	2080 00
9.	Payroll Taxes	250 00	374 00	499 00	624 00
10.	Workmen's Comp.	86 00	86 00	86 00	86 00
11.	Light and Power	40 00	40 00	40 00	40 00
12.	Direct Supplies	250 00	250 00	250 00	250 00
13.	Repairs to equipment (2% of Investment)	20 00	20 00	20 00	20 00
14.	Personal Property Tax	60 00	60 00	60 00	60 00
15.	**SUB-TOTAL**	5893 00	8513 00	11134 00	13755 00
16.	General Factory Expense (10%)	589 00	851 00	1113 00	1375 00
17.	TOTAL MFG. COST	6482 00	9364 00	12247 00	15130 00
18.	Administrative & Selling Overhead (35%)	2269 00	3277 00	4286 00	5295 00
19.	TOTAL COSTS	8751 00	12641 00	16533 00	20425 00
	Manufacturing costs per productive hour based on operating activity of:				
20.	85% of 40 hr. week........1659.......hrs.	5 27	7 62	9 97	12 31
21.	75% of 40 hr. week, 1464 hrs.	5 98	8 63	11 29	13 95
22.	60% of 40 hr. week, 1171 hrs.	7 47	10 80	14 12	17 44

2

Hourly Costs for Pasteup Preparation

1. **Hourly cost rate**
2. **Analyzing the hourly cost**
3. **Time sheet**

HOURLY COSTS FOR PASTEUP PREPARATION

Those who begin to work for a company preparing pasteups are often surprised when they learn that the charges for their services are significantly higher than the pay they receive. This must be so to cover all overhead expenses, supplies, the employer's matching social security payment, etc. The hourly cost would be higher, but the investment in a Pasteup Department is generally lower than other departments in a printing operation where machinery depreciation must be figured in the cost.

Understanding what it costs to produce pasteup work can be enlightening, and can help individuals meet the challenge to produce pasteups quickly and efficiently, yet render quality work.

Furthermore, one must know cost in order to charge for a particular pasteup job. Remember, we are selling time and very often we are asked to estimate the time required on a particular job so that the work may be quoted in advance of preparation. Knowledge of the time required can be most helpful in any operation.

Since we are selling time, it is important that we bill out the work at cost plus markup. It is often difficult to establish fixed charges for jobs, because the preparation time can vary a great deal. A charge of $35.00 to compose and paste up an 8 1/2" x 11" form could be low or high. Some forms are very simple and some very complex when $35.00 would hardly pay for the composition.

Let's examine the hourly cost for pasteup preparation in detail.

Analyzing the Hourly Cost

The hourly cost rate analysis has four columns of figures. The first column for a $2.00 per hour pay scale, the second $3.00, third $4.00 and fourth $5.00. These hourly pay rates are presented to give an idea of the final actual cost of pasteup work for each $1.00 per hour increase in the hourly pay.

The cost figures can vary in geographical areas. Other cost items may need to be included. Payments made toward insurance, for example, are not shown in the cost analysis. The personal property tax item on line 14 may not be a cost in some states. Consider this analysis as basic and conservative. The analysis assumes that the Graphic Artist works 40 hours per week and receives two weeks vacation plus six paid holidays during the year.

Let's take a look at the manufacturing cost per productive hour as shown on lines 20, 21 and 22. On line 20 we assume that we are able to charge out 85 percent of our time to a customer. This means that 34 hours out of the 40 hours in the week are chargeable hours. For each day we would bill out an average of 6.8 hours. What we are saying here is that we cannot bill out 100 percent of our time because of the minutes in a day when we have to be away from our desk, discuss a job, correct our own mistakes, encounter slack periods, etc.

On line 21 we show a 75-percent productive time hourly cost. Here we would sell an average of six hours per day or 30 hours per week. The 60 percent figures are for 4.8 hours per day and 24 hours per week. How do you arrive at which figures to use? Keeping records of chargeable time to indicate how much chargeable time is expected. Some days will be 100-percent days, while others can be less. It is the average for a period of a month or a year that will prove a true picture of the percentage of productive hours.

It is revealing to note that time is very important to our business. To be efficient in our work is necessary in order to produce with speed and accuracy.

Time Sheet

A record of time for pasteup work should be recorded on a Daily Time Sheet which can be used for billing purposes. A study of these time records can produce information regarding the time required for work, so that estimating similar types of jobs can be realistic and easier. Some companies have established production norms which those in pasteup are expected to achieve or surpass. A length of time may be suggested to produce, let's say, a 32-page booklet. The job ticket may indicate 15 minutes per page pasting up the booklet from furnished composition proofs. The goal should be to try and beat the norm time, and thus become as efficient as possible and achieve a great deal of personal satisfaction. Extreme haste in pasteup work is not always advisable because we know that a good job is the first consideration, and that if it isn't done right the first time, it can be more costly to do it over on non-chargeable time.

The Daily Time Sheet figures are used to post to a Job Cost Sheet. When the work is completed, the time may be totaled and multiplied by the hourly selling rate for billing purposes.

DAILY TIME SHEET						
Name _____				Date _____		
JOB NO.	CUSTOMER	Kind of Work	Charge-able	Non Charge-able	TIME	
					IN ___	OUT ___
					IN ___	OUT ___
					IN ___	OUT ___
					IN ___	OUT ___
					IN ___	OUT ___
					IN ___	OUT ___
					IN ___	OUT ___
					IN ___	OUT ___
					IN ___	OUT ___
					IN ___	OUT ___
					IN ___	OUT ___
					IN ___	OUT ___
					IN ___	OUT ___
					IN ___	OUT ___
					IN ___	OUT ___
					IN ___	OUT ___
		TOTAL				

PHOTOTYPESETTING	STRIKE-ON COMPOSITION	PREPARATION		MINUTES		
01 Recording	10 Composing	20 Pasteup	24 Proofs	5 min. = .1 hr.	25 min. = .4 hr.	45 min. = .8 hr.
02 Customer Alterations	11 Customer Alterations	21 Layout	25 Creative Services	10 min. = .2 hr.	30 min. = .5 hr.	50 min. = .8 hr.
03 Proofs	12 Proofs	22 Art Work	26 Clean up	15 min. = .3 hr.	35 min. = .6 hr.	55 min. = .9 hr.
		23 Customer Alterations	27 Idle	20 min. = .3 hr.	40 min. = .7 hr.	60 min. =1.0 hr.

Verified and approved by:

3

Basic Steps of Pasteup Preparation

1. **The basic steps**
2. **Case history applying the basic steps**

BASIC STEPS OF PASTEUP PREPARATION

1. PLAN ROUGH LAYOUT OR COMPREHENSIVE LAYOUT.
2. MARKUP FOR COMPOSITION.
3. SET/KEYBOARD.
4. PHOTOCOPY GALLEY, TWO SETS.
5. PROOFREAD ONE GALLEY PHOTOCOPY.
6. DUMMY JOB WITH SECOND SET.
7. PHOTOCOPY DUMMY FOR CHECKOUT BY CUSTOMER.
8. CORRECT GALLEY OUTPUT.
9. TRIM GALLEY OUTPUT.
10. WAX COAT GALLEY OUTPUT AND DISPLAY.
11. PREPARE BASE. USE PREPRINTED BASE SHEET.
12. DRAW GUIDELINES.
13. INK RULE.
14. FINAL TRIMS, POSITION, SQUARE UP, BURNISH.
15. APPLY BORDER TAPES.
16. APPLY WINDOWS AND/OR SCREENED PRINTS.
17. PREPARE OVERLAY.
18. PHOTOCOPY FINISHED PASTEUP.
19. IMPOSITION ON PIN COPY FLAT.
20. FINAL SILVERPRINT PROOF.

1. PLAN

Plan the job on grid planning paper.

In order to visualize the printing job, start by preparing a printing plan. This plan might be prepared on a sheet of tissue, or on a sheet of grid planning paper (following the system suggested in this book). This plan would use blue-lined grid paper, and the plan is drawn in black pencil for good visibility.

For newspaper ad work this plan might be more comprehensive and take the form of a partial pasteup where the clip art and other photo elements are actually pasted in position. Then a blue-penciled indication of the type size and placement is drawn so that type may be set to fit the blue-penciled areas. Following this the type proof material is pasted on that partial pasteup.

2. MARK

Mark up the manuscript to specify the type size, style and leading.

Someone will need to take the manuscript and mark it up to indicate the style, size and width of the composition to be set. This markup is most often done by someone in a supervisory capacity whose experience will aid him in the selection and evaluation of type. For example, a manuscript might have its body marked up as follows:

$$22 \text{ picas}, \frac{10}{11} \text{ Univers Med.; or } 22 \text{ picas}, \frac{10}{11} \text{ Univers Med.}_{3}$$

The example would mean that the type should be set 22 picas wide in 10-point Univers Medium type style on an 11-point base. This will place an extra point of leading between the lines of type. The second example showing the "3" would indicate three-point leading between paragraphs.

Copy should be double-spaced on 8 1/2″ x 11″ sheets and typed on one side only. It might be copy for a publication, form, letterhead, folder, newspaper, etc. The condition of this manuscript will have a great deal of influence on the work involved in pasteup. Copy that is hastily prepared without careful editing will mean that there will be changes and corrections after the composition is set. A good, well-edited manuscript will save a lot of pasteup time.

3. SET

Set composition.

4. PHOTOCOPY GALLEY

The composition should be proofread and corrected before it is pasted down on the base. To avoid marking on the output, two copies should be made on a photocopy machine. One photocopy can then be marked for corrections using the standard proofreader's marks.

5. PROOFREAD GALLEY PHOTOCOPY

Proofread one of the photocopies of the galleys. Mark the corrections, additions and alterations.

6. DUMMY

Use the second photocopy to paste up a dummy on grid planning paper following the plan. Sometimes the photocopy is pasted directly on the plan previously prepared on the grid planning paper.

7. PHOTOCOPY DUMMY

Make photocopy of the dummy to show customer job for his approval. Keep the original pasted-up dummy in your own office.

8. CORRECT GALLEY

Wax the corrections, place on cutting board, knife-cut vertically and horizontally, and with tweezers or blade pick up corrections and position on galley. Burnish.

9. TRIM

Hand-trim or machine-trim the galley proof.

Newspaper galleys are trimmed on motorized cutting wheel devices. The galleys are long and involve considerable volume, and trimming must be on a production basis. For the smaller commercial jobs, trimming is done by hand using art knife, or preferably a desk top trimmer.

10. WAX COMPOSITION OUTPUT AND DISPLAY

Wax-coat galley output. Place on wall display.

After strips of composition output have been waxed, press them on the wall so they hang on display next to your desk or table. Other material needed for future assembly can be placed on the wall as well. Visualize how this simple idea can help you organize material for pasteup, because all of the pieces are seen at a glance on display, rather than searching or leafing through folders. This "stick-on-the-wall" technique is a simple idea but most helpful to swiftly reach for a strip, page number, heading, caption, or screened print to assemble on the base sheet. You may prefer to attach a sheet of 4' x 8' acrylic or other plastic material on which to place waxed strips and pieces. Just a slight pressure with the thumb will hold a strip of waxed output on the wall display.

An adhesive coater or waxer is a neccessity for production pasteup. The coating of wax applied to the back of composition will provide tack when the composition is burnished down in position on the pasteup. Wax is to be preferred over rubber cement because it is faster and provides a cleaner finished pasteup. Pasteups have greater longevity with wax.

11. PREPARE BASE

Tape down pre-printed base sheet, draw guidelines and ink trim marks.

The pasteup base is pre-printed in non photo blue, generally on heavy paper or light card stock. The guidelines should be drawn in light blue or light gray.

12. DRAW GUIDELINES

13. INK

Ink-rule lines if required.

Because ink and wax will not mix, it is difficult to ink on a pasteup where wax has been exposed to the surface. It is necessary that inking be done on the surface before any waxed elements come in contact with the base.

14. FINAL TRIMS, POSITION, SQUARE, BURNISH

Pick up elements from cutting board using tweezers as much as possible. Place on pasteup in position following the dummy prepared on the grid paper. Adjust and square elements. Burnish.

15. TAPES

Apply border tapes if required.

16. WINDOWS/PRINTS

Apply windows and/or screened prints.

Paste pre-screened halftone prints directly on the pasteup, or place windows on the pasteup so that a clear area will result on the negative to allow the stripper to lay in a screened negative behind this clear "window" on the film. Windows may be necessary for reverses too.

17. OVERLAY

Cut overlay if required.

An acetate overlay may be necessary for producing a second color or a tint area. If the color separation of the job is a *simple separation* an overlay should not be made. Merely indicate the second color with a tissue so the camera operator will know what elements will be in the second color.

18. PHOTOCOPY FINISHED PASTEUP

In order to be certain there is no final error, it is wise to prepare a photocopy of the final corrected pasteup. This photocopy is then submitted for a final approval of the preparation. Work should be proofread and corrected before it is submitted to the customer; however, the customer should proofread the work as well, and initial an "OK" on this photocopy.

By using the photocopier we can keep the original pasteup in-house to avoid excessive handling and transportation out of the department.

19. IMPOSITION

It may be necessary to take steps in pasteup to prepare the job for imposition in signature form or printing multiple impositions on a flat for the camera. A study of the system will give insight into this procedure to create a fast efficient method of imposition.

20. FINAL PHOTOCOPY OR SILVERPRINT

The final proof might be a silverprint, brown print or blue-line print. This print is made from the plate-ready negative, and contains all halftones, tints and other stripins. You may be able to photocopy your final pasteup if you have pre-screened prints positioned directly on the pasteup, and the job does not require stripping.

The steps are basic

The 20 steps for a pasteup are basic. Some of the steps may be skipped depending on the particular type of job performed.

Have these basic steps before you when preparing a pasteup from start to finish. It will be difficult to go wrong if you follow the procedure, and you will find less chance for errors to occur. These steps provide opportunity for checks and double checks and the final proof should not require any adjustment unless the author changes his mind.

Is it complete?

A pasteup is not complete if the camera operator has to ask questions about a pasteup. All instructions should be written so the camera operator will know what result is required. For instance, if an overlay is on the pasteup that requires a 20-percent tint, this percentage of tint indication should be written on the flap's tape hinge. Other instructions should appear in writing on a tissue overlay sheet.

An actual case history . . . a publication is born . . .

THE NEBRASKA MASONIC NEWS

Here is the step by step preparation to achieve a camera-ready publication, four pages, 8 1/2" x 11" page size. This analysis follows the basic steps.

1. PLAN

Determined the complete specifications of the publication which were as follows.

a. Body type style . . . . Palatino
b. Size and leading . . . . . . Ten on eleven point
c. Column width . . . . 14 picas (three-column format)
   (Two columns) . . . . 29 picas
d. Captions . . . . Eight on nine point Univers
e. Headlines . . . . Univers medium and bold
f. Paragraphs . . . . Indent one pica
g. Paragraph leading . . . . None
h. Space between columns . . . . One Pica

2. MARK

The double-spaced typewritten manuscript was marked-up to reflect the type sizes, etc. One article was set 12 picas so it could be boxed. Several other articles were set two-column due to the nature of the material.

3. SET

Type was set on phototypesetter to produce photo proofs on photo paper.

4. PHOTOCOPY GALLEY

Two sets of photocopy prints made of the photo-proof galleys.

5. PROOFREAD GALLEY PHOTOCOPY

First set of photocopy prints proofread and marked using proofreader's marks.

6. DUMMY

Second set of photocopy prints were waxed and assembled on sheets of grid planning paper to make up a dummy of the four-page publication. On this dummy, the headlines were penciled so they could be set when corrections were made on the galleys. Time required to prepare dummy: two hours, 15 minutes.

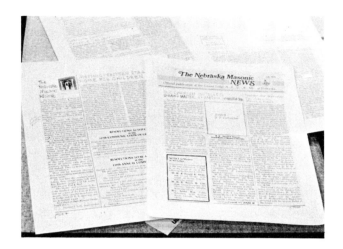

7. PHOTOCOPY DUMMY

Made photocopy proofs of the dummy. Original dummy on the grid paper remained in the shop. A sheet of 11″ x 17″ paper was folded to 8 1/2″ x 11″ and the photocopy proof was waxed onto this paper to make a clean dummy for customer approval. This copy was delivered to the customer for his OK. He also received the galley to check for any additional errors not found during first reading. Customer was requested to mark any typos or alterations on the galley, rather than on the dummy proof because the photocomp is in galley form and it's faster to locate and change by setting corrections marked on the galley.

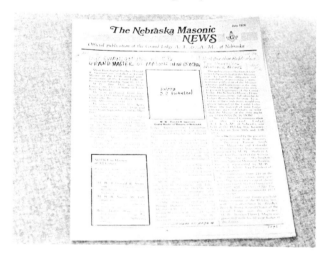

8. CORRECT GALLEY

There were several typographical errors, four lines of missing copy, and one author's alteration. The corrections were set, waxed and positioned on the galleys.

9. TRIM

The galleys which had been corrected were trimmed on the trimmer.

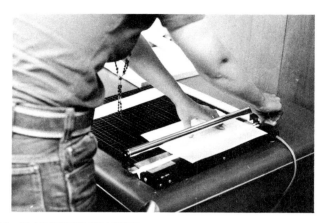

10. GALLEYS WAXED

The galleys were waxed on a mechanical waxer along with the headlines which were set at the time the corrections were set.

11. PREPARE BASE

Regular prepared base sheets with light blue pica grid lines were used; therefore, no guideline preparation or planning was necessary.

12. DRAW GUIDELINES

13. INK

No inking was required.

14. FINAL TRIMS, POSITION, SQUARE, BURNISH

By checking with the original dummy it was simple to place all the type proof elements in exact position by referring to the grid lines which match the planning paper. Elements were squared and burnished using the small board system, and pasting up each page on an individual base sheet. Time: two hours, 50 minutes. (This time will be less on future issues, because some time was spent on the nameplate that will not require attention in the future.)

15. TAPES

Hairline border tape was applied between columns where required to separate articles.

16. WINDOW/PRINTS

One photo appears on page one. A window of red plastic was placed in position to accommodate the proportion of the portrait. A 133-line halftone negative was later stripped in the window of the line negative.

17. OVERLAY

No overlays were required for this issue.

18. PHOTOCOPY FINISHED PASTEUP

19. IMPOSITION

Pages were punched at the bottom using the punch system for imposition on a flat. The same flat will be used for all future issues.

The flat is a standard publication flat used for 8 1/2" x 11" page-size publications without bleed.

20. FINAL PHOTOCOPY OR SILVERPRINT

The negative was shot, film halftone placed on the window, and a blue-line print was made for the final proof for customer's OK. Had pre-screened prints been used on this job, the final proof would have been produced on the photocopier.

Comments . . .

A very clean manuscript was provided for this job. Only one author's alteration! The cost of the alteration was $7.00. It is interesting to point out that while the customer had the dummy and galley at his office, he telephoned to question the arrangement of the type on the dummy. It was a very simple matter to view the *original* pasted dummy on the grid paper and discuss the job on the phone. This is one very good reason to retain this original dummy at your office.

Had the customer revised the layout and shifted articles, it would have been a simple matter to do all the adjusting while the work was in dummy form. The best time to get planning done is before pasteup actually takes place.

4
Pasteup—A Total System

1. **THE NEED FOR PLANNING**
2. **PRE-PRINTED BASE SHEETS**
3. **WORKING FROM THE CENTER**
4. **METHODS OF TRANSFERRING THE LOCATIONS OF ELEMENTS FROM A LAYOUT TO A BASE SHEET**
Dividers, measuring, clear grid, centering rule.
5. **WHEN JOBS ARE NOT PLANNED ON GRID PAPER**
6. **USING A PLASTIC GRID FOR PASTE-UP WORK**
7. **THE PICA GRID**
8. **PASTEUP METHODS IN BRIEF**
Clear plastic grid, printed grid, grid planning paper, the board system, summary.
9. **TWO-ACROSS PASTEUP FOR MULTI-PAGE PREPARATION**
10. **FILM MAKE-UP**
11. **BASE SHEETS FOR PASTEUP**
110-lb. index, mirror finish, dull coated enamel, illustration board, special sheets.
12. **TRIM MARKS**
13. **FORMS—PLANNING, RULING, COMPOSING AND PASTEUP**

PASTEUP—A TOTAL SYSTEM

It is so important to place pasteup into a total system because someone can be taught a definite procedure on "how to do it." Instead of giving someone a job to prepare for the camera and saying, "Here, paste it up," he can receive definite instructions on an exact system to follow. By following the system, it is easier to *learn* and easier to *teach*.

If this "Graham System" can be taught as an established system that can be adopted by our industry, we can then think alike, and those taught in the schools will come out with the proper training and use the system to prepare pasteups.

This system should be taught in schools of:
Graphic Arts
Commercial Art
Advertising
Journalism
Secretarial Science
Business Administration
Office Management

THE NEED FOR PLANNING

Have you ever had someone give you copy from which to prepare a pasteup that was in such poor condition that you could not figure out what he wanted?

Was it one of those scrawled pencil layouts on the sheet of yellow tablet paper?

This type of communication makes pasteup work very difficult, and further emphasizes the need for planning our pasteups as part of our total system.

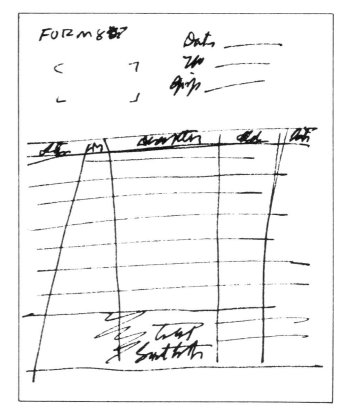

Don't prepare a pasteup from a poor printing plan.

The poor rough drafts and manuscript copy in deplorable condition make pasteup preparation very time-consuming and difficult to prepare accurately to satisfy the customer. When we go ahead and do the pasteup from these careless layouts, we generally find that we must drastically alter the final pasteup through no fault of our own.

Basically the total system of pasteup begins by thinking in terms of picas, that is, six lines per inch. Even someone who is not familiar with picas can still work with the system which corresponds to typewriter spacing. Therefore: six picas equal one inch. One pica equals 12 points.*

To proceed with the system we need to prepare a printing plan from which we will prepare the pasteup. These plans should be prepared whenever possible on pica GRID PLANNING PAPER. If the job is drawn up and planned on this grid planning paper and then you do the final pasteup on a matching pre-printed base sheet, you have a system that follows through from the planning state to the finished pasteup.

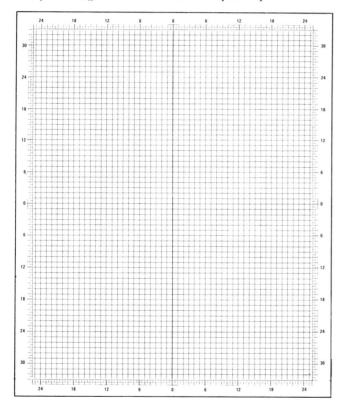

The planning sheets are pica-grid and printed in light blue. It is easy to follow the light blue guide lines on the planning paper, even without the use of a straight-edge. Those people involved in planning printing should have a pad of planning paper for their initial preparation.

* It is acknowledged that a true pica is very slightly under one-sixth of an inch. However, this variation may be disregarded so that typewriter spacing and the pica are one in the same. Anyone preparing pasteups will find no problems in the creation of pasteups measuring a pica as one-sixth of an inch.

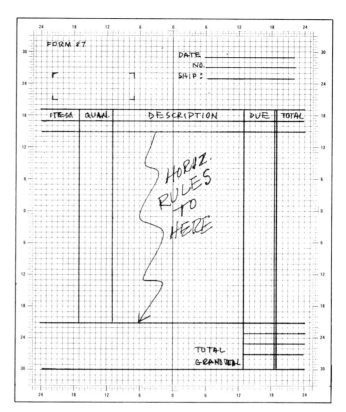

Plan printing on Grid Planning Paper
for quickness and accuracy.

Thus, pasteup actually begins with the individual who creates, inspires or prepares the printing job. This person might be a printer's customer, or someone in the printing prep department who plans jobs for composition and pasteup.

When jobs come into a shop in an unworkable fashion, it is far better to plan it out first, before composing and pasteup. This plan can then get approval *before* going ahead with time-consuming and expensive typesetting and preparation.

PRE-PRINTED BASE SHEETS

The pre-printed base sheets on which you paste up should correspond to the grid planning paper. By looking at the location of lines, copy blocks, illustrations, etc. on the grid paper, you can then render the complete pasteup on the corresponding base sheet.

The base sheets should be printed in non-reproducing blue ink with the pica border and center lines in both directions. The border paper base sheet ties in with the grid planning paper because the border edges are exactly the same as on the planning paper, but without the grid. The grid can be printed on the base sheet if desired. Normally the grid is not printed on the base where inking may be done. For publication work, when no ruling is anticipated, the grid may be helpful to align columns of type, etc.

Your pasteup base sheet inventory should contain an ample supply of these pre-printed base sheets along with larger sheets of blank stock for those special jobs that will require preparation which will not conform to the regular pica-bordered base sheet.

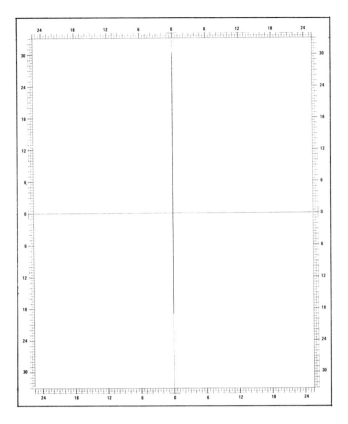

Base sheets printed with non-repro blue ink save time in pasteup preparation.

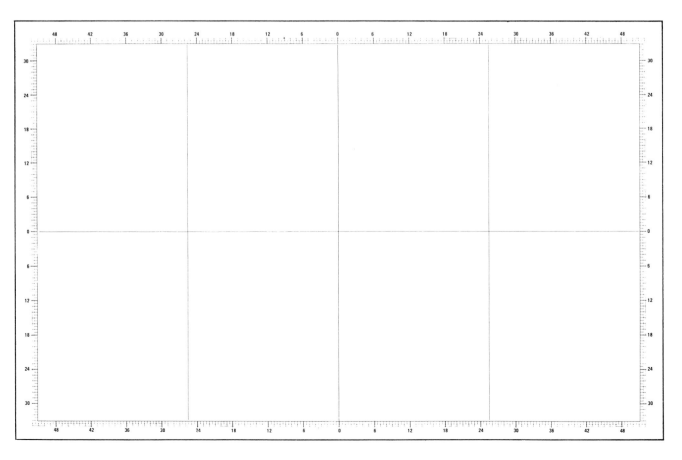

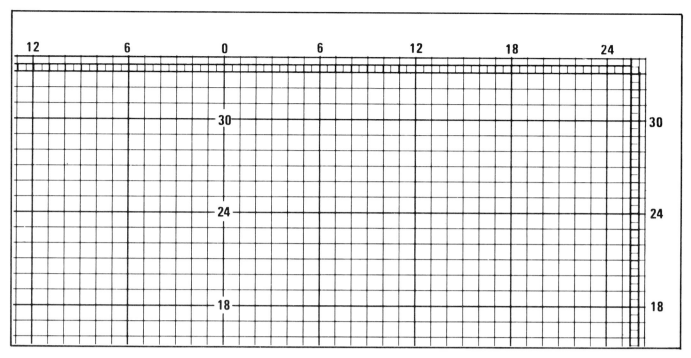

A pica grid is ideal for pasteup planning.
It should have measurements indicating spacing
from left and right of zero.

WORKING FROM THE CENTER

The base sheets and the grid planning paper should be designed with "0" at the centers in both directions.

The pica measurements run from left and right of center horizontally. The "0" is at the center point vertically, and the picas are measured from "0".

In all pasteup preparation work from centers, you'll be able to center material and position columns and other elements faster and easier. Working from centers will take a bit of practice and mental adjustment, but your effort will pay off, because after a few trials you'll find that it is much easier.

When you are going to type a simple form or letter for reproduction, it is so much easier to type on the border paper with the center marks in position.

As you type your lines, you always know where you are located on the sheet. You can center copy with ease. For instance, it is very simple to start typing at 18 picas at left of zero, then type to 18 on the right of zero and you know that your copy is centered. Furthermore, you always know where the center is located by the zero and the center line.

The 80 lb. base sheet paper on the dull coated enamel is ideal for use in preparing typed jobs that are for reproduction. As you become familiar with the pica incrementation, you'll find that using this paper is part of your thinking. Your prep work will be easier and faster.

Some typists have taped a centered-pica scale over the scale on the typewriter, and always center the paper in the center of the platen. This scale becomes an additional aid in placement of copy on your prepared base sheet.

METHODS OF TRANSFERRING THE LOCATIONS OF ELEMENTS FROM A LAYOUT TO A BASE SHEET

1. Dividers

A pair of flexible or fixed screw-type dividers can be used to obtain a dimension from a layout and then transfer this dimension to the base sheet. By using a non-repro pencil the guidelines can be placed on the base sheet where the divider points are placed to coincide with the location of the elements on the layout. For entire jobs, this plan is generally not recommended, but can be handy on some occasions.

2. Measuring with a ruler

To measure a distance of an element with a ruler, then measure the same distance on the base sheet is slow and not recommended.

3. Using a clear grid

By placing the clear plastic grid over the layout, you can see the locations of all the elements and then transfer these dimensions to the base sheet quickly. By far the best method, because you get a visual picture of the work, and can place it on the base quickly and accurately.

4. Use of the centering rule

The Graham Color-Coded Centering Rule is an excellent plotting instrument to transfer dimensions. On some jobs the rule will prove an additional aid to use in combination with the other transfer methods. The rule, as well as the grid, ties in with the measurements on the base sheet.

WHEN JOBS ARE NOT PLANNED ON GRID PAPER

You can appreciate the desirability of work that has been planned on the grid paper, but naturally layouts will be presented to you for pasteup preparation on regular paper, and you want to take advantage of this grid system.

Therefore, we can use a *clear plastic grid* which can be placed over any layout presented for preparation, and we automatically convert the page into a visible layout with the grid imposed.

USING A PLASTIC GRID FOR PASTEUP WORK

The clear plastic grid can help you save a lot of time in pasteup preparation.

You can transfer locations of elements from a layout to the base sheet.

It is fast, accurate and visible. Using the grid will take a little practice because you must get accustomed to working with the squares, but as you use it you will find that the grid becomes a familiar "picture" when

The clear plastic grid can be placed over any layout for converting the layout into a printing plan.

Guidelines can be positioned on the base sheet according to the layout.
Measuring is not necessary.

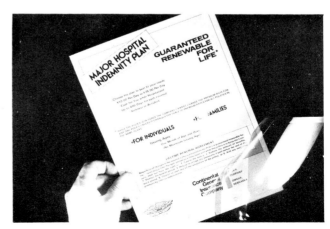

The completed pasteup is camera-ready.

The clear plastic grid matches the grid planning paper.

placed over a layout that you want to transfer to a base sheet.

The grid becomes a part of your system.

When you are going to plan your own job, you can plan it on the grid planning paper which is the same as the plastic grid. It is all part of the *total* system. Use the same planning grid, then use the bordered paper for your pasteup base sheet.

THE PICA GRID

A grid with pica squares is ideal for general pasteup. Picas are the printer's measure. Type is set in pica width. Columns of type are thought of in terms of picas. A standard typewriter is six lines to the inch which ties-in with the pica system. Particularly, when preparing forms, the spacing should be designed so that the final printed form can be used in the typewriter, and the carriage returns will make it simple to type the next fill-in portion, and the succeeding portions on the form.

Becoming familiar with picas and thinking in terms of six lines to the inch is not difficult, and it will be helpful in the preparation of all printed material.

PASTEUP METHODS IN BRIEF

Clear plastic grid

1. Place grid over any layout or typewritten material. Note measurements of elements at border, then pencil non photo guidelines on base sheet to correspond to layout.

2. Place clear plastic grid over any layout. Place on window of photo copier and make a copy that can be referred to while drawing in the guidelines on the base sheet. Even though some layouts have multi-color patches, the reproduction can often reproduce sufficiently to view and obtain the locations of the elements.

3. Place clear plastic grid on light table. Put blank base sheet over clear grid, and use grid lines as guide for pasteup.

Printed Grid

1. Print grid in light non-reproducing blue ink on the base sheet. Paste the elements on the grid sheet on light table. Alignment can be accomplished by placing and aligning by use of the grid lines.

2. Print grid in black ink on base sheet. Place sheet on light table with printed grid face down on glass so blank side is uppermost. With light you can see the grid to align and place copy elements. Base sheet should not be too heavy stock. Stock weight from 80-lb. paper to 110-lb. index is satisfactory. You are doing the pasteup on the blank side of the stock and using the grid lines on back side for the guide. Advantage: you have use of

grid without being printed on face of base sheet. Base sheet can be moved about easily on the light table and grid will always be in the same location because it's printed on the back.

Grid Planning Paper

Plan job on grid paper, and draw guidelines following locations of elements as planned on grid paper. Eliminate the need for measuring. Planning is done with the idea in mind that the job will be pasted up on a base sheet which conforms to the planning paper.

The Board System

This simplified system is described in detail in another section of this book.

Summary

The reason you are using the grid for aid in pasteup preparation is to eliminate the need to measure any distances to locate elements on a pasteup. The result is speed and efficiency to prepare a pasteup.

TWO-ACROSS PASTEUP FOR MULTI-PAGE PREPARATION

Often confusion and frustration can occur when preparing multi-page book pasteup, because Graphic Artists are often requested to get pages camera-ready two-across facing each other as they will print on the press. It is much easier and more convenient to paste pages two-across exactly as they appear in the book. For example, a booklet, 8 1/2″ x 11″ page size should be prepared with the cover and outside back cover together side by side on one spread. Now, pages two and three should be prepared side by side, then four and five, six and seven, eight and nine, etc. These spreads are viewed as one reads the pages in the book. All crossover rules can be produced conveniently, crossover heads can be aligned with confidence and the spread is seen as it appears in the book. These double spreads will prove convenient so that crossovers will align properly. After the pages are completed and approved and the pages are ready to go to camera for negatives, it is a simple matter to cut the pages in half so that individual 8 1/2″ x 11″ single pages can be reassembled to abut next to each other to shoot on camera as they will print on the press. Better yet . . . punch pages at the bottom margin on center so that pages can be dropped on a pin copy flat to photograph according to the imposition requirements.

It will also be apparent that the preprinted two-across base sheet will provide easier preparation, and easier placement in juxtaposition after cutting the pages apart. Furthermore, it will also assure correct

	1971	1972	1973	1974	1975	1976	1977	1978	1979
FINANCIAL REPORT									
Income	$ 25	$ 30	$ 33	$ 38	$ 42	$ 44	$ 41	$ 48	$ 51
Expense	20	28	28	33	36	39	40	37	46
Sales	100	120	110	130	108	116	121	125	136
Budget	52	58	59	56	52	59	54	55	56
Equity	10	12	23	21	19	16	14	18	17
Shares	20	21	23	21	26	27	29	19	23
Index	5	4	6	5	7	6	5	4	6

Page 6   Page 7

Punch pages for imposition.   Cut here after pasteup.

Two-across multi page preparation as pages are viewed, not as they are printed.

---

alignment to assure registration of the critical crossover copy.

FILM MAKE-UP

When manuscripts are submitted that are in perfect condition, and all editing has been done to perfection, it may be possible to use positive film make-up on the light table. The print-outs on photo-typesetting equipment can be made to produce a film positive of the type.

Take for example, a book such as a paperback book. Each page contains a fixed number of lines at a given width. A perfectly edited book of this nature may be set on film, so that each page is complete on film with the page number in position. These film positives can be used to expose directly on a positive-working offset plate.

The imposition of these pages may be accomplished by placing them in position on a clear film base that is over a grid on the light table. The pages are affixed with the emulsion side up using clear tape or clear adhesive. The emulsion is up so that this emulsion side will

contact to the sensitized plate surface. All placement of pages is according to the grid lines, and each page is positioned according to the planned layout for the signature.

Typographical errors must be corrected on the film positive. To handle this type of work, lines can be cut in by hand and mortised in position.

BASE SHEETS FOR PASTEUP

There is need for a variety of base sheet paper stock to use for pasteup, because some thickness and weights of paper are considerations. Cost of the base sheet stock can also be a consideration The newspaper putting out hundreds of pages every week, will want to use a lower cost stock, and it is handled under a controlled situation, and generally it is not used again.

Some recommended paper stocks to use for base sheets for pasteup preparation include:

1. A good grade of 110-lb. index.

2. Mirror finish 65-lb. cover stock (such as Kromekote).

3. Dull coated 80-lb. enamel (best quality).

4. 50, 60, or 70-lb. offset paper.

5. Transluscent papers and films.

110-lb. index

For general pasteup work such as publications and book pages, I would recommend a stock such as 110-lb. index. This weight is convenient to use on a drawing board and stiff enough to hold waxed proof material without much danger of pop-off if handled carefully and the burnishing is properly done.

Mirror finish 65-lb. cover stock

The mirror finish on stock such as Kromekote, Lusterkote or Mead Mark I, will provide an excellent surface for ink-ruling lines using technical fountain pens of the Rapidograph type. The ink will not absorb into the paper, but dry on the surface to provide clean sharp ruled lines for forms, charts and graphs in particular.

There may be some difficulty marking guidelines on the slick mirror surface with a pencil; therefore, it is necessary to use a ballpoint or plastic tip pen containing non-photo blue ink. These non-reproducible guidelines should be controlled to mark as light as possible, as heavy pressure with the ballpoint could produce a darker blue line that may appear on plates or negatives. Draw them as faint as possible.

Dull coated 80-lb. enamel (best quality)

A good combination stock for ruling and composition can be found by using a high grade, dull-coated enamel stock. Many of these papers rule very well *and* can be placed in carbon ribbon composing equipment to provide sharp reproduction of keyboarded direct impression composition. With this paper, the ruling can be done first or last.

A form can be ruled, placed in the composer and the information typed directly in place. Or the composition can be done first and the ruling drawn in place afterward.

Furthermore, the stock in 80-lb. weight has good transluscency for light-table use. The carbon impression from the composing will adhere to the surface in the larger and smaller point sizes, and corrections can be made during typing by using correction fluid or white-out tape, if desired.

Illustration Board

While illustration board may be found practical for certain pasteup applications, it is generally not used for pasteup preparation involving the techniques suggested in this book. A few reasons include:

1. The thickness of illustration board creates a raised

surface and the t-square blade is not flat across the surface.

2. Higher cost.

3. Difficulty to punch for pin register preparation.

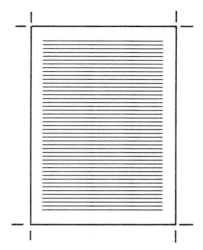

TRIM MARKS

Trim marks will be required on pasteups used in a camera to produce film negative. These trim marks serve the platemaker, the press operator and bindery personnel.

The platemaker will use these marks, visible on the negative, to square up and mask the negative on the light table to position on the plate to print in the correct position according to the paper size.

The press operator will position the printed matter on the page according to the trim marks, and use them to determine that the printing is straight on the sheet. They also aid in the positioning of additional colors of ink on the sheet.

The folder operator will fold the press sheets according to the trim marks and the cutter operator will trim the press sheets according to these marks.

There are several important rules to remember when placing trim marks on the pasteup.

1. Make the marks very thin short black rules for greater accuracy.

2. Place the marks outside of the finished area. The marks must not show after the job is trimmed in the cutter.

These trim marks should not be confused with circular bullseye register marks which are positioned on base sheets to use to register overlay negatives with base negatives. When pasteups with overlays are prepared, you'll need both trim marks and register marks for completeness.

FORMS—PLANNING, RULING, COMPOSING AND PASTEUP

Step 1   Use the grid planning paper to draw the form as required. This plan would have pencil lines on the blue grid paper. Type and sizes of type would show on the plan. (NOTE: Step 1 is the same in all cases.)

Step 2	Step 3	Step 4	Step 5	Comments
Place sheet of ruling paper over this plan. Place on light table and rule with technical pen and t-square.	Set text matter in a block, wax and place on a cutting board and cut apart words, lines with art knife.	Pick up elements and place in position using tweezers. Burnish.	Make negative.	Fast method with skill. Plexiglas pasteup board ideal for this work.
Type composition on sheet of composition and ruling paper, and place all elements in exact position while typing.	Lightly pencil in guidelines where inked rules required.	Ink-rule lines with technical fountain pen.	Make negative.	Good when composition heavy and few rules.
Make photocopy of the form on the grid planning paper for later reference and proofreading.	Set text matter in a type-set block, wax and place on cutting board and cut apart words, lines with art knife.	Pick up elements and place in position on the grid plan sheet over the penciled words. Burnish.	Place frosted acetate drafting film over copy and rule lines. Shoot negative of base, then negative of overlay and double burn on plate.	Fast method with skill.
Place sheet of ruling paper over the plan. Place on light table and rule with technical pen and t-square.	Place ink-ruled sheet in strike-on machine and type information in position according to the plan.	Make negative.		Good when composition light and many rules.
Type composition and use ruling font to place rules in position with repeat key.	Make negative.			Good. Machine skill required. Machine must be in exact alignment or rules can be broken and uneven.

5

The Board System for Pasteup

1. **Board Sizes**
2. **Advantages**
3. **A workable system**
4. **It's portable**
MATERIALS FOR THE BOARDS
1. **The clear plastic board**
ACCURACY
THE PIN REGISTER PASTEUP BOARD
ULTRA-THIN STEEL BLADE T-SQUARE
**THE GRAHAM DUAL ALIGNMENT
   PASTEUP BOARD**

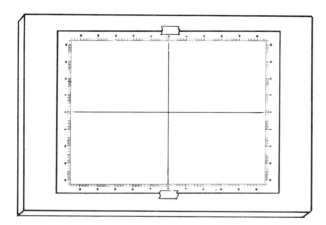

*Two pieces of tape
will hold the base sheet
to the board.*

THE BOARD SYSTEM FOR PASTEUP

Basically this system involves placing a base sheet on a board, then applying waxed proof material to the base sheet while aligning the pieces using the t-square held against the edge of the board. Furthermore, ink lines are easily ruled on paper or film vertically or horizontally by positioning the t-square head on any side of the pasteup board. The Board System eliminates the need for a triangle which is often awkward to hold against the t-square while trying to rule a line against the triangle's edge.

The board with a base sheet taped to it, can be moved and turned to any convenient angle deemed comfortable for whatever pasteup, ruling or application required. The Graphic Artist can sit on a stool, chair or stand up and work with the board on any surface. Whatever comfortable position the artist wishes to assume will be allowed with the Graham Board System.

*Preparing pasteups on boards
is convenient, comfortable
and faster.*

BOARD SIZES

11-3/4″ x 15-3/4″

Use for pages 8 1/2″ x 11″, 9″ x 12″ and 8 1/2″ x 14″ and smaller pages.

13″ x 19-3/4″

Use for preparation of 11″ x 17″ and two-across 8 1/2″ x 11″ spreads. A t-square to accommodate this distance should be on hand.

19 1/2″ x 24″

Use for 17″ x 22″ preparations and two-across 11″ x 17″ spreads. A 24″ t-square should be used with this board.

These board sizes will provide convenient surfaces for a variety of page sizes and spread arrangements. Pre-printed base sheets can be placed on the boards and pasteups using the t-square to aid in alignment, as a ruling edge and as a cutting guide edge.

THICKNESS

If the boards are 3/8″ thickness or more, the t-square head will move freely along the edges of the board. If thinner materials are used, small stick-on bumpers can be placed near the board's corners and at other spots to elevate the board to a convenient thickness. Thinner materials have the advantage of providing a lighter weight board, especially when using acrylic.

Advantages

The advantages of preparing pasteups using the board system are numerous.

1. With the pasteup base corner-taped on the boards, the t-square can be used in *both directions*.

2. The pasteup is not removed from the board until it is proofread and checked if desired. This saves picking up and squaring up a job over and over.

3. If a pasteup is on a board and partially completed, it may be put aside temporarily. Another board can be used for another pasteup. Have you ever been interrupted during the work on a particular job, with the request that you "drop everything" to work on the rush job? When this happens, all you do is put your board with pasteup aside, pick up another board and work on the new job. You need only pick up the previously used board to get back to the other job for completion. You need not disturb the pasteup already being worked on. No picking up and repositioning is necessary. Photocopies and proofreading can often be handled while the pasteup is on the board.

4. Your pasteup receives a minimum of handling during preparation. You can get away with using lighter weight stock for base sheets.

5. When working with the board, it can be turned at the most convenient angle to avoid awkward positions of working at big drawing tables. For instance, think of how difficult and uncomfortable it is to rule vertical lines on a base sheet fastened to a light table, while you try to manipulate t-square and triangle! With your base sheet on the board you can turn it so you are comfortable as you rule your lines.

6. If you are pasting up pages for books, catalogs, magazines and other publications, you can prepare one page or double spreads. You can paste up a page partially, and work on another page on another board. You need not disturb the page you worked on partially. Think of the time you can save on this procedure alone. You will find a full discussion on imposing these individual publication pages for camera-ready placement in another portion of this book.

A workable system

Even newspaper pages can be prepared on boards by making the boards about 1/2-in. larger than the newspaper page perimeter.

When the smaller boards are used, pasteup work may be performed while seated before a regular office desk and have plenty of drawer space to keep all of the necessary tools, inks, pens and accessories.

It's portable

Many printers are inclined to take some of their pasteup work home to work on in the evening. The board system will prove ideal for this as the system is the ultimate in portability.

You can take a half-completed pasteup home while it is still on the board without picking it off and repositioning.

Furthermore, it is an ideal system for teaching pasteup in shop or school, because a student needs only his board with other tools to handle his pasteup practice at his desk or table. Working with the boards at school for practice can be followed for practical pasteup in the field.

MATERIALS FOR BOARDS

Wood

Inexpensive boards may be prepared using 3/8″ smooth plywood with edges sealed with a penetrating varnish for durability. Utmost care must be taken when sawing out these boards to assure 90 degree accuracy.

3/8″ Acrylic

The 3/8″ acrylic boards can be cut accurately, then milled on a milling machine to assure an extremely precision pasteup board. The need for milling becomes

A clear plastic board is ideal for use with a light table in combination with a clear plastic grid.

apparent when preparing pasteups when one wants to use the t-square on at least two sides of the board to take advantage of the movability of the boards for convenience.

3/16″-1/8″ Acrylic

These thinner clear plastic sheets can be used for boards by affixing stick-on bumpers near the corners and other places as needed to elevate the board yet provide a firm surface.

The Clear Acrylic Board

There is a great advantage to using a clear acrylic material for a pasteup board.

It can be used at a desk for pasteup preparation, yet may be placed on a light table to allow the light source to illuminate the copy on the base sheet when required. Truly the ultimate in versatility! For example, a plastic grid may be taped on the acrylic board. A translucent base sheet is taped on top of the grid. The grid aids to align copy horizontally and vertically. It now becomes important to have at least several clear boards at the desk for pasteup preparation.

ACCURACY

When pasteup boards are manufactured for use in the board system, it is most important that they be made

so the sides are 90 degrees.

The reason for this accuracy is because you want the advantage of using the t-square on any side of the board at any time. This is part of the efficiency of the system.

Home made boards may not prove successful due to inaccurate cutting, and it may be an advantage to purchase boards that are manufactured to close tolerance.

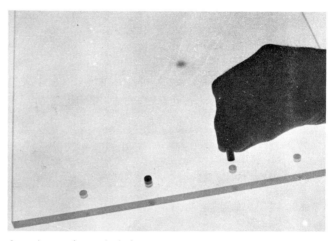

Inserting steel pegs in holes to form posts to accommodate base sheet.

Placing base sheet on pegs for automatic alignment on board.

THE PI REGISTER PASTEUP BOARD

To provide additional versatility and precision in the preparation of pasteups, precision holes can be drilled near the edge of the acrylic board so that base sheets can be punched near the edge to match the drilled holes. By inserting 1/4″ diameter steel pegs, 1/2″ length, the holes in the base sheet can be positioned on the pegs which will automatically position the base sheet on the board so that it is square with the sides. If desired, the base sheet can be taped and the pegs removed for ease in moving the t-square around the board without interference. All material positioned on the base sheet can now be placed parallel to the holes. If desired these holes can later be used to position the page for imposition on a pin copy board.

A further advantage of the pin register board, is that punched overlay materials can be placed on the pegs to prepare in register to the base pasteup. Overlays can be removed and replaced in precise register. This procedure eliminates the need to tape-hinge overlays on pages which are often inconvenient and cumbersome. When the pasteup is sent to the camera, the overlay may be secured to the base with 1/4″ diameter dowls, .060″ thick. These thin dowels will not harm the copyboard glass, but act to hold the overlay in register during photographic procedures.

The Pin Register Pasteup Board will prove convenient when revising pasteups. Peg the pasteup on the board and revise as necessary. Every time the pasteup is placed on the pegs, the positioning is exactly the same as it was originally prepared when positioned on the pegs.

ULTRA-THIN STEEL BLADE T-SQUARE

In connection with the board system, it is important that we locate a t-square that is completely compatible with the system.

We need a thin, strong versatile steel t-square for pasteup preparation.

The proper t-square should be:

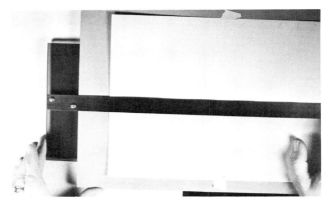

A thin steel t-square is essential for ruling, squaring and cutting.

1. Light weight for ease in handling;
2. Steel edged for *cutting, ruling and squaring;*
3. Thin steel so that alignment of small elements can be accomplished accurately.

A t-square of this type is available on the market.

Technical fountain pens, such as the Rapidograph, will work beautifully with the Ultra-thin steel t-square. If the pen is held correctly, all ruling can be performed quickly and accurately.

When using the plastic points, which are used for the very bold lines, lift glides can be pressed under the blade to raise the ruling edge higher to prevent blotting and smearing. It is quick and easy to place these lifts under the t-square blade.

Graham Dual Alignment Pasteup Board

THE GRAHAM DUAL ALIGNMENT PASTEUP BOARD

For those who prefer not to use a t-square, the Dual Alignment Board can provide quick easy alignment of copy on a base sheet. It is an acrylic board 19-3/4″ x

14-1/2″, and a steel angle similar to a carpenter's square or drafting arm is moved along raised guide edges at the side and bottom. It is made to slant about 10 degrees and may be used on light table. It is drilled for pin registration of base sheets and overlays.

6
Manuscript Preparation

Special Sheets

MANUSCRIPT PREPARATION

The condition of the original manuscript is probably one of the greatest influences on the outcome and cost of setting up a printing job.

Handwritten and overcorrected manuscripts result in guess work, mistakes and slow keyboarding on the part of the typesetter. The final result is the need for excessive alterations adding to the cost of the job and delays in production.

The time to make *author's alterations* is while the job is in manuscript form. Careful serious checking of the original typewritten material will eliminate the need for making alterations on the final output.

Andrew R. Alaways, a typesetter in Washington, D.C., points out that "little things mean a lot" when preparing a manuscript for composition. He states that alterations can cost between $4.00 and $10.00 for each. Typing a manuscript in an office might cost $8.00 per hour, but typesetting will cost $30.00 per hour plus all the delays and misunderstandings.

Here are some important points to remember when preparing a manuscript for typesetting:

1. Clean the keys of the typewriter.
2. Double space all copy.
3. Never hyphenate a word at the end of a line.
4. Use one side of the paper only.
5. Express all measurements in picas and points.
6. Submit copy in groups according to type style, if applicable.
7. Minimize spacing changes, however minor. Minimize need for modular leading and "leading out" of paragraphs of pages.
8. Use standard proofreading symbols.
9. Mark changes with colored pen or pencil on the photocopy galleys.
10. Understand what is standard and what is special.
11. Use discretion as to number of typefaces specified.
12. Key copy to the plan (layout). Number the copy areas on the plan to correspond with numbered blocks on the layout. This saves time in verbal instructions, composition and proofreading.

13. Layouts should be drawn to exact dimensions or proportion.
14. Use an extra tissue overlay sheet if neccessary to provide further information.
15. Photocopy proofs should be marked "OK" or "OK as corrected" and initialed by the person authorized to pass on the work.
16. If a revised photocopy proof is required, request should be made when first photocopy proof is returned.

Special sheets

It may be advisable to preprint special sheets to use for manuscript typing. Parallel lines can be printed on the sheets and information typed between the lines. From this experience, it is known that each typewritten line will be about the same as an output line.

J. S. Paluch Co., Inc. provides its customers with special sheets for manuscript preparation for church bulletin printing. Illustrated is an actual manuscript page.

Eat 6 pt.
Eat 7 pt.
Eat 8 pt.
Eat 9 pt.
Eat 10 pt.
Eat 11 pt.
Eat 12 pt.
Eat 14 pt.
Eat 16 pt.
Eat 18 pt.
Eat 20 pt.
Eat 22 pt.
Eat 24 pt.
Eat 28 pt.
Eat 32 pt.
Eat 36 pt.
Eat 40 pt.
Eat 44 pt.
Eat 48 pt.
Eat 56 pt.
Eat 60 pt.
Eat 72 pt.

Photocomposition Comparative Type Sizes and Leading Scale

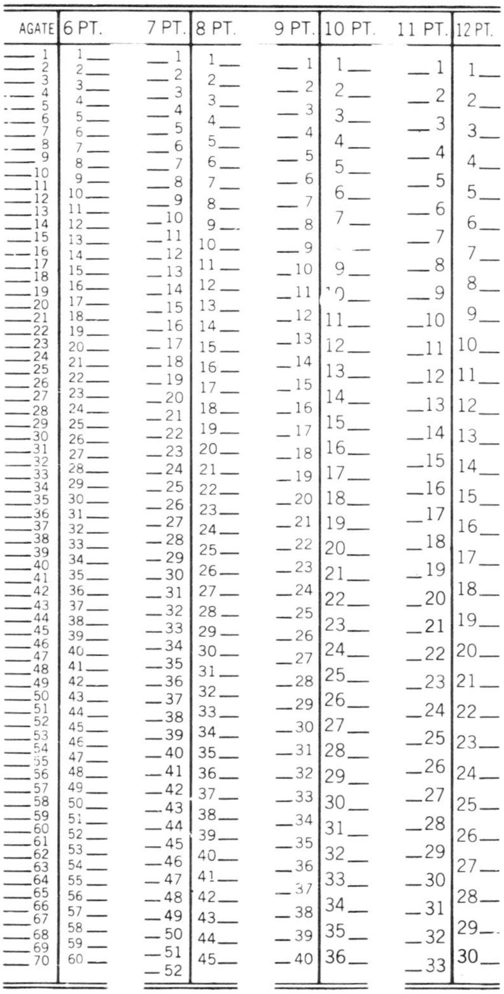
AGATE
6 PT.
7 PT.
8 PT.
9 PT.
10 PT.
11 PT.
12 PT.

Leading Scale

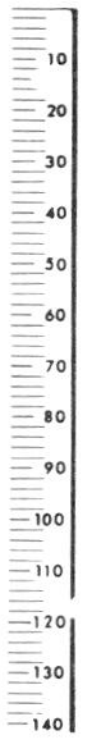
10
20
30
40
50
60
70
80
90
100
110
120
130
140

7
Composition

**METHODS OF PRODUCING
COMPOSITION FOR OFFSET PRINTING**
Hot metal
Phototypesetting
Strike-on
Flush left and flush right
Headlines
COPYFITTING
Points and picas
Method of copyfitting
Copyfitting on the IBM Composer
Copyfitting figures time
Copyfitting problem
The square inch method
**Setting type to facilitate easier splicing and
     correcting**
Copyfitting Aids and devices

METHODS OF PRODUCING COMPOSITION
FOR OFFSET PRINTING

There are many pieces of equipment on the market built to achieve composition ready for pasteup. These break down into three basic categories: (1) Hot Metal (2) Phototypesetting (3) Strike-on.

Hot Metal Typesetting

The Linotype machine has been one of several very popular slug casting machines which provides typesetting for letterpress printing. The type is set by using a keyboard which drops matrices into a holder to be cast in lead. Hot metal can be used to provide composition for pasteup. After the type is set, a reproduction must be made on a proof press to produce a suitable proof of the composition for pasteup.

More and more hot metal has been replaced with photo-composition and strike-on composition. Nearly all newspapers have converted to cold methods of typesetting.

Phototypesetting

Phototypesetting provides composition in the form of a photographic proof on photo-sensitive paper. These proofs are ready for pasteup after development through a processor. The output on a phototypesetter can be either on film positives or paper. The positives can be stripped up on a light table to expose on positive-working offset printing plates.

Generally the output is on paper due to the ease in making corrections and adding illustrations, headings, pictures, and other elements on the printed page.

The phototypesetting system involves two stages, input and output. The input is prepared at a typewriter keyboard to produce a punched paper tape, magnetic tape or floppy disk. The paper tape is automatically punched with a series of holes unique to the character depressed on the keyboard. The prepared tape is run through an output unit where these signals are converted into photographic images through a system of lenses and shutters to expose the characters through a photo matrix on photosensitive paper. The tapes move rapidly through the output to produce lines of type flush left and flush right automatically.

Some phototypesetting equipment is of the direct input variety which exposes the characters after each line is recorded on the keyboard.

Phototypesetting has made great advances in recent years and has proved to have many advantages. Some of the advantages are:

1. The output is camera-ready proof copy ready for pasteup.

2. The image is of high quality.

3. Capability of mixing a wide range of faces and sizes on one machine.

4. Less storage space is required. Pasteups can be stored in files to eliminate the need for metal galleys.

5. A compact space-saving system.

6. Faster than hot metal, particularly on complex composition.

7. Can be used in an improved environment. Tiled or carpeted floors can provide pleasant and comfortable working conditions.

8. The output of the equipment is the fastest.

Typesetting on paper or on film

Those of us doing pasteup work are concerned with

composition produced to give us a proof copy on paper. Phototypesetting equipment can produce its images directly on film to produce a sharp positive film image.

These print-out positives of the type can be assembled on a grid on a light table to form a "flat" for direct exposure to positive-working plates without need of an intermediate negative. This system works well for those producing straight typeset books, booklets and novels when the manuscripts will not be altered.

It should be pointed out however, that using the positives is the exception and not the rule, because it fits specialized applications. To use film positives to try to produce ordinary publications would involve more

The operator is preparing a perforated strip of paper tape when keyboarding the composition.

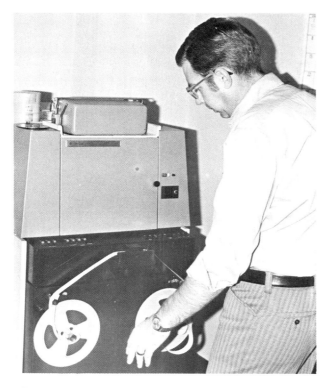

The perforated tape is placed on a print-out unit to produce the photographic images on photo-sensitive paper.

time stripping together the positive film batches. These pieces of film are mortised and fitted laboriously to form a composite with all of its cuts and edges. This composite is used to make a contact negative which can require considerable opaquing.

There is strong logic that favors the use of paper. In 25 years in the printing business it was found that film makeup for a variety of printing jobs was never practical. Alterations and changes are annoying enough when working with paper.

Strike-on composition

Typesetting or composition for offset printing can be produced on a variety of composing equipment. The simplest machine for typesetting is the ordinary typewriter. A typewriter is very useful for composition work, but it is important to use a machine that is in good condition which will produce a clean sharp impression. So often, people set up jobs for printing with typewriters which are out of alignment, have worn platens and they type copy using worn ribbons which produce light copy difficult to photograph.

Good printing quality can be produced if the typewriter impresses sharp black characters. The best typewriter to use is one which is properly adjusted and uses a carbon ribbon. The carbon ribbon is used once, and each character typed is of the same density. After copy is typed for a job, and a week later a correction is pasted in, the density of the characters will be the same. Fabric ribbons get light with use, and print fuzzier images. Carbon ribbons produce sharper and blacker images.

The IBM Composer and the Varityper use a carbon ribbon and have features to allow changes in type styles and sizes. Both have systems attached to simplify justification on the right margins. The Composer is avail-

A carbon-ribbon impression using a strike-on typewriter, Composer, or Varityper, provides a black consistent impression for better reproduction.

able with a magnetic tape system so that justified composition can be produced automatically from the tapes.

Years ago during the emergence of offset printing shops, many used ordinary typewriters and would "justify" the margins of publications to imitate typesetting. Another trick was to reduce typewriter comp about 25% so that it looked sharper and gave a better appearance.

Flush left and flush right or "justification" of typewriter composition

Many attempts have been made to produce justified typewriter composition with a single typing.

One idea was the use of a sheet of die cut paper strips mounted on a backing sheet and lines are typed on the strips. Each line is lifted up and stretched to the right hand justification point. The surface is a stretch-type paper.

Some years ago a French device called the Optype was on the market which photographed each line of type and reduced or enlarged the individual lines to the desired width.

As a practical matter, justification of typewritten matter using a standard typewriter means the material must be typed twice.

To type composition on a typewriter for flush left and right, first determine the width of the column you wish to type. With sheet of paper in the typewriter, measure from the left margin out to the point of the right margin. Place a pencil dot at the right margin on the paper. Most typewriters have a small notch on the metal or plastic strip in front of the platen. Place a pencil point in this notch and roll the platen in line with the pencil dot to produce a line parallel to the left hand margin. This is good procedure, because if you draw a line on the paper first, then try to place it in the typewriter, you'll have difficulty getting it perfectly parallel from top to bottom. Using the pencil point in the notch assures exact alignment with the margin.

Proceed to type your composition allowing each line to fall short of reaching the penciled line on the right. In the spaces that remain, type "i" in each space. Some typists use "x" or "/" but that's a matter of preference. It's what is easy for you to type, and what is easy to count quickly. The letter "i" is convenient to strike and it's easy to count.

After the rough type is completed, go back through and retype the material putting in extra spaces between words so the line will end up flush left and flush right. Some prefer to tab over on the same paper with the rough typing and type the justified line. The reason is that the words are fresh in mind and that's the best time to do the second justified typing . Some typists will go through the rough typing and with a colored pencil

mark between words where they will leave extra spaces. This is not good procedure, because you are taking time to make all these marks. Practice for the technique should be to glance at the number of i's and to remember the number of spaces needed to place between words. After a time it's surprising how quickly a typist can justify lines by glancing at the i's and remembering the count.

When justifying in this manner, make the lines look better by avoiding "rivers of white." That is, placing all of the extra spaces so that the space falls under another space in the line above. At times this cannot be avoided during final typing. Generally, place a required extra space after a period or comma or other punctuation

```
        The practice of typography, if it
be followed faithfully, is hard work
and full of detail, full of pettyiii
restrictions, full of drudgery, andi
not greatly rewarded as men nowiiiii
count rewards. There are times wheni
we need to bring to it all the his-i
tory and art and feeling that we can
to make it bearable. But in theiiiii
light of history, and of art, and of
knowledge and of man's achievement,i
it is as interesting a work asiiiiii
exists--a broad and humanizing em-ii
ployment which can indeed be fol-iii
lowed merely as a trade, but whichii
if perfected into an art, or eveniii
broadened into a profession, williiii
perpetually open new horizons to our
eyes and new opportunities to ouriii
hands.
                        --D.B.Updikeiiii
```

```
        The practice of typography, if it
be followed faithfully, is hard work
and  full of detail,  full of  petty
restrictions,  full of drudgery, and
not  greatly  rewarded  as  men  now
count  rewards.  There are times when
we  need  to bring to it all the his-
tory and art and feeling that we can
to  make  it  bearable.  But  in the
light of history, and of art, and of
knowledge  and of man's achievement,
it  is  as  interesting  a  work  as
exists----a broad and humanizing em-
ployment  which  can  indeed be fol-
lowed  merely  as a trade,  but which
if  perfected  into  an art,  or even
broadened  into  a  profession,  will
perpetually  open new horizons to our
eyes  and  new  opportunities to our
hands.
                              --D.B.Updike
```

*Type copy to a target point
and place i's to compensate for the blank spaces.
When retyping, allow extra spaces between words
to "justify" to right hand margin.*

that occurs in the typewritten line. Extra space after punctuation seems to give a more logical appearance and not as noticeable as being extra space.

HEADLINES

Headlines can be produced using templates and lettering scribers with pen points to ink the letters.

Very popular today are photo-lettering systems using devices which will reduce and enlarge from the film strips of the alphabets. Some of the devices on the market are the Strip-Printer, Headliner, Photo-Typositor and Film-O-Type. Not all will enlarge or reduce but they will produce sharp lettering by exposing the characters individually from film matrices. These machines are hand operated, and the characters are exposed on strips of photosensitive paper or film.

While some phototypesetters are used to keyboard headlines and other large display type, display headings may also be set using sheets of acetate letters or dry transfer lettering. Naturally it will take more time to handset, but often attractive hand letter styles of type may be useful and necessary.

Acetate Lettering and Graphic Art Aids

These acetate cut-out self adhesive sheets of lettering, symbols, shading and other arts aids are cut out with an art knife, lifted and positioned on a guide line. The pressure sensitive coating will cause the letter to adhere.

Acetate letters can be positioned on the edge of a ruler for fast convenient alignment.

Dry Transfer Lettering and Graphic Art Aids

Dry transfer letters can be applied to almost any surface. A few uses include lettering for slide art, cells, layouts, signs and pasteups. To apply dry transfer type, first determine the length of a line using a tissue sheet and soft pencil. Rule a faint guideline on a sheet, place bottom of letter even with the rule and rub with stylus, ball point pen or burnishing stick. Place backing sheet

Rub the dry transfer letters with burnisher to transfer to surface.

over finished characters and re-burnish entire surface, then gently erase pencil lines.

Spacing

Using one of the acetate lettering sheets such as Formatt or Artype will be necessary from time to time. Aligning and spacing this type correctly is an absolute necessity for professional pasteup preparation.

Most beginners to pasteup seem to have trouble learning how to space letters with precision.

It should be pointed out that when placing acetate letters one after another to form a word, it is the volume of space between the characters that determines their placement. The volume of space should be about the same between each two letters. This rule may not seem to apply to some type styles, but it is worth mentioning to control spacing carefully, and remain conscious of its importance.

The volume of space between letters should be about equal optically.

If you should add space between characters to letterspace, the spacing rule still applies. When working with all-caps you might enhance a line of type in certain situations by the use of letterspacing:

Normal: PASTEUP ACHIEVEMENT
Letterspaced: P A S T E U P   A C H I E V E M E N T

Letterspace only all-caps in display lines. Do not letterspace condensed letters. If you have to letterspace condensed, then why would you consider using condensed type?

Kerning

The hand compositor using metal foundry type to set up letters was restricted in spacing to some degree, because he had to butt the type characters one next to the other. Note that in the word "AVALON" as illustrated, the spacing between "A" and "V" would be wide if set in foundry type. When using acetate lettering, note how its appearance can be improved if some of the letters are "tucked" a bit to occupy some of the white space. We can set tighter lines for what is often considered a better-looking design or arrangement. This tucking is referred to as "kerning" characters.

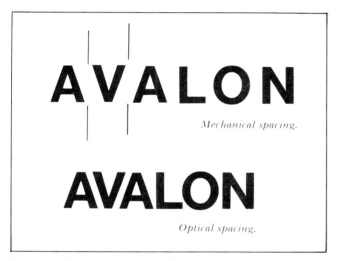

Mechanical spacing.

Optical spacing.

Snug your letters together to avoid awkward spacing. Kern letters when required.

Spacing between words

What is the rule for spacing between words? Many typographers would use one-third the type size. If the type is 36-point, you would then allow 12 points of space between the words.

There is a trend today to set type with the letters very close to each other, and if this is the situation when you set your transfer type, cut down the word spacing to one fourth the type size. If the type size is 48-point you would allow 12 points; 36-point, nine points; 24-point, six points.

You can achieve better-looking lines, too, by watching some of the characteristics of the words you set. For instance, if a word ends in a w or v, you might want to reduce the space. If a word ends or begins with an ascending letter, a slightly narrower space may look better.

COPYFITTING

Points and picas

Points and picas are the printer's unit of measure, and you should think in terms of points and picas because this measure is used with all typesetting systems, including the IBM Composer. For practical purposes note that:

Six picas = one inch

One pica = 12 points

The standard typewriter is designed to produce six single spaced lines per inch, hence each line is a pica.

When designing a form to be used in a typewriter, it is important that it be designed to accommodate typewriter spacing. An IBM Composer will produce typewriter spacing when the rachet is set on 12 points. (12 points = one pica). Even though a smaller type is used, such as eight or 10 point, the composer will move 12 points with each carriage return.

It is simple to convert any number of pica lines to points. For instance, six inches equal 36 picas and 36 picas equal 432 points (36 x 12 = 432). If you were going to set type in nine point solid, you need only divide nine into 432 and you would get a result of 48. ($432 \div 9 = 48$). Thus 48 lines of nine point type would fit into 36 picas.

To save time in doing the arithmetic, a line gauge will visually indicate the number of lines in a given amount of space.

Without a line gauge the number of lines are determined by measuring the depth of the type in picas and multiplying as follows, the answer is the number of lines:

6-point type = picas times 2

8-point type = picas times 1.5

9-point type = picas times 1.33

10-point type = picas times 1.2

12-point type = picas times 1.0

Method of copyfitting

To determine how many lines of type will be set from a manuscript, you should have knowledge of some system that is quick and simple. Let's examine a system called the *Character Count Method.*

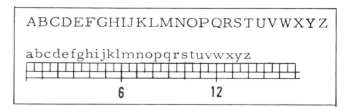

Every size and style of type will have a character

CHARACTERS PER PICA CHART

HANDY COPY-FITTING CHART—The basic number of characters per pica followed across to the pica width to be set will give the number of characters that will set in the pica measure. By dividing the number of characters of one line into the total number of characters in copy will give the total number of lines.

Char. Per Pica ↓	5	6	7	8	9	10	11	12	13	14	15	16	17	18	19	20	21	22	23	24	25	26	27	28	29	30	31	32	33	34	35	Char. Per Pica ↓
5.7	28	34	39	45	51	57	62	68	74	79	85	91	97	102	108	114	119	125	131	136	142	148	154	159	165	171	176	182	187	193	199	5.7
5.6	28	33	39	45	50	56	61	67	72	78	84	89	95	100	106	112	117	123	129	134	140	145	151	156	162	168	173	179	184	190	196	5.6
5.5	27	33	38	44	49	55	60	66	71	77	82	88	93	99	104	110	115	121	126	132	137	143	148	154	159	165	170	176	181	186	192	5.5
5.4	27	32	37	43	48	54	59	64	70	75	81	86	92	97	103	108	113	119	124	130	135	140	146	151	156	162	167	172	178	184	190	5.4
5.3	26	31	37	42	47	53	58	63	69	74	79	84	90	95	100	106	111	116	122	127	132	137	143	148	153	159	164	169	174	180	186	5.3
5.2	26	31	36	41	46	52	57	62	67	72	78	83	88	94	99	104	109	114	119	124	130	135	140	145	150	156	161	166	171	176	182	5.2
5.1	25	30	35	40	45	51	56	61	66	71	76	81	86	92	97	102	107	112	117	122	127	132	137	142	148	153	158	163	167	172	178	5.1
5.0	25	30	35	40	45	50	55	60	65	70	75	80	85	90	95	100	105	110	115	122	125	130	135	140	145	150	155	160	165	170	175	5.0
4.9	24	29	34	39	44	49	54	59	63	68	73	78	83	88	93	98	103	108	112	117	122	127	132	137	142	147	151	156	161	166	171	4.9
4.8	24	28	33	38	43	48	52	57	62	67	72	76	81	86	91	96	100	105	110	115	120	124	129	134	139	144	148	153	157	162	167	4.8
4.7	23	28	32	37	42	47	51	56	61	65	70	75	79	84	89	94	98	103	108	112	117	122	126	131	136	141	145	150	154	158	163	4.7
4.6	23	27	32	36	41	46	50	55	60	64	69	73	78	82	87	92	96	101	105	110	115	119	124	129	133	138	142	147	151	156	160	4.6
4.5	22	27	31	36	40	45	49	54	59	63	67	72	76	81	85	90	94	99	103	108	112	117	121	126	130	135	139	144	148	152	157	4.5
4.4	22	26	30	35	39	44	48	52	57	61	66	70	74	79	84	88	92	96	101	105	110	114	118	123	127	132	136	140	144	148	154	4.4
4.3	21	25	30	34	38	43	47	51	55	60	64	68	73	78	82	86	90	94	99	103	107	111	116	120	124	129	133	137	141	146	151	4.3
4.2	21	25	29	33	37	42	46	50	54	58	63	67	71	75	79	84	88	92	96	100	105	109	113	117	121	126	130	134	138	142	147	4.2
4.1	20	24	28	32	36	41	45	49	53	57	61	65	69	74	78	82	86	90	94	98	102	106	110	114	119	123	127	131	134	138	143	4.1
4.0	20	24	28	32	36	40	44	48	52	56	60	64	68	72	76	80	84	88	92	96	100	104	108	112	116	120	124	128	132	136	140	4.0
3.9	19	23	27	31	35	39	42	46	50	54	58	62	66	70	74	78	81	85	89	93	97	101	105	109	113	117	120	124	128	132	136	3.9
3.8	19	22	26	30	34	38	41	45	49	53	57	60	64	68	72	76	79	83	87	91	95	98	102	106	110	114	117	121	124	128	132	3.8
3.7	18	22	25	29	33	37	40	44	48	51	55	59	63	66	70	74	77	81	85	88	92	96	100	103	107	111	114	118	122	126	129	3.7
3.6	18	21	25	28	32	36	39	43	46	50	54	57	61	64	68	72	75	79	82	86	90	93	97	100	104	108	111	115	118	122	125	3.6
3.5	17	21	24	28	31	35	38	42	45	49	52	56	59	63	66	70	73	77	80	84	87	91	94	98	101	105	108	112	115	118	121	3.5
3.4	17	20	23	27	30	34	37	40	44	47	51	54	57	61	65	68	71	74	78	81	85	88	91	95	98	102	105	108	111	114	119	3.4
3.3	16	19	23	26	29	33	36	39	42	46	49	52	56	59	62	66	69	72	76	79	82	85	89	92	95	99	102	105	108	112	116	3.3
3.2	16	19	22	25	28	32	35	38	41	44	48	51	54	57	61	64	67	70	73	76	80	83	86	89	92	96	99	102	105	108	112	3.2
3.1	15	18	21	24	27	31	34	37	40	43	46	49	52	56	59	62	65	68	71	74	77	80	83	86	89	93	96	99	101	104	108	3.1
3.0	15	18	21	24	27	30	33	36	39	42	45	48	51	54	57	60	63	66	69	72	75	78	81	84	87	90	93	96	99	102	105	3.0
2.9	14	17	20	23	26	29	31	34	37	40	43	46	49	52	55	58	60	63	66	69	72	75	78	81	84	87	89	92	95	98	101	2.9
2.8	14	16	19	22	25	28	30	33	36	39	42	44	47	50	53	56	58	61	64	67	70	72	75	78	81	84	86	89	91	94	97	2.8
2.7	13	16	18	21	24	27	29	32	35	37	40	43	45	48	51	54	56	59	62	64	67	70	72	75	78	81	83	86	88	90	93	2.7
2.6	13	15	18	20	23	26	28	31	33	36	39	41	44	46	49	52	54	57	59	62	65	67	70	72	75	78	80	83	85	88	90	2.6
2.5	12	15	17	20	22	25	27	30	32	35	37	40	42	45	47	50	52	55	57	60	62	65	67	70	72	75	77	80	82	84	87	2.5
2.4	12	14	16	19	21	24	26	28	31	33	36	38	40	43	45	48	50	52	55	57	60	62	64	67	69	72	74	76	78	80	83	2.4
2.3	11	13	16	18	20	23	25	27	29	32	34	36	39	41	43	46	48	50	53	55	57	59	62	64	66	69	71	73	75	78	80	2.3
2.2	11	13	15	17	19	22	24	26	28	30	33	35	37	39	41	44	46	48	50	52	55	57	59	61	63	66	68	70	72	74	76	2.2
2.1	10	12	14	16	18	21	23	25	27	29	31	33	35	37	39	42	44	46	48	50	52	54	56	58	60	63	65	67	68	70	72	2.1
2.0	10	12	14	16	18	20	22	24	26	28	30	32	34	36	38	40	42	44	46	48	50	52	54	56	58	60	62	64	66	68	70	2.0
1.9	9	11	13	15	17	19	20	22	24	26	28	30	32	34	36	38	39	41	43	45	47	49	51	53	55	57	58	60	62	64	66	1.9
1.8	9	10	12	14	16	18	19	21	23	25	27	28	30	32	34	36	37	39	41	43	45	46	48	50	52	54	55	57	59	61	63	1.8
1.7	8	10	11	13	15	17	18	20	22	23	25	27	28	30	32	34	35	37	39	40	42	44	45	47	49	51	53	54	56	57	59	1.7
1.6	8	9	11	12	14	16	17	19	20	22	24	25	27	28	30	32	33	35	36	38	40	41	43	44	46	48	49	51	52	54	55	1.6
1.5	7	9	10	12	13	15	16	18	19	21	22	24	25	27	28	30	31	33	34	36	37	39	40	42	43	45	46	48	49	50	52	1.5
1.4	7	8	9	11	12	14	15	16	17	19	21	22	23	25	26	28	29	30	32	33	35	36	37	39	40	42	43	44	46	47	48	1.4
1.3	6	7	9	10	11	13	14	15	16	18	19	20	22	23	24	26	27	28	30	31	32	33	35	36	37	39	40	41	42	44	45	1.3
1.2	6	7	8	9	10	12	13	14	15	16	18	19	20	21	22	24	25	26	27	28	30	31	32	33	34	36	37	38	39	40	42	1.2
1.1	5	6	7	8	9	10	12	13	14	15	16	17	18	19	20	22	23	24	25	26	27	28	29	30	31	33	34	35	36	37	38	1.1
6.0	5	6	7	8	9	10	11	12	13	14	15	16	17	18	19	20	21	22	23	24	25	26	27	28	29	30	31	32	33	34	35	6.0

count which refers to the average number of characters that will fit into one pica. This count is referred to as "Characters per pica," or "cpp."

Take a look at the average number of characters in one pica of IBM Executive Typewriter composition, modern type style:

We know that:

Six picas = one inch. One pica = 12 points.

There are 26 letters in the alphabet, and let us add 2.5 more characters to this alphabet to account for punctuation marks used with the lower case alphabet. We have a figure of 26 + 2.5 = 28.5 which we can call k (constant).

We can now set up a simple formula to figure the characters per pica for the modern type style:

$$\frac{k(constant)}{lower\ case\ alphabet\ length\ in\ picas} = characters\ per\ pica$$

The measurement of our modern type face lower case line is 14.25 picas.

To figure the characters per pica for our modern type we can proceed as follows using the formula:

$$\frac{28.5}{14.25} = 2.0\ characters\ per\ pica$$

To determine the characters per pica, first measure the lower case line from the left of the "a" to the right of the "z." Use a pica scale for reasonable accuracy, but for greatest accuracy a point-scale should be used.

Type style books will often indicate the characters per pica for available type faces. Manufacturers of typesetting equipment will provide this information in their specifications. It is well to understand how this was figured to have a thorough understanding of copyfitting.

To estimate how many lines of type will be required for a manuscript, first determine the number of characters in the manuscript. To do this count the number of characters in an average typewritten line in the manuscript and count the number of lines. Let's assume a manuscript contains 30,000 characters. It is to be set in eight-point type, 12 picas wide. The character count is 2.5 (cpp) for our type style.

If our type is to be set 12 picas wide, we can multiply 12 x 2.5 which tells us that one line will require 30 characters.

12 picas x 2.5 cpp = 30 characters in one line

Our 30,000 character manuscript will therefore require 1,000 lines of type figured as follows:

30,000 characters ÷ 30 characters in one line = 1,000 lines

Now that you know the number of lines you will know exactly the full depth of the type without leading.

A line gauge will aid to determine the amount of leading necessary to fit the space on the layout.

Copyfitting on the IBM Composer

Composition produced on the IBM Composer can be fit to an area using the character per pica system. The characters per pica are as follows:

BLUE sector composition ..3.3 characters per pica
YELLOW sector composition ....2.9 characters per pica
RED sector composition....2.5 characters per pica

Copyfitting figures time

The technique of copyfitting is not only useful to determine how much space the composition will take, but also to determine how much time a job will take to be set. These time estimates are important to printers who must estimate printing costs by examining a manuscript and layout to provide an advanced estimate.

If an operator can compose at the rate of 60 words per minute, theoretically, maximum production would be 18,000 keystrokes per hour. (Figuring an average of five characters per word). Let's figure a 75% net productivity, therefore, we would have 13,500 characters per hour as a net. The 30,000 character manuscript would be composed in 2.22 hours.

Some patience in advanced figuring for copyfitting can pay dividends on many printing jobs in order to do a better job of getting the proper leading, and size of type required before the job is set. Without proper planning, a job may be set only to discover that you *wished* you had set in a larger or smaller size to look best on your pasteup.

The line gauge will tell you the number of lines of type in a given amount of space.

Copyfitting problem

Determine how many lines of type will result from the following typewritten manuscript.

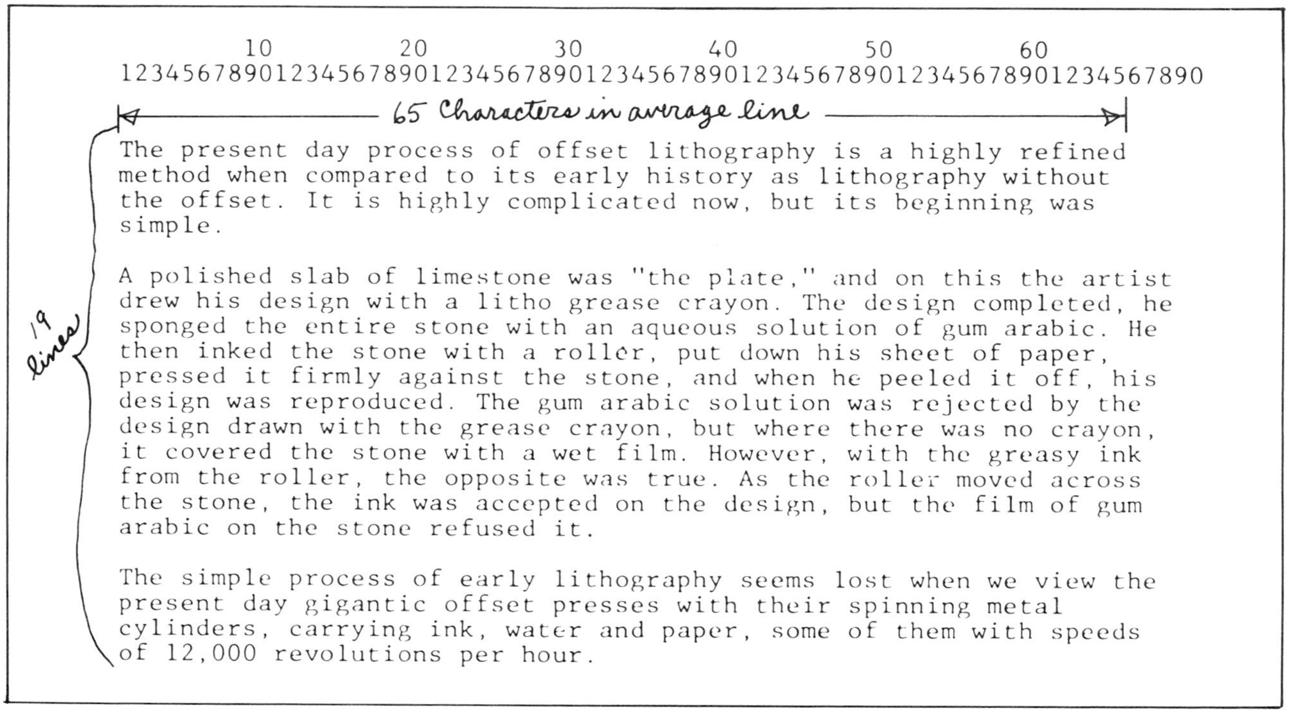

10 20 30 40 50 60
1234567890123456789012345678901234567890123456789012345678901234567890
65 Characters in average line
19 lines

The present day process of offset lithography is a highly refined method when compared to its early history as lithography without the offset. It is highly complicated now, but its beginning was simple.

A polished slab of limestone was "the plate," and on this the artist drew his design with a litho grease crayon. The design completed, he sponged the entire stone with an aqueous solution of gum arabic. He then inked the stone with a roller, put down his sheet of paper, pressed it firmly against the stone, and when he peeled it off, his design was reproduced. The gum arabic solution was rejected by the design drawn with the grease crayon, but where there was no crayon, it covered the stone with a wet film. However, with the greasy ink from the roller, the opposite was true. As the roller moved across the stone, the ink was accepted on the design, but the film of gum arabic on the stone refused it.

The simple process of early lithography seems lost when we view the present day gigantic offset presses with their spinning metal cylinders, carrying ink, water and paper, some of them with speeds of 12,000 revolutions per hour.

Other requirements:
Type size and style . . . . 10-point De Vinne
Pica width to be set . . . . 17 picas
Characters per pica . . . . 2.7 cpp

Let us simplify solving this problem by setting up a simple form so that we can easily follow the steps required to determine the number of output lines we can expect.

Lines in manuscript	19
	x
Average characters per manuscript line	65
	=
Characters in manuscript	1,235
Type: De Vinne, Characters per pica	2.7
	x
Type line width in picas	17
	=
Characters in one line	45.9

$$45.9 \overline{)1235.0} = 26.9 \text{ Lines}$$

We can usually work within a tolerance of a few lines for most printing jobs. After we determine the number of lines, we may want to decide on the line leading and the paragraph leading for the job in order to fill a given area of space with the type we have selected. A line gauge is placed on the space on the layout to visually note how 26 lines would space if set 10-on-10, 10-on-11, 10-on-12 or whatever other leading between lines and paragraphs we may want to use. After figuring these lines, you may determine that the type could be set in a larger point size to fill the space . . . or you may have discovered that you would require a smaller point size. This is the advantage of determining the number of lines before you spend money having type set, only to find that you wished you had specified differently.

> The present-day process of offset lithography is a highly refined method when compared to its early history as lithography without the offset. It is highly complicated now, but its beginning was simple.
>
> A polished slab of limestone was "the plate", and on this the artist drew his design with a litho grease crayon. The design completed, he sponged the entire stone with an aqueous solution of gum arabic. He then inked the stone with a roller, put down his sheet of paper, pressed it firmly against the stone, and when he peeled it off, his design was reproduced. The gum arabic solution was rejected by the design drawn with the grease crayon, but where there was no crayon, it covered the stone with a wet film. However, with the greasy ink from the roller, the opposite was true. As the roller moved across the stone, the ink was accepted on the design, but the film of gum arabic on the stone refused it.
>
> The simple process of early lithography seems lost when we view the present day gigantic offset presses with their spinning metal cylinders, carrying ink, water and paper, some of them with speeds of 12,000 revolutions per hour.

The square inch method.

Another method of estimating copy fit which is not as accurate as the character count method, but it can be convenient to use for quick estimating, is called the Square Inch Method and the formula is as follows:

To determine the number of typeset words which will fit in one square inch, you can use a previously printed job to get this information or the type style book.

1. Determine the number of words in the manuscript.

2. Determine the number of words of type (to be set) in one square inch.

3. Divide as follows:

$$\frac{\text{Number of words in manuscript}}{\text{Number of words in one sq. inch}} = \frac{\text{Number of square}}{\text{inches job will make}}$$

For example:

$$\frac{\text{40,000 words in manuscript}}{\text{20 words in one square inch}} = \frac{\text{2,000 sq. inches of}}{\text{composition}}$$

To find the number of square inches you merely multiply the length times the width. If the type area is 4" x 5" then the number of square inches would be 20.

Setting type to facilitate easier splicing and correcting

1. Body type looks better with at least one point of leading between lines and the space will allow a cutting area between lines to help prevent damage to type ascenders and descenders. Type set solid, or without leading, will require extra care in cutting and correcting.

2. Set correction type using the same leading specifi-cations as on the original typeset material.

3. Set type without extra leading between paragraphs. Lines of type will be consistent for the entire text. Splicing will be easier because the type, when placed on a grid, will fit to the grid. If space between paragraphs is the equivalent of a typeset line you will also have consistency of vertical spacing. A full line of space between paragraphs may be considered "too much," but it is the style used by a few newspapers to facilitate fast cuts between paragraphs when fitting columns of body type. This suggestion is not intended to overrule any aesthetic commitment you have regarding space between paragraphs, but to suggest a specification which will make splicing and correcting easier.

Copyfitting Wall Chart

Copyfitting aids and devices

In the graphic art marketplace there are sold a variety of copyfitting books, charts, and dials which will assist the compositor to fit type after counting the characters in the manuscript.

The copyfitting wall chart will tell the number of lines of type which will occupy any space from 10 to 36 picas wide. Any typeface can be used because it is only necessary to measure the number of characters per inch by measuring the type with a ruler and locating this number on the wall chart. Next locate the number of typewritten characters in the original manuscript under the heading. "Characters in Manuscript." Move across the chart under the "Pica Width" heading to read the number of lines.

Copyfitting calculators operate in the same manner. By feeding in to the device the characters and type width factor, the number of lines can be read.

8
Proofreading

PROOFREADING
Proofreader's marks

Whenever you proofread your pasteups, always use the proofreader's marks. Don't invent your own special hieroglyphics that you think are better than those adopted and used by the printing industry.

Furthermore, don't worry that someone else doesn't know what the marks mean. It's everybody's responsibility to use the correct marks, and it's everybody's job to understand these marks.

Study the proofreader's marks carefully and memorize them so you can use them unconsciously when proofreading.

Proofreading Responsibility

Often the proofreading responsibility falls on personnel in the pasteup department. You find that you must read the "galleys," make corrections on them, and proofread again on the final pasteup.

Proofreading is a very necessary and important part of the printing business, and there is a great deal of satisfaction in knowing that the printing job is error-free. Printing buyers can get very annoyed at finding lots of typographical errors, and will change printers when they see their copy persistently set full of mistakes.

There are reasons why we must take the proofreading responsibility ourselves rather than place the responsibility on the customer. Very often a customer is not a good proofreader. A buyer may proofread a job and give it a final OK. After the job is printed and it contains errors, everybody feels bad—you and the customer.

It is important that a good relationship exist between printer and customer. A printer must make the printing buyer look good at all times. The printer must proof the material, and check and double check.

The question comes up as to the cost of proofreading. The proofreading cost must be included in the chargeable time for the job in line with the hourly cost rate figure. Good proofreading practices by a printer can put him out ahead of the competition. Furthermore, this service is a good selling point when soliciting for new business.

The mechanics of proofreading

When you have galleys of photocomposition or strike-on composition to proofread against an original manuscript, you may be using the two-person approach to proofreading. One person reads the manuscript to the other who holds the proof composition. This is not a good method.

First, you are using two people. Secondly, the one who is listening can unconsciously tend to relax mentally and miss errors. Furthermore, some symbols are not easy to convey when one person talks to the other.

One person should sit and proofread along with manuscript and photocopy proofs. Read a line, phrase or sentence on the proof and then read it on the manuscript. Proofreading becomes a one-person responsibility. With practice one person can become very proficient at catching those mistakes which will always be with us. It is a matter of concentration and keeping your mind on what you are doing.

Should you change the copy

The question comes up . . . "Should I or can I change the customer's copy?"

The answer to this would be, "Yes, if you absolutely know you are right." When you know a word is misspelled or that a grammatical error is present, you should make these corrections if you know you're right.

Be careful about grammar. It can be tricky, because common usage does not always mean the copy is incorrect.

Knowledge of grammar and spelling is important to us in pasteup so we can better serve our customers.

How do you mark the corrections?

Proofs of photocomposition or from the strike-on composers can be duplicated on a photocopy machine. It is advisable to proofread on these photocopy prints

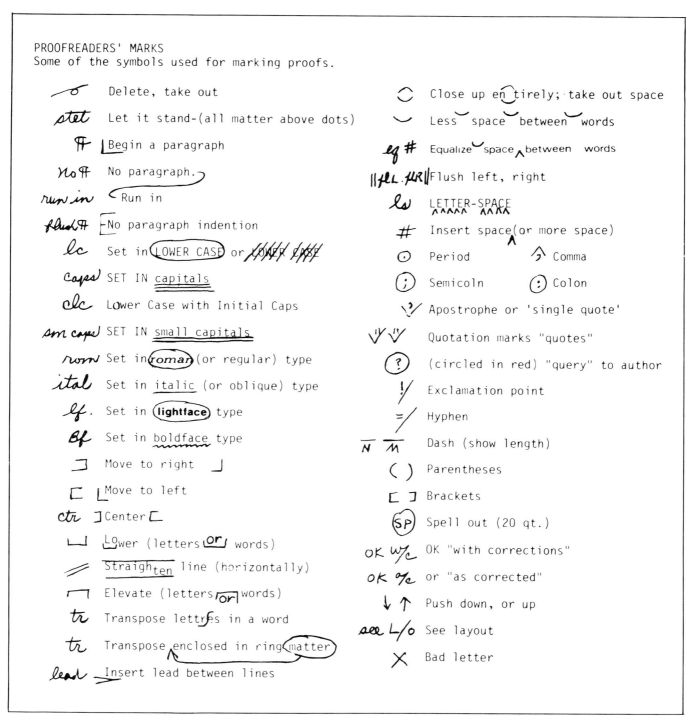

PROOFREADERS' MARKS
Some of the symbols used for marking proofs.

Delete, take out

stet   Let it stand-(all matter above dots)

Begin a paragraph

No ¶   No paragraph.

run in   Run in

flush ¶   No paragraph indention

lc   Set in LOWER CASE or LOWER CASE

Caps   SET IN capitals

clc   Lower Case with Initial Caps

sm caps   SET IN small capitals

rom   Set in roman (or regular) type

ital   Set in italic (or oblique) type

lf.   Set in lightface type

bf   Set in boldface type

Move to right

Move to left

ctr   Center

Lower (letters or words)

Straighten line (horizontally)

Elevate (letters or words)

tr   Transpose lettres in a word

tr   Transpose enclosed in ring matter

lead   Insert lead between lines

Close up entirely; take out space

Less space between words

eq #   Equalize space between words

flL. flR   Flush left, right

ls   LETTER-SPACE

Insert space (or more space)

⊙ Period   Comma

Semicoln   Colon

Apostrophe or 'single quote'

Quotation marks "quotes"

(?) (circled in red) "query" to author

Exclamation point

Hyphen

N M Dash (show length)

( ) Parentheses

[ ] Brackets

(SP) Spell out (20 qt.)

OK w/c   OK "with corrections"

OK o/c   or "as corrected"

↓ ↑ Push down, or up

see L/o   See layout

✗ Bad letter

and mark the corrections on the prints rather than proofread directly on the galley photo output which will be used for pasteup. Check for correctness of type size and leading.

Make the correction marks with a red ballpoint pen or red pencil so they will show good contrast for easy correction.

This is the preferred system of proofreading composition from photocopies, because the output gets less handling.

Marks made on the output can result in problems and a poor appearance on the pasteup. Damage can occur to the type and marks may pick up on camera.

If an occasional necessity requires that proofreading be done directly on the photocomposition, place the proofreader's marks in the margins of the proof to left or right of the column. Use one of the light blue non-reproducing felt tip pens or pencils for this. You can indicate the error with a mark in the line, and then write the proofreading symbol in the white space margin. Most of the light blue marks will trim off after waxing.

After you have pasted up your page, a photocopy of the page should be made for final proofreading and checking to see that all corrections were properly made on the galleys.

Summary

1. Take proofreading responsibility as chargeable time.

2. Proofreading is a one-person job.

3. Change only if you know you are right.

4. Proofread and mark on photocopy prints of the composition output.

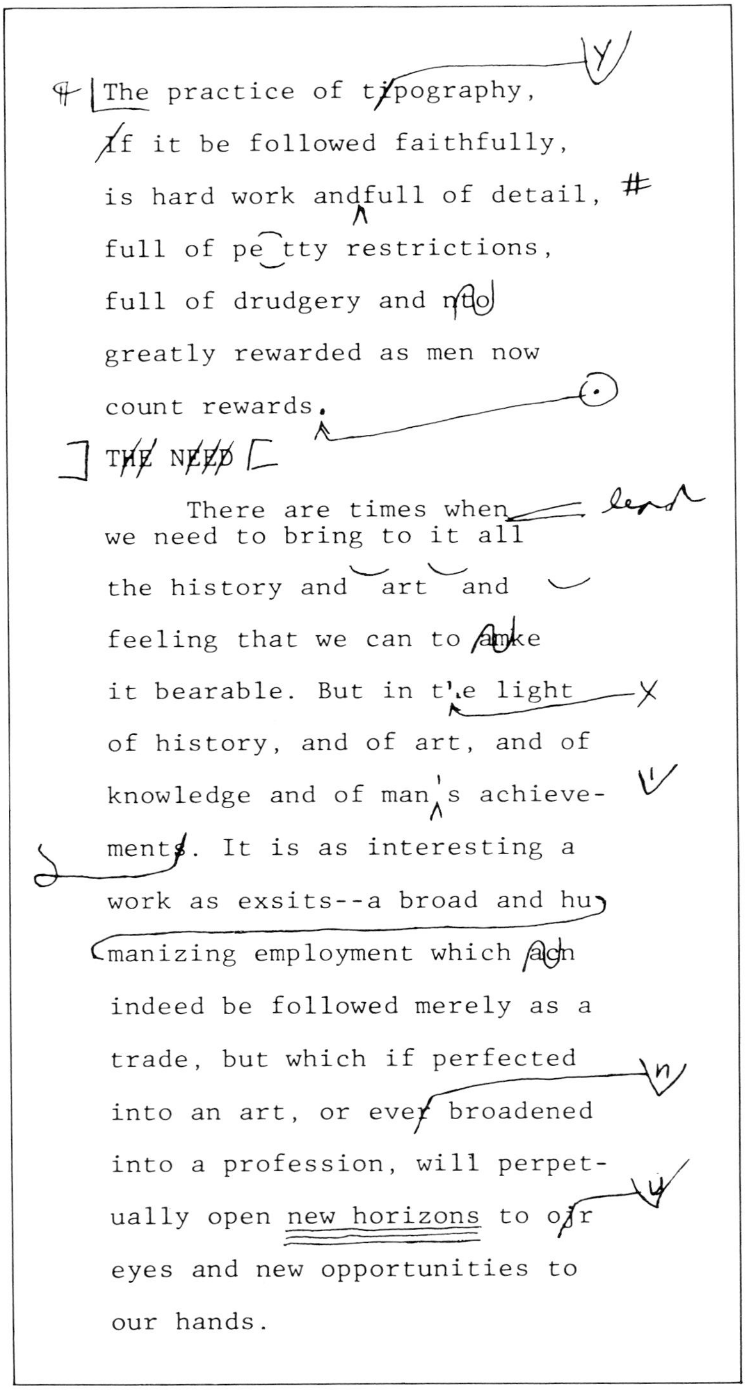

The practice of typography,

If it be followed faithfully,

is hard work andfull of detail,

full of pe tty restrictions,

full of drudgery and not

greatly rewarded as men now

count rewards.

THE NEED

There are times when
we need to bring to it all

the history and art and

feeling that we can to make

it bearable. But in t'.e light

of history, and of art, and of

knowledge and of man's achieve-

ments. It is as interesting a

work as exsits--a broad and hu

manizing employment which may

indeed be followed merely as a

trade, but which if perfected

into an art, or ever broadened

into a profession, will perpet-

ually open new horizons to our

eyes and new opportunities to

our hands.

9
Tools of the Pasteup Trade

TOOLS OF THE PASTEUP TRADE

It has been suggested that you prepare your pasteups at a regular desk unless you must work on extremely large pasteups when you would work at a large drafting table.

All tools of the trade should be kept in the drawers or on top of the desk while being used. You must become efficient in your method of handling tools and materials. Keep your tools in the same place all the time.

There are many tools and materials for the pasteup field, and all are not mentioned here. Nevertheless, those mentioned here are very basic to all pasteup and should be considered useful for any pasteup department.

There is a finesse to handling tools. The more you handle them, the more they become familiar to you and easier to use. It is best not to economize on tools, but get those that can produce a good quality job. For example, don't use single-edged razor blades for your cutting on pasteups. Holding this blade, and trying to cut with it is not desirable. Learn to use the art knife with the sharp angled blade. How can you efficiently cut an overlay on masking film with a razor blade? Use the knife that offers opportunity for skill development.

You can acquire skills with tools using methods not recommended. This occurs when you practice over a long period of time learning with the tools you may have "picked up on your own."

The tools recommended here are recommended for those who start in the business and for those who have been in the business.

PASTEUP BOARDS, SMALL, MEDIUM, AND LARGE

The use of pasteup boards is described under the Board System section of this book. The boards can vary in size depending on the size and type of work produced. You should have a clear plastic board and several wood ones. They are used for general pasteup so that you can prepare pasteups conveniently and use the t-square in both directions and eliminate the need for a triangle.

THIN STEEL BLADE T-SQUARES

The t-square with a perfectly smooth thin steel edge is ideal for squaring up work, cutting waxed elements, and ruling with ballpoint or Rapidograph pens. The regular steel Rapidograph points rule perfectly against the edge. The t-square provides an ideal edge for a combination of uses necessary for pasteup: squaring up, ruling and cutting.

The color patches on the Graham rule are in relative position on each side of zero.

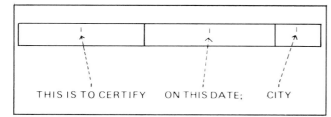

Match the center of the lines or blocks of copy to the center of the area in which it is placed.

THE GRAHAM COLOR-CODED CENTERING RULE

The Graham Color-Coded Centering Rule was designed for pasteup layout to use with the Graham Total System, and to provide the fastest method of centering type blocks, heads and areas on the base sheet.

This rule should be used consistently for all pasteup work so that you become accustomed to it and gain efficiency and speed through its use.

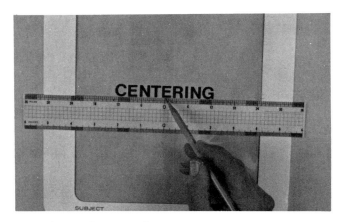

*A pencil dot will indicate the center
of the line of type
when using the Graham
Color Coded Centering Rule.*

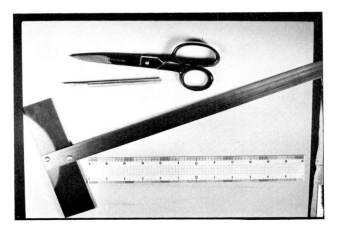

*Pasteup board with scissors, art knife,
t-square and Graham Color Coded Centering rule.*

What are the characteristics of the rule? The color patches are in relative position on each side of zero. Three picas to the left of zero and three picas to the right, the color is blue. The next three picas the color is yellow, then red, then green. When you place the rule under a line of type, merely adjust the color patches and you quickly find the center noting the color patches at the edge of the line of type.

After you've moved the rule to make the color equidistant on each side of the rule corresponding to the line of type, place a pencil dot at the center point of the type line. A good spot to place the dot is just above the line. This dot should be so light it will not photograph.

Use as a plotting device

The centering rule makes an excellent plotting scale to take measurements from an existing layout. By placing the rule on a layout it is only necessary to read the measurements of the elements, then locate these measurements on the border measurement on the pre-printed base sheet. Then draw the guidelines. When the centering rule is placed on the layout, be sure it is exactly in the center of the layout so you will be reading from left or right of zero. Use the pica scale and become familiar with the pica system when using the centering rule.

STANDARD 18″ INCH AND PICA RULE

SCISSORS

A pair of quality scissors is an important asset.

ART KNIFE

This is the ideal knife for pasteup work. One popular brand is the X-acto knife. Use the sharp angled blade for best results.

SWIVEL KNIFE

A knife especially convenient for cutting overlays using the ruby or amber cutting film. The knife blade swivels to make it easier to follow curved lines.

Swivel knife for cutting irregular shapes in peel coat masking film.

TWEEZERS

Pointed tweezers

These tweezers are used to handle small correction lines and words. The tweezers offer better control of the piece while you handle it when placing in position.

Self-closing tweezers

Pointed tweezers which open when you squeeze them, and close when you let loose. These can be used to grip small pieces of copy.

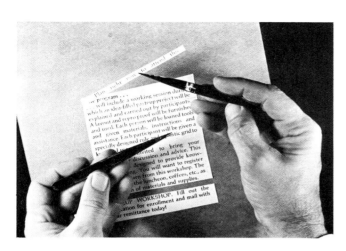

Pointed tweezers and self-closing pointed tweezers.

COMPASS

A compass that will hold a technical fountain-pen point section is helpful for inking circles. Some compasses will hold a swivel knife for cutting on overlay film.

Compass with point section for inking lines.

PLAIN DIVIDER, 5-inch

These flexible dividers are used to take a measurement from one source and transfer to your pasteup. They flex easily, yet hold position snugly while you use them.

SCREW-TYPE DIVIDER

This divider has a thumb screw so it can be opened to the correct distance, and the points will remain securely in position. Suppose you want to mark a series of consistent measurements along the edge of a page to space lines on a form. Merely set the distance on the

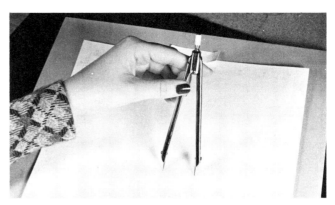

Flexible dividers.

small dividers and "walk" the dividers down the edge of the paper. You can rule lines according to the point marks.

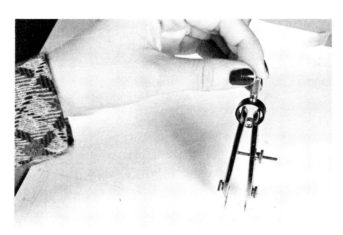

Small screw-type dividers.

PLASTIC TRIANGLE

Both 45- and 30-60 degree triangles are handy for pasteup. Or one of the 8-in. adjustable-type triangles is ideal. You can adjust it to any angle required.

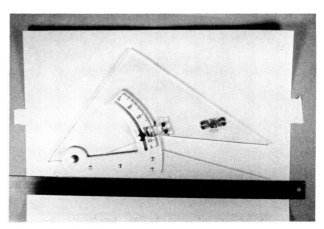

Adjustable triangle.

WHITE PAPER TAPE

This is a versatile, white, flat-back paper tape which has dozens of uses for pasteup work. You can cover up an unwanted spot, tape pasteups together, hinge flaps and hold down base sheets on the boards. Another advantage to this tape is that you can write on its surface. When you hinge a flap, you can write instructions on the tape hinge. This white tape is a substitute for drafting tape for pasteup.

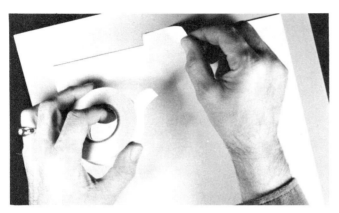

White paper type for pasteup.

WAXER

A waxer of some type should be available for use in pasteup preparation. See the section on waxers for a discussion of waxing and waxers.

Waxer.

WHITE GLUE STICK

A convenient stick of glue for making up dummies and for sticking down some little bits and pieces that require permanent adhesion. You'll find a hundred uses for these sticks in your pasteup work.

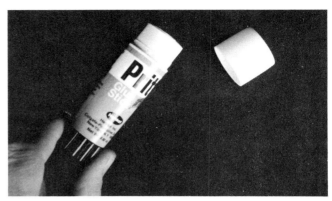

White glue stick.

SPRAY ADHESIVE, REMOVABLE TYPE

Sometimes you need a pressure sensitive coating on the back of proof copy, especially when pasting up on positive film.

Spray adhesive.

RUBBER CEMENT

While not recommended for pasteup work, it is handy to have at the desk for some occasions.

GRAPHIC WHITE

A white paint that can be used to cover blobs, edges, whiting out on photos, etc. A good grade is important so that it covers well. It should be water soluble for pasteup work.

BRUSHES

Art brushes are used for whiting and touching up with black and for general use in pasteup. No. 2 and No. 4 size brushes are excellent for most pasteup retouch work.

Q-TIPS

Use to dip in solutions. Clean off wax from a pasteup surface using rubber cement thinner. You can dip in Windex and clean inked lines from polyester film.

ERASER

A soft rubber eraser of good quality for erasing on pasteup surface is best.

6H PENCIL FOR GUIDELINES PLANNING

A hard 6H pencil will provide sharp light gray non-photo lines when not pressed too hard. It is a good pencil to use for planning jobs on a base sheet. The hard lead stays sharp, makes a thin guideline for close accurate planning.

LIGHT BLUE NON-REPRODUCING PENCIL

For making corrections on pasteups so that marks will not show on camera. They can be used for guideline work, but don't stay sharp and lines are difficult to erase.

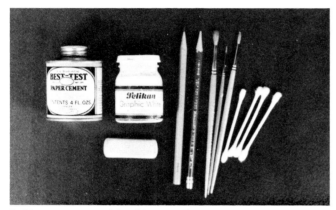

Rubber cement, graphic white, pencil eraser, 6-H pencil, light blue pencil, brushes and Q-tips.

TECHNICAL FOUNTAIN PENS

Several pens should be on hand for ruling jobs. The most popular point section is probably a 00 point. A good variety of points to have for pasteup would include, 00, 0, 1 and 2.

Rapidograph pen with black ink.

BLACK FOUNTAIN PEN INK

Be sure to get the ink designed for the technical fountain pen. Some India inks can cause the pen to clog in a short period of time.

BALLPOINT PEN, FINE BLACK

Good for limited form preparation, ruling trim marks.

Ballpoint pens for ruling. Fine black.

FELT-TIP PEN WITH POINTED TIP, BLACK INK

Handy for marking the edges of reverses that have been pasted down on red areas. You want the edges blackened so they will not pick up as a thin line on camera. The felt-tip pen is ideal for this type of touch-up work.

Felt tip pen (black) to touch up reverses, etc.

TEMPLATES

These templates are available in a variety of shapes and sizes for use with the technical fountain pen. Ellipses, circles and squares are a few of the templates available.

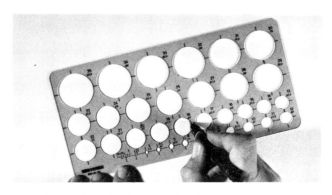

Templates such as the circle template here.

BURNISHING TOOLS

Burnishing roller

A narrow roller makes burnishing waxed proof copy to the base sheet easier than ever. The roller can roll over larger areas of a pasteup for faster burnishing and more secure burnishing of the proof copy. Teflon makes an excellent roller surface material.

Burnishing stick

A small plastic or wood stick necessary for some small burnishing jobs.

Burnishing roller, teflon.

LINE GAUGE

This gauge will tell you exactly how many lines of type will fit into a given area. It has marks indicating all sizes of type and leading.

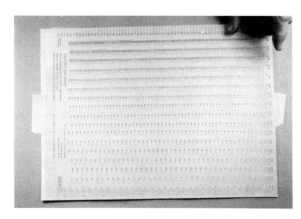

Line gauge.

PROPORTION DIAL

This dial will tell you the measurement of a photograph after it is reduced by the camera. Position dimensions of photo on dial, then turn dial to reduced width size and read the finished height dimension.

Proportion dial.

SCALE-O-GRAPH

This device makes it possible to frame a segment of a photo and enlarge or reduce automatically without computation. See a complete discussion of this device in the layout section.

Scale-O-Graph.

VIEWER-MAGNIFIER

Sometimes called a linen tester, these little 5.0 power magnifiers are important to check dot patterns, align borders, type, etc.

Viewer-magnifier.

MECHANICAL DRAWING INSTRUMENTS

A set of mechanical drawing instruments can be a good investment. Use the mechanical drawing compass and ruling pen to fill with thinned down graphic white to rule white lines as needed on pasteups or for outline work.

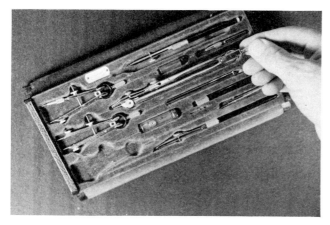

Mechanical drawing instruments.

MATTE FIXATIVE

A light spray of this fixative on cold-type composition proofs will prevent smearing of the carbon impression. Also use for spraying chalk layouts.

Matte fixative protects layouts and strike-on composition.

BUFFER SHEET

This is a sheet of paper or plastic to place over the copy so you can burnish on its surface rather than directly on the proof copy surface. The best material for a buffer sheet is clear Mylar or Cronar or other polyester film. This material resists any wax sticking to its surface and will not scratch. A handy size is an 8 1/2" x 11" sheet. Put a piece of white tape on one corner and keep this side uppermost at all times when you use the sheet.

You will always keep the same side up after continual usage.

Carbon ribbon impression copy may require a buffer sheet unless you use a Teflon roller carefully.

Polyester buffer sheet for use when burnishing.

PLASTIC REGISTER DOWELS

A supply of these handy dowels can be used on pasteups to pin overlays in register, or for the pasteup punch system. Dowels fit snugly in 1/4-in. holes.

Plastic dowels.

PUNCH FOR PIN REGISTER PASTEUP

To further add to the efficiency of pasteup preparation, it is useful on some pasteup preparations to punch base sheets and overlay materials in order to register overlays and prepare for later imposition. A good punch with 1/4" fixed holes to match with a drilled pasteup board is ideal. A four-hole punch is preferred to punch sheets to hold materials in register.

It must have a center line scribed down the center because pin register is based on a center system in the imposition methods taught in this text.

A very desirable punch configuration is 2-3/4″ on center and 7″ on center. Some punches are available with a step-over peg so that an additional series of holes can be punched along the edge of a wide base sheet.

Precision punch with center line.

CUTTING BOARDS

Several sizes and thickness of cutting boards are necessary to make final trims on waxed strips of composition and other waxed pieces. The waxed strips are placed on the cutting board, then using the art knife and a steel or plastic straight edge, the copy can be cut apart and trimmed as required before placement on the pasteup. The cutting board is a backer for cutting, and the best cutting boards are those made of a softer type of plastic material such as vinyl or poly plastic. These surfaces will allow easy pick up of the pieces from the cutting board for placement on the base sheet. The plastic material will help to save on knife blades because the blade tip goes into the surface slightly. Glass surfaces, for example, dull blades quickly.

THICK AND THIN CUTTING BOARDS

It's convenient to have on hand a thick cutting board so that a t-square can be used against the side for a series of parallel cuts for some cutting work. Thinner sheets of plastic are also necessary to use as backers when it's necessary to place strips of waxed copy in orderly sequence for cutting out as the pasteup work progresses on a particular job.

POLY CUTTING BOARD, 3/8″ THICK

The poly material makes an excellent cutting board.

After the board is scored with knife cuts, it can be scrubbed with a steel wool pad or fine grit paper to close up the cut marks.

VINYL CUTTING BOARDS, .010 thickness

These sheets make excellent thin backers.

TRANSPARENT OR TRANSLUCENT CUTTING BOARDS

When cutting on a light table for correction splicing and alignment of overmounting correct lines, the clear type of cutting board is useful. Soft clear plastic materials are available in thin sheets as well as thick sheets as may be required.

OTHER MATERIALS FOR CUTTING BOARDS

While the above mentioned materials are considered the best, other materials used in the past are aluminum sheets, slick card stock, rubber-type surfaces and linoleum floor covering sheets.

Cutting board.

CUTTING GUIDES

When cutting between lines of type material, a 1/8″ thick clear plastic strip is necessary so that the graphic artist can see exactly where the knife will cut. Type may be set without leading and the ascenders and descenders from line to line are nearly touching. These cuts must be carefully executed so type will not be damaged. Plastic straight edges are available clear on one edge and an embedded steel strip on the other side.

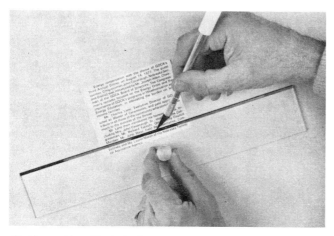

Cutting guide with steel edge.

FILMS FOR PASTEUP

Red Window Vinyl

This red vinyl is good for making windows on pasteups. You can cut the window to size and wax the vinyl to stick down on base sheets.

Ruby and amber cutting film

Ideal for overlay work. You cut through the film coating surface and remove the film. What remains on the base is photographable. While amber is easier to see

Cut-mask film.

through, it is a good idea to have both colors because for multiple overlays it is best to make one on red and the other amber for easier viewing.

Frosted and clear polyester film

This film can be used for overlay work, particularly when you want to ink rule lines over a pasteup. It can also be used for an overlay in combination with the self-adhesive red masking film which will adhere to its surface.

Red blockout film

This is a transparent red self-adhesive film which can be placed on a pasteup, and cut with a knife. Place on pasteup and cut to render an area photographable. The red photographs the same as black. You get clean, sharp edges with this material. A substitute for painting on the pasteup with black ink.

TRIMMERS

A good trimmer is essential for production pasteup work. The trimmer is used to trim off the excess paper along the sides of composition strips. Therefore, trimming is accomplished quickly and accurately and consistently before waxing. For high production in the newspaper field, high speed motorized trimmers are used to trim both edges of composition strips swiftly and accurately.

Many prep departments will find the wheel-type trimmer safe and convenient. The cutting wheel quickly cuts the excess paper while the strip is held in position. This trimmer is available with an edgelight accessory so that light will transmit along the paper edge to view the trim. This light can be useful when it may become necessary to trim copy face down in the event copy is trimmed after it is waxed on the back.

Another trimmer is the Safe-Trim which has a cutting blade at the edge of a hinged board. By placing copy under the blade and pushing on the board, the copy is cut exactly where positioned. Torsion springs

Cutting wheel trimmer.

return the board to its original position. This device is like having a giant pair of scissors on top of a desk. It's available 17″ and 34″ wide.

These two trimmers, while excellent for trimming paper strips, are used extensively to trim overlay films of all types to sizes needed for various pasteup uses.

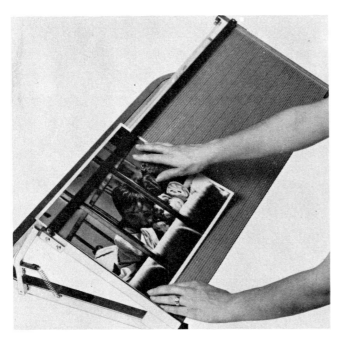

The Safe-Trim trimmer.

Portable light box unit.

TRACING PAD

A 14″ x 17″ or larger tissue pad will provide sheets to hinge over pasteups. Also use for tracing, layout work, planning and placing over pasteups to keep them clean.

LIGHT TABLE

A light table such as one of the desk top models is ideal for handy access when a light source is necessary.

GRID

A clear plastic pica grid is necessary to use to tie in with the system using pre-printed base sheets.

Clear grid.

GRID PLANNING PAPER

This is the grid paper that ties in with your base sheets. It has pica squares. It is used for planning jobs prior to pasteup to make the final pasteup work go faster.

Assorted base sheets and grid planning paper.

PASTEUP BASE SHEETS

Composition and ruling paper

A high-quality, dull-coated enamel paper stock is especially good for ruling and composition. You can rule with technical pens and ink on this surface and can compose on it with carbon ribbon typewriter or composer. It is a multi-purpose paper stock for a variety of jobs involving ruling and composition.

110 lb. index

A good grade of 110-lb. white index is good for general pasteup of book pages, etc. The waxed proofs stick well to its surface and it's not too expensive and is a tough light weight card stock.

Mirror finish

Jobs that require a better quality base sheet can be pasted up on Kromekote, Lusterkote or Mead Mark I card stocks in the 65 lb. weight. You can ink on this surface extremely well. There is a bit more ability to slide your waxed proof copy but this can be an advantage. Proper burnishing will cause the copy to stick tightly to the surface.

The surface of this mirror finished stock stays clean with repeated handling due to its slick surface.

Paper

Regular sheets of 70-lb. white offset paper can be used for base sheets when the cost of the paper is a factor and when you want the lighter weight to use over a light table. For newspaper work where pasteups are short-lived, a paper base sheet is generally used.

LIQUIDS

A small jar of each of the following products will be helpful and make your work easier.

Rubber cement thinner

Probably the most useful solvent in pasteup. Use for cleaning wax from tools. You can remove a waxed-down proof from a base sheet with this thinner. Squirt a little on the edge of the waxed-down proof and as you pull it off add more thinner to dissolve wax. You can also squirt thinner on the back of the base sheet and it will soak through to release waxed-down proof copy. Useful to clean wax from the top roller of the waxer.

Ammonia

Use to clean technical pens. Keep small jar and partly fill with ammonia and soak pen parts in jar to dissolve ink. A bit of ammonia in the bottom of a small jar will dissolve ink from the tip of a non-working pen. Let point soak in the ammonia for a few moments . . . shake and start to use.

Liquid eraser

Use as ink remover with Q-tip to dissolve ink on acetate overlays. Windex can be substituted to clean off ink.

Water

A jar of water is needed to clean brushes and to use with the water-soluble graphic white.

BORDER TAPES

An assortment of border tapes should be available for solid and pattern designs to use for borders, column rules, etc.

REGISTER MARKS

A sheet of register marks on clear pressure-sensitive film is needed to position on pasteups and on overlays to make it easy for the stripper to position negatives in registration with the overlay.

10
Sticking Proofs to the Base Sheet

1. **Waxer and waxing**
   The mechanical waxer
   The hand waxer
   Tips on waxing and waxers
   1. **Wax bleeds through newsprint**
   2. **Electric timers useful**
   3. **Making waxed proofs adhere to the base sheet**
   4. **Removing waxed proofs from the base sheet**
2. **Glue stick**
3. **Pressure sensitive coaters**
   The Adheser
   Spray adhesive
4. **Tape**
5. **Rubber cement**

STICKING PROOF COPY TO THE BASE SHEET

Copy must be fastened to a base sheet by using some adhesive that will do a good job of holding, yet give us the opportunity to reposition the copy if necessary and allow "slidability." For many years, rubber cement was the adhesive used for pasteup. Today, wax coaters provide us with a method of adhering copy quickly and efficiently, and the results are cleaner pasteups which result in negatives free of specs and dirty edges.

Let's examine various products that provide us with adhesive methods for pasteup, because there can be advantages to each of these adhesives for pasteup applications.

Waxers and waxing

The use of wax as a pasteup adhesive has made pasteup production faster, cleaner, easier and more economical. A proof is run through the waxer to receive a coating of wax on the back. This proof will not stick to a surface unless burnished down, therefore handling this waxed sheet is very convenient.

A bit of proof material can be burnished down on a base sheet, but can be removed and repositioned if desired. It has excellent longevity. The author has had waxed pasteups dating back to 1959, and the elements can be lifted and repositioned with the same wax coating! Wax is very clean. There is no need for cleanup work.

The Mechanical Waxer

Motorized mechanical waxing machines are designed to put a coating of wax on the back of proof copy. This wax coated proof, when properly burnished, will adhere tightly to a base sheet.

The wax coater sits on a table. It holds a reservoir of melted wax controlled by a thermostat. This liquid is conveyed to a roller when the switch is turned on to rotate the rollers. When you allow a sheet of proof copy to run through the machine, the roller coats the back of the copy with either a striped coating or complete surface coating. Some machines are available with floor switches so that you can start the unit by stepping on a foot pedal.

The advantages of this type of mechanical waxer are speed and convenience. You turn on the switch, run the proofs through the machine. The wax coating on the paper stays semi-hard, and can be handled. It will not stick to a surface until burnished. This is one of the convenient features of wax. It does not require a sheet of release paper against the wax coating. The waxed proofs can be placed on cutting boards ready for trimming. Your proofs go through the mechanical waxer in seconds, and you are ready to use them immediately.

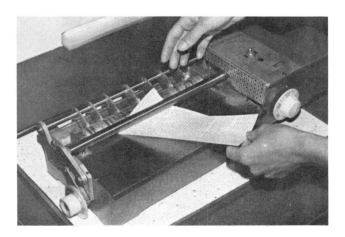

Motorized mechanical waxing machine.

These mechanical waxers will sell for $228.00 and up. As for the wax, be sure to use that which is recommended by the manufacturer to achieve best results and prevent mechanical problems. Wax sells for around $2.00 per pound.

A few popular brands of mechanical waxers include: Artwaxer, Daige, Shaefer, Multigraph, Potdevin, Challenge and Goodkin.

The Hand Waxer

If your pasteup work is rather limited, yet you want to use wax for adhesion, you can purchase an inexpensive, yet very satisfactory hand waxer called the Lectro-Stik. With this convenient unit you can roll a coating of wax 1 1/2-in. wide on the back of proof copy. The device plugs into an electrical outlet and can remain plugged in permanently.

Some shops will have a hand waxer in addition to the mechanical waxer so the graphic artist can use it at his own desk.

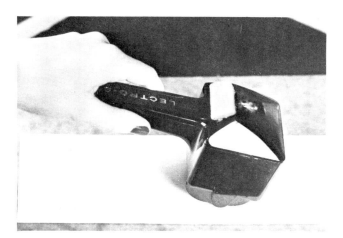

Lectro-stik Hand waxer.

Tips on Waxing and Waxers

WAX BLEEDS THROUGH NEWSPRINT. Have you waxed thin paper through your mechanical waxer? It might be a phone book ad, news clipping or tissue sheet. Did the wax bleed through the paper? The bleed-through was caused by the wax temperature. Wax that is too hot will bleed through thin paper. Keep the temperature adjusted as low as possible so the wax temperature is just above its melting point (about 150°).

A blank sheet of paper can be waxed on both sides and the thin paper copy placed on this double-coated paper. This eliminates the need to run the original piece through the wax coater.

ELECTRIC TIMERS USEFUL. Very often users of equipment do not like to keep electrical equipment in the "on" position regularly. In this instance, you can purchase an inexpensive timer device from any department store. Set the timer to turn on and off at the desired times, and you'll have your waxer or other equipment requiring "warm-up" ready to go when you arrive at work.

MAKING WAXED PROOF COPY ADHERE TO THE BASE SHEET. A tight bond of the elements on the pasteup base sheet is most important to save time at the opaque table. Curled copy can cause shadows which show up on film.

Never add anything to the wax in your machine to attempt to get better adhesion. Use only the brands of waxes recommended by the manufacturer of the waxer you own. Waxed proofs will adhere securely to a base sheet with proper burnishing. Burnishing should be accomplished with one of the burnishing tools available for pasteup. These tools consist of the following:

Burnishing stick or bone.

There are plastic, bone and hardwood sticks with beveled edges so that you can rub on the face of a wax-coated proof. Rub carefully so you'll not damage the proof surface if you use one of these sticks. On carbon impression copy, you'll want to place a buffer sheet on which to burnish. The best buffer sheet on which to burnish is clear polyester film such as Mylar or Cronar. With the clear film you can see through and know exactly where you are burnishing. Put a piece of tape in the corner of this buffer sheet so that you always keep the same side uppermost as you continue to use it.

Burnishing bone.

Burnishing roller.

The best roller to use for burnishing is similar to those used as seam rollers for wallpaper. It is better to burnish with a roller because it is faster and you can get more pressure easier. Use a narrow roller about one inch wide. Teflon rollers are the best, because you can often avoid the use of the buffer sheet on carbon impression copy if you are careful. Teflon resists picking up foreign particles more so than other materials.

Burnishing roller.

Using a buffer sheet

A buffer sheet is placed on top of a waxed pasteup and the burnishing tool is rubbed on top of this sheet.

An ideal buffer sheet material is a sheet of transparent polyester film approximately 8 1/2″ x 11″. It is placed on the pasteup and a burnishing bone or roller can press down pieces of copy on the pasteup to insure good adhesion of waxed proof material.

REMOVING WAXED PROOFS FROM THE BASE SHEET.

Your waxed-down proof may be tightly stuck and your attempt to remove it may cause a layer of the base sheet to tear. There are several methods of softening the wax so that copy can be removed easily.

Heat

Generally you can pull off the waxed-down copy by pulling *slowly* from one edge. If there is too much resistance, try placing the pasteup on the top of the mechanical waxer to allow the heat from the waxer to warm the wax slightly so that removal is easy. If very large sections of waxed-down proofs must be removed, you can use one of the commercial hand-held hair dryers and direct warm air on the face of the pasteup to soften the wax enough to allow removal.

Solvent release agent

An excellent solvent for wax is rubber cement thinner.

The thinner can be applied to the back side of the base sheet, and it will penetrate through the base to allow easy release of the waxed-down element. You can also use a small eye-dropper to apply drops of thinner to the edges of the element and pull off the copy and continue dropping more thinner as you pull away the proof.

When you remove waxed pieces from the base sheet, there is a residue of wax remaining. To remove this residue coating, wipe it with cheesecloth. This material has enough abrasive quality to rub the wax off quickly. Rubber cement thinner can be rubbed on the base sheet as well to clean the base thoroughly.

Glue stick

These little glue sticks should be in every graphic artists desk. It's a white transparent adhesive in stick form, and useful for last minute spot pasteup of page numbers and last minute word changes on the final pasteup. While the adhesive is permanent, you do have time to adjust small bits for positioning before it dries completely. A permanent adhesive for a tiny piece can be desirable for some jobs.

Glue stick for small corrections.

PRESSURE-SENSITIVE COATERS

The Adheser

An adhesive-coating device is available to apply a pressure-sensitive adhesive to the back of proof copy. It is called the Adheser, and it produces a thin film coating. A sheet of release paper is placed on the back of the sheets after they pass through the unit. After copy is positioned on the pasteup it can be lifted without any adhesive remaining on the base sheet. It requires little or no burnishing.

This adhesive coating has proved effective for adhering film to film when preparing film positive assembly. Film positive make up is not widely used except in some specialized applications.

The Adheser.

Spray adhesive

Spray adhesive can be very useful in pasteup work. There are instances where very small bits and pieces need to be positioned on a form. This adhesive can be sprayed on the back of the proof copy to apply a thin coating. The proof can be placed on a sheet of acetate film which will act as a release base. You can cut through the proof to the acetate and lift off the elements and place them on the base sheet.

Be sure that you use a *removable adhesive* when working with these sprays. Check the container before you buy to be certain that you do not get a permanent adhesive. You want the ability to lift off the proof from base and reposition it if necessary.

Tape

Do not use clear tape or other tapes to hold down edges of elements on a pasteup. It is slower, and your elements are only partly held to the base sheet. The tape that is sticky on both sides can be placed on the back of elements for placement on the base. This is not recommended, because it is a very slow method and you lack the ability to move copy after positioning. Tape adhesives can discolor and deteriorate in time. Tapes are not recommended.

Rubber cement

At times rubber cement is handy, but inferior for pasteup work. The edges of your proof copy can pick up dirt, and can require time-consuming clean-up with a "rubber cement pick-up." Many shops have eliminated the use of rubber cement. Rubber cement pasteups kept in storage for years will deteriorate and the copy will fall off. Avoid rubber cement pasteup if you want to develop speed and efficiency. Continually reaching for the brush applicator is sufficient reason not to use it. Even the one-coat type does not offer the same opportunity for development of technique as does wax.

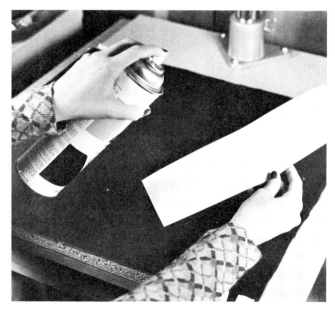

Spray adhesive, removable type.

Edge clean-up of rubber cement.
with rubber cement pickup.

11
Ruling, Tapes, Borders and Corners

RULED LINES FOR PRINTING
TECHNICAL PENS
THE ROUNDED CORNER SITUATION
BORDER TAPES

RULED LINES FOR PRINTING

On many printing jobs, rules are required. Business forms will often require many rules which must be placed accurately in the required positions.

Rules may be designated between columns of a publication, between articles, or even placed on a page to enhance the appearance of the layout.

How do you get rules on the page?

Rules may be placed on a job by using one of the following devices, materials or methods.

1. Strike-on

Rules may be placed on a page by using a strike-on machine such as the typewriter, Composer or Varityper.

2. Exposed

The rules may be exposed on photo-sensitive paper or film on phototypesetting equipment.

3. Scribed

Scribing rules on the film negative using scribing tools so the scribed negative can be exposed on the offset plate for printing.

4. Ink rules

Rules may be inked on paper using a pen especially designed for ruling with liquid ink or with a fine-point ballpoint pen.

5. Border tape

Border tape can be placed on the pasteup to produce ruled lines on a pasteup. Tape is sold in a wide range of line widths to accommodate practically every need.

Scribing lines on film vs. inking lines on the pasteup.

There is a preference to prepare ruled printed material on a pasteup rather than film scribing.

No one would disagree with the perfection achieved by scribing lines on film, but with the advent of photo-direct printing systems only a pasteup can be used. Furthermore, ruling on paper has these advantages:

1. Lower cost of preparation.

2. Alterations can be made on a pasteup, while a scribed negative may require rescribing when alterations are needed.

Film scribing ruled lines

Quality scribing tools are available for use in scribing a variety of line widths on a film negative. These scribers have precision loop-type points that actually cut lines out of any emulsion with a light clean stroke. These lines expose perfectly on a litho plate.

A technique often used by form specialists involves scribing directly on the emulsion side of a sheet of raw undeveloped film on a light table. This film is translucent and can be scribed while positioned over a comprehensive form layout being viewed through the film.

When the scribing is complete, the film is developed in the normal manner to provide a negative of the ruled lines. The exposed film will develop black, and the emulsion you have removed by scribing will be clear. The type matter is prepared on a pasteup to match the ruling and a negative is then exposed in register on the same plate to provide a combination of the rules and type.

Scribe Coat Film

This is a polyester film base with a red or rust coating which can be scribed with a needle point to produce perfect rules to expose directly on an offset plate as would be done with a negative. A scribing point is positioned against a straight edge moving lightly to remove a coating on the scribe coat film. The scribe points can be pointed or ground to any desired bluntness to produce lines of any desired width.

A sheet of scribe coat film is placed on a board, and the form is drawn on the coated surface with a pencil. The lines are scribed on the drawn lines using a scribing point. This point penetrates the coating. Type matter to match the ruling is prepared on a separate sheet in register. A negative produced from this pasteup is then exposed to the plate in register with the scribed sheet. Scribe coat film is a K and E product.

Scribing lines on scribe coat film.

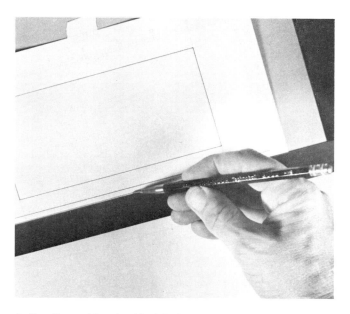

Ruling lines with a fine black ball point pen.

Ballpoints for ruling

Ballpoint pens can be used to produce a good camera-ready ruling job.

Be sure to rule on a high-quality, dull-coated enamel paper or a mirror-finished stock such as Kromekote. This will provide you with a good ruling surface. Using some uncoated papers can cause lint pickup on the point of the ball.

Select a *fine point* black pen, often referred to as a "bookkeeping pen." Be sure the ink in the brand pen you try is a good dense black as some black pens produce grayish lines. A few pens that work well for ruling are the Bic, Technoball and Cross . . . all fine black. Draw the pen against the straight edge with a smooth, even stroke for the entire line length. Do *not* push the pen in a backward motion. Exert enough pressure to produce good lines and maintain this pressure consistently for the entire ruling job.

While the ballpoint produces good lines, you are limited to one line width, while other technical ink ruling pens have points in a variety of line widths for an assortment of line thicknesses.

Don't use the ballpoint for too long a time, because as the ball wears, the point can roll on excessive ink through the "loose" ball. After limited usage in the pasteup department, send the used pens to others to use for general office writing. Keep your ballpoints fresh to produce the best ruling results.

Cleaning ballpoint tips

Sometimes an excess of ink from the ballpoint will show when you start to make a rule.

Before you make a rule, poke the ballpoint into the surface of a piece of tightly woven carpet about 3″ x 3″. This action will clean off the tip so the rule will begin without the little blob.

Ink ruling lines for forms, on pasteups

Anyone preparing pasteups needs to acquire the knack of ruling lines with a technical fountain pen using a dense black ink. These pens are ideal for ruling, available with points of various line widths and carry a generous supply of ink.

RAPIDOGRAPH PEN LINE WIDTHS

PEN NUMBER	COLOR CODING	LINE WIDTH
No. 5x0	pink	micro
No. 4x0	lavender	ultra super fine
No. 3x0	beige	super fine
No. 00	gold ochre	extra extra fine
No. 0	grey	extra fine
No. 1	brown	fine
No. 2	red	medium
No. 2½	light blue	medium broad
No. 3	green	broad
No. 4	orange	extra broad
No. 6	cordovan brown	extra extra broad
No. 7	cerise red	super broad
No. 8	royal blue	ultra super broad
No. 9	emerald green	macro

THE RAPIDOGRAPH TECHNICAL PEN

The Rapidograph pen is a technical fountain pen which contains a plastic cartridge to hold "India-type" ink. This fountain pen is widely used for graphic arts ruling because it has many advantages over the old style drafting pen with the screw-type adjustment.

1. The Rapidograph pen provides uniform lines for forms. You can rule a form one day and later on add more lines, and you know that the line width will be the *same* when you use the same point.

2. You'll not run out of ink in the middle of a rule. Keep the pen more than half full of ink. Remember how aggravating it was to refill the old drafting pen and hope the rules would be exactly the same?

Ink ruling lines with a Rapidograph pen.

Care and use of the pen

The ink in this technical pen flows through a small tube point. This point can become clogged when the pen is not used regularly, and it may take some effort to coax the ink to begin flowing. Here are some tips and ideas that can be helpful in the day-to-day usage of this ruling instrument.

The various elements of the Rapidograph pen.

Use the correct ink

Do not use an ink that is too heavy-bodied, but one that is designed to flow properly in the pen. Some India inks have a heavier consistency and would need to be thinned with distilled water.

Keep the cartridge at least half full.

If the flow of ink is too heavy or if a small drop of ink forms at the tip of the writing tube, you may need to refill the cartridge. The pen functions best if the cartridge is at least half full.

Use the pen regularly

The best way to keep the pen working properly is to use it. If the pen sets a long time without being used, the ink can evaporate in the pen and harden in the point to retard or stop the flow of ink. If you use the pen infrequently, take the pen apart and wash it out with water and leave it stored in your desk without ink in it.

Why you shake the pen to start the flow of ink.

There is a cleaning wire in the tube pen point. When you shake the pen, the wire will help eject carbon particles contained in drawing ink.

If the ink does not start to flow right away, replace the cap on the pen, and tap the cap end on the palm of your hand. Then turn the pen end for end and tap again on the palm. Keep repeating this procedure a few times to get the point opened up. This action moves the weight with the cleaning wire back and forth firmly.

Cleaning procedure

When the pen is not to be used for an extended period of time, remove the ink and thoroughly wash all parts clean, allow to dry, and then reassemble. If the point section, through neglect, contains dried ink residue, thoroughly clean with Rapido-Eze pen cleaner or household ammonia. Then flush out with lukewarm water. An occasional thorough cleaning of the pen is recommended.

Pen parts can be soaked in ammonia to clean them, particularly the point section. Be sure to wash out all of the ammonia with water before filling and using the pen.

Oil the pen parts.

Take the technical pen completely apart and apply a coating of household machine oil inside the ink cartridge and inside and outside of the point section.

The oil coating acts to prevent the ink from adhering to the pen parts. The pen is usable for a longer period of time without the need to clean so often. The ink level in the capsule is always visible because the oil prevents the ink from clinging to the sidewalls of the capsule. When it comes time to clean the pen, it will clean up more easily because of the oil coating.

When oiling the point section, take the weight out, dip it in oil, and use a cotton swab to oil the threads and the inside of the point section including the tube point as well. Exception: Do not take the cleaning wire out of any point smaller than 00 point size. Clean and oil these point sizes intact as the wire is so fine that it is extremely difficult to re-insert the wire.

Oil any new pen before using and oil any older pen after thorough cleaning and drying. Once oiled, fill the pen with ink in the usual manner. A bit of oil may flow from the tip for a moment or two. Practice rule until the ink is flowing smoothly from the tip.

This idea has been tested and proved an excellent aid in maintaining a pen in good working order for a longer period of time.

Kind of paper for ruling

You can rule on practically any kind of paper to obtain an inked ruled line. Soft, porous paper surfaces are not best for ruling. A hard, smooth finish is best for a sharp line and to prevent the point from picking up surface lint.

Rapidograph pen rules will look particularly sharp on mirror-finished stock such as Kromekote or Lusterkote or a dull coated enamel. The advantages of these papers for ruling are many.

1. The ink is not absorbed into the paper but stays on the surface to dry and produce a sharp-edged rule.

2. The pen glides over the surface smoothly to faithfully reproduce ruled lines in the line width according to the point used.

Use a light touch of the pen when using the stainless steel points. The plastic points for the wider line widths may require slight pressure. Too much pressure on the steel points will tend to clog the tip from surface coatings.

A good quality 80-lb. dull-coated enamel provides a surface on which to rule Rapidograph lines and for use in a strike-on machine such as the IBM Composer. Thus you can compose and then ink rule or ink rule and then compose, depending on the particular job you have to prepare. Furthermore the pen rules perfectly on a variety of acetate and polyester film surfaces when required.

To fill the pen.

Unscrew Cap E. Remove clamp C, and separate cartridge D from assembled replacement point and body assembly (A and B). Fill cartridge D from special filler bottle (or dropper stopper) to within 1/4-in. of the lip of cartridge in order to leave sufficient air space for reattachment of assembly. Insert the replacement point and body assembly A and B into the cartridge. Reattach and tighten the screw-clamp C. Replace cap E. Place holder over cartridge and tighten with clockwise motion.

To change to another drawing point section, unscrew holder from the point section counterclockwise. Hold clamp C while removing holder so that clamp is not removed along with holder. Keep point up when separating cartridge from point section to prevent spillage of ink remaining in cartridge. Keep point clean and replace cap immediately after use to prevent ink from drying in point.

Ultrasonic cleaner

For the greatest efficiency in maintaining technical pens, the Ultrasonic Cleaner will clean off dried ink with sound waves which travel into the inner parts of the point section when the nib is emersed into a solution in the Ultrasonic unit.

Humidified Revolving Selector

A plastic unit contains the point sections superbly organized. It provides safe and humidified storage for open pens which are always ready for use even after work interruptions. A liquid humectant is poured on a plastic sponge in the base of the unit to keep moisture in the covered humidor so pens will not dry out.

The Humidified Revolving Selector to contain pens and keep them working for long periods because of the humidified conditioning.

E   A   B   C   D

THE ROUNDED-CORNER SITUATION

A form, a publication page or any page of printed literature can often be enhanced with a border which has four rounded corners.

There is a quick easy method of producing rounded corners without skill, yet render them perfect.

First draw the straight border ruled lines of the outside border. Use a technical pen such as the Rapidograph with the point size you want to use to obtain the boldness or lightness you desire. After the border is ruled, remove the point section of the pen and place it in a compass which will accommodate the point section. Ink a circle which has the circumference to obtain the degree of corner curvature you desire. A circle template is also convenient to use for drawing circles with the Rapidograph pen.

Wax coat the circle on the back and cut into four equal parts. Burnish down a quadrant of circle to exactly match to border lines. Carefully performed at each of the four corners, this technique will produce precise borders with rounded corners which are absolutely indetectable where the tangent meets the straight line.

The fact that you have used the same pen point to produce the border as you used to draw the circle, means the exact same line width will be produced all around the border. This method is fast, accurate and requires no whiting-out.

This technique is a better method than trying to use a compass to draw arcs at each corner and then try to connect the edges of the circle with a ruled line. Remember to keep your pasteup clean and use a lighter weight stock for the circle, such as 80-lb. dull-coated enamel, so that you are not pasting down excessive stock thickness

Applying a corner quadrant to form a perfect rounded corner.

which may cause the possibility of a shadow pickup on the negative.

When you cut out the circle's quadrants as illustrated by the dotted lines, be certain to cut squarely. Do not trim close to the circumference of the circle. You want the extra paper at the edge of the quadrant to cover the corner lines you originally drew.

Different circle diameters produce different corner curvatures. What size circle you will use for your corner is determined by your own artistic evaluation.

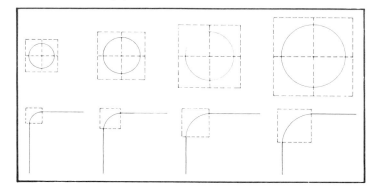

Note how neatly the same circle corner method will apply to those situations where you need to make those little angle marks on forms to designate where to type an address to show through a window in an envelope.

Merely draw a square or use a square from a sheet of acetate sorts and cut into four quadrants. This is much easier than trying to draw the perfect angles to get each one exact.

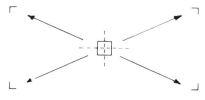

By blacking the outer edges of the quadrant, and cutting out our circle we can come up with other interesting corner variations.

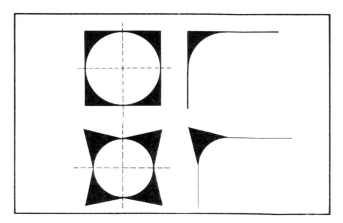

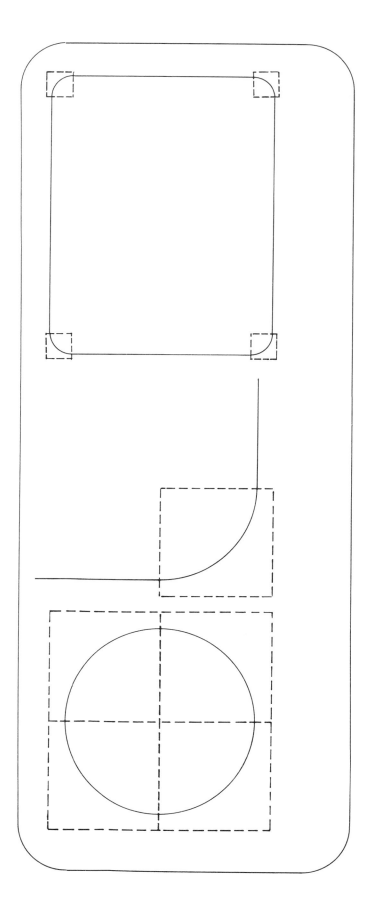

A solid circle when cut into quadrants produces a reverse corner. By putting down a square patch of red masking film, then placing a reverse quadrant at each corner, you will produce a perfect reverse rounded corner. Very handy for brochure preparation and overlay production when these reverse corners are required.

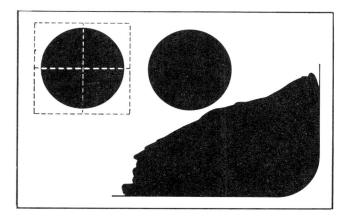

By drawing two circles in juxtaposition and cutting the areas shown on the dotted lines we produce an interesting corner quickly and easily. Additional embellishments can be added such as the wedge illustrated.

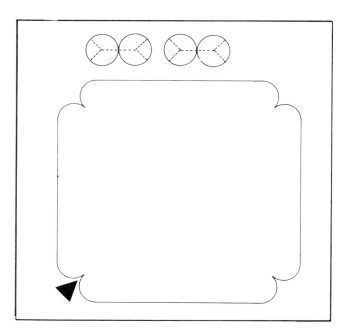

Inverted rounded corners are easily produced by allowing the circle quadrant to *cover* the corner rule. Trim away the small wedges as illustrated with the dashed line above. Flick away these little wedge pieces and you'll have perfectly aligned inverted corners produced mechanically.

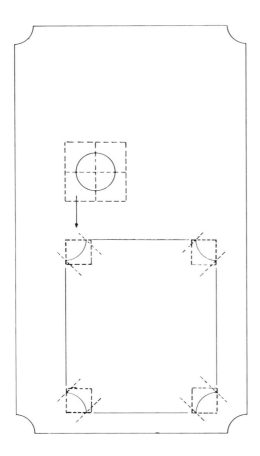

Other variations or additions to this inverted corner technique can add interest to the border design. The border tape bullets positioned in the corner areas can add weight to corners.

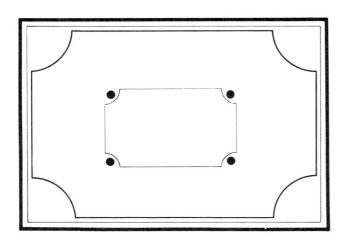

BORDER TAPES

Pressure-sensitive border tapes are sold in rolls in various widths and designs.

These tapes are time-savers and will enhance printed matter particularly for ads in magazines and newspapers.

Applying border tape.

First blue-line the area to be bordered. Pull off a length of tape longer than required and hold taut with fingers of each hand. Do not stretch the tape, but place it down on the guideline, and with your fingers lightly rub the tape so it will adhere in position. Allow the corners to overlap. Using the art knife, cut a 45-degree angle at the corner and remove the over-hanging pieces, so that the corner forms a neat mitre as in a picture frame corner.

An excellent knife blade to use for cutting the 45-degree angle is the rounded-type knife blade, because you can rock the rounded edge of the blade at the corner, instead of drawing a blade across the tape to disturb your alignment. Keep a rounded-blade knife at your desk if you prepare a larger volume of border work with tape.

This 45-degree technique works well with all of the solid tapes and the overlapping patterns. If tapes have broken patterns, such as dots and stars, the tape can be placed with the design running from the corner without the need to overlap for the mitred corner technique.

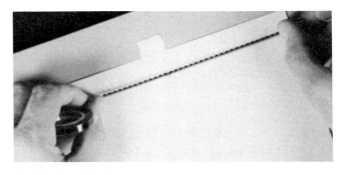

Application of border tape.

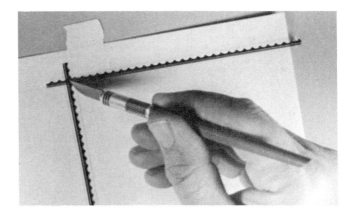

Angle cutting the corner to produce a mitred corner.

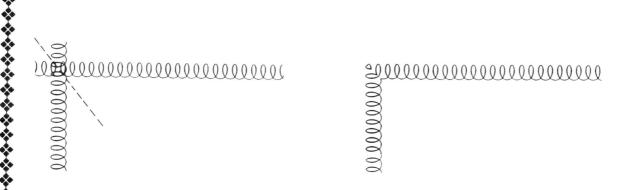

Several different border tapes are shown with the corner overlap, then after cutting at a 45-degree angle and the excess tape removed, neat, mitred corners result.

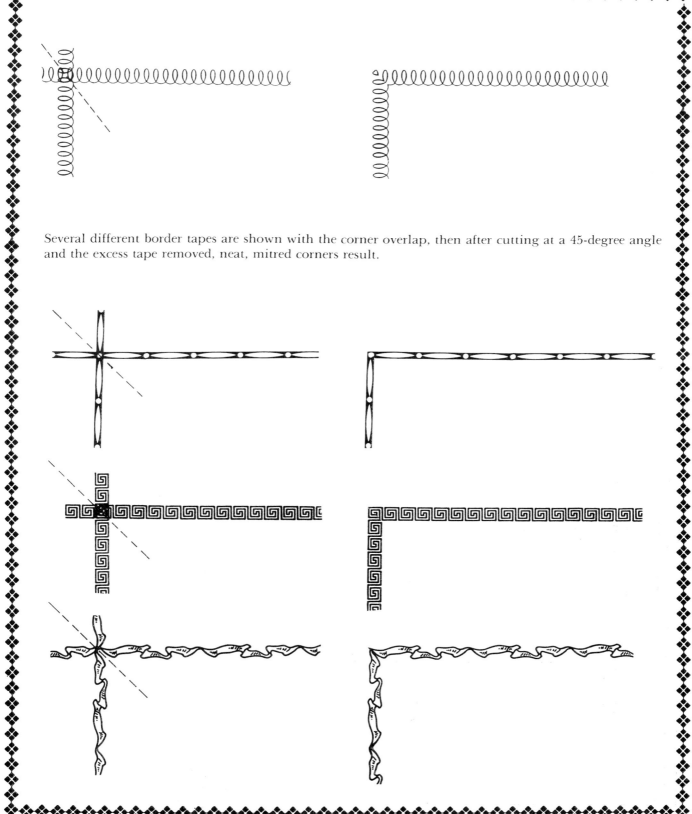

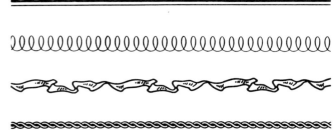

Some border tapes are made up of separate individual designs printed closely together to form a continuous repeated element.

Other tapes connect continuous designs or variations of rules. These designs lend themselves to the mitred corner technique.

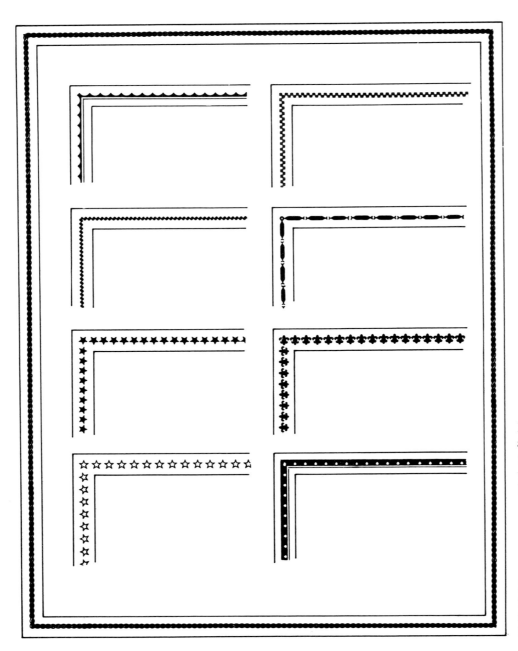

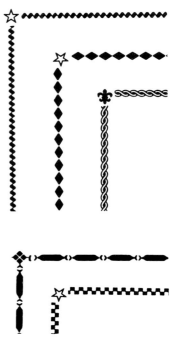

By combining both tape patterns and using an individual tape element in the corner, we can produce attractive border arrangements.

Border tapes can be combined with tape or inked solid ruled lines to produce attractive heavier border designs.

12
Cropping and Proportion

Cropping Photos
Understanding Proportion
Proportion Aids

The reduced size of the halftone.

CROPPING PHOTOS

Crop your photographs to use only the main point of interest in the picture. The only exception would be the necessity to use more area of the photo to fill a space on a publication page due to layout and type fitting adjustments.

UNDERSTANDING PROPORTION

To understand proportion think of a perfect square that you want to reduce. When the perfect square is placed in the camera copyboard and the camera set to reduce, the width of the square will be precisely the same as the height. A photograph 8" x 8" if reduced 50 percent will result in a finished size 4" x 4".

If you have a page of copy 17" x 22" and want to reduce it 50 percent, the final reduced size will be 8 1/2" x 11". Those new to proportioning work will often think that a 50 percent reduction of a 17" x 22" sheet will result in 11" x 17".

PROPORTION AIDS
The tissue overlay diagonal method

Hinge a sheet of tissue over a photograph. With a *soft* lead pencil or felt tip pen, draw an outline on the tissue of the picture area that you want to use. Draw a diagonal line from the lower left to upper right corner (B) of this area (C). Measure from the left of the box and mark on the base line the distance of the width of the final size (D). At this point draw a vertical line (E). The height of the vertical line from the base is the height of the final size photo (F). Photos can be enlarged or reduced, and the proportion is the same.

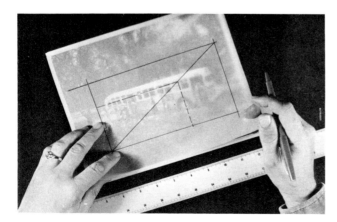

A tissue over the photograph.

The proportion dial

The proportion dial is a device which quickly determines the final size of photographs or art.

To determine the proportion using the dial, set two dimensions of original opposite each other. Read any two dimensions that are opposite each other as the final proportional height and width.

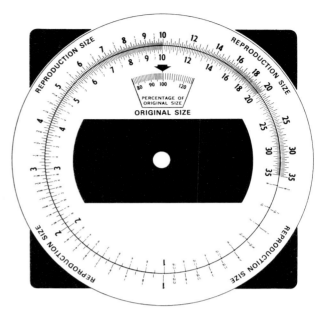

The proportion dial.

The Scale-O-Graph

With this device you can frame the most desirable segment of the art to be reproduced, and once set to a proportion, it will enlarge or reduce automatically without computation.

Place the Scale-O-Graph on a photo, select the most effective composition and block in the proportion.

The plastic arms can slide freely on a diagonal bar and maintain the pre-set proportion. A pencil outline can be drawn on a layout using the Scale-O-Graph opening as a guide, or the outline may be drawn lightly on a red window material or PMT print.

Using the Scale-O-Graph.

13

Pasteup for Halftones

THE HALFTONE TO PRINT A PHOTOGRAPH

To print a photograph on a piece of paper using ink and an offset plate, we must use a dot pattern so that ink will pick up on these little dots and form the various shades of light and dark on the picture.

Why does it work? It is easier to grasp if you consider the construction of a single dot. It appears generally as the drawing on the illustration.

K. W. Beattie, author of an offset camera course explains simply how it works:

The variation in density of each individual dot from light to dark permits the transmission of exposure light to vary with the density of the original photo. For example, the amount of light reflected from the man's white shirt collar would be about the maximum amount of light for a portrait print. Properly exposed, the halftone would only show an intermittent dot in that white area. But in the other areas of the picture which reflected varying degrees less, the amount of light

acting on the film after passing through the screen would create dots of smaller sizes simply because they had been "underexposed" as it were. The screen ruling provides so many dots (17,689 to the square inch for 133-line screens) each is exposed in proportion to the density of the original photograph. The result is a HALF tone or an optical illusion which the eye accommodates and accepts as a reasonable likeness of the original. It is an illusion as much as the motion in the movies or the scan lines of the TV screen.

Halftone screens can be very coarse such as 65-line generally used by some newspapers: other popular screens are 85-, 100- 120- and 133-line screen. The finer the screen, the closer the dots are to each other to give a greater density to the halftone reproduction. Screen selection would depend on type of press, paper, skills of the camera personnel and press operators.

Coarse dot halftone.

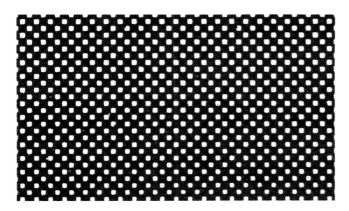

Enlargement of round dot screen.

CARE OF PHOTOGRAPHS

Crop marks should be drawn in the white perimeter area of a photograph using a red grease pencil. Wood encased pencils used for projection marking can be used. The marks rub off when re-cropping is neccessary or unblemished photos must be returned to the customer.

Other rules to remember:

Paper clips should never be used on photographs. The emulsion of a print is soft and the mark left by a paper clip can photograph in the litho camera.

Pencil marks on the back of an unmounted photograph make an indentation. If marking is absolutely necessary, use a very soft pencil marking lightly.

Rubber stamps do not ordinarily damage a print. However, the wood portion may get tilted in stamping and the hard edge may emboss a print. Rubber stamp ink does not dry fast and smearing can occur.

Rolling of prints (if absolutely necessary) should be done with the print surface on the outside. If the emulsion does crack slightly it will close up when the print is flattened. Best to avoid this problem by mounting the print and shipping flat.

Mailing without protection is dangerous to prints. Merely marking of "Do Not Fold" is not enough. Prints should be placed between two heavy pieces of cardboard. Some standard mailers are too thin.

Face to face mailing or handling of prints from one department to another should be avoided. Dirt particles may get in between prints and damage not only one print but two at the same time.

Finger prints can cause much damage to a print. Oil from the finger can stay on the print surface and if strong enough can show up on a halftone negative.

Film Halftone

Halftones are exposed on photographic film which is used to contact against the sensitized offset plate for printing. This film halftone is stripped-in on a negative in proper position so that the placement is correct according to the printing plan.

Years ago, halftones were positioned in a base negative by mortising them into place. In other words, the area where the halftone was to be placed, was cut out with a knife, then the halftone negative seated in this open area, and red tape run around the edges. This work was done carefully so that the emulsion side of the negative was flat and smooth. Later it was discovered that a black or red patch or "window" could be placed on a pasteup to produce a clear area on the negative and then a halftone negative on thin-base could merely be edge-taped on the window for exposure to the offset plate.

Other methods of exposing halftones to offset plates include a common practice of cutting out windows in correct position on orange masking paper. This separate stripped-up halftone sheet is exposed to the offset plate separately from the base line negative. This double-burn method would combine the line and halftones on one plate. For this procedure, the pasteup should show an outline of the halftone area, or corner marks. The stripper then knows where the halftone is to be positioned. With this method a pin registration system must be used to assure proper relative registration of the base negative and overlay when exposing on the plate. An advantage to this method: you can have your type extremely close to the picture without fear of distortion caused by the extra thickness on the window method.

Thin-base film halftones on windows of line negative.

THE WINDOW . . . what it does

We know that red photographs the same as black on our film negative. If we put a patch of red on our pasteup, that patch will come up clear on the negative.

This is what we want, because a screened halftone negative can be placed on this window to provide a quick simple method of placing a halftone in position on a negative. The window system using the red vinyl or masking film is practical because of the use of thin-base film for halftones. This thin film adds a small amount of extra thickness to the negative and will not distort copy or type if a few precautions are taken during the pasteup preparation.

Keep type away from the edge of the window

If your captions or type and art elements are nearly touching the window, there can be noticeable distortion

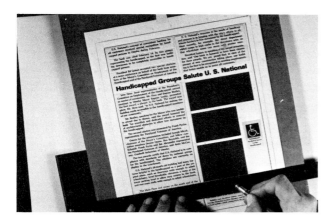

Windows on the pasteup.

of the type due to the buildup of the extra thickness caused by the halftone laid on the emulsion side of the negative. If you *must* get your type almost touching the window, the stripper can make an extra base negative, and strip all the halftones to one base, and use the other negative for the line work. These two negatives would be doubled-burned in register onto the offset plate . . . one for the line and one for the halftones. This system eliminates any double thicknesses. Some strippers cut out openings on orange masking paper and tape the halftones to this mask. This halftone-orange paper piece is exposed to the plate in register with the line film negative. This double exposure combines the line material with the halftones on a single offset plate so that all will print together.

Materials to use to make windows

You could use india ink and paint a black patch to produce a clear window on the negative. The disadvantage of this method is that it takes a lot of time and the coverage of india ink can be spotty and thin in spots and often this patch will have to be painted over several times. Naturally, a poor coverage of black will not produce a perfectly clear window which is essential for the window system.

Red or black paper.

In order to cut costs some use red or black pieces of paper for windows. Extra care must be taken with paper because the edges can nick and be fuzzy.

Red masking/blockout film

This is thin dull finished red plastic film with a pressure sensitive coating on the back. It is transparent and is handy and convenient to use for windows and has dozens of other uses in the pasteup department. For windows, you need only lightly pencil the outline of the halftone on the pasteup, then place the film over

this area, then cut through the film surface, and peel away the outer excess, to leave a sharp red window that will produce a perfectly clear window. This material lends itself to cutting out irregular shaped windows quickly and easily. Red masking film has dozens of uses in pasteup work, and these uses are discussed elsewhere in this book.

Red window vinyl

This red, dull-finished plastic film is .005 thickness. It cuts perfectly with a wheel-type trimmer producing clean sharp edges for perfect windows. This material is desirable for those who do newspaper work or publications requiring a large volume of windows. It is very economical, costing a good deal less than the pressure-sensitive red masking film. It lends itself to the fastest method of producing windows on a pasteup.

Placing red vinyl window on pasteup.

The Rapid Window System

Here is a fast system of scaling your photos and cutting your windows to exact size.

Materials and equipment required

To use this system you will need the following:
1. Sheets of red window vinyl.
2. Trimmer.
3. Scale-O-Graph.
4. Waxer

The Scale-O-Graph is a mechanical device that is used to crop and scale photos.

By using the Scale-O-Graph you can crop and scale your photo in seconds. The Scale-O-Graph is placed on photo and the most effective composition is determined, and the proportion is locked in by tightening the knobs on the corners of the L-shaped arms. Although the knobs have been tightened, the arms will slide apart or together to accurately scale the photo area and maintain the exact proportion.

Scale-O-Graph placed on glossy photograph.

Adjusted and locked in position after cropping.

Marking on the red window vinyl.

Trimming vinyl on the trimmer.

Waxing the piece of red vinyl.

After the Scale-O-Graph is adjusted to the window size, the instrument is placed on a piece of red window vinyl. The edges of the photo area are marked with a pencil directly on the vinyl.

The piece of marked vinyl is placed in the trimmer which has a cutting wheel that is drawn along the line on the vinyl, cutting clearly and accurately. The Edge-light accessory sold with the trimmer is highly recommended as the illumination under the cutting edge provides excellent visibility for accurate cutting and trimming.

After cutting out the window, it is waxed by running through a motor driven waxing machine, or by using a hand waxer.

It is now only necessary to position the waxed red

Positioning red window on pasteup.

vinyl piece on the pasteup, burnish down firmly, and the window has been placed on the pasteup in a jiffy.

This system may take a bit of practice to get used to working with the Scale-O-Graph and trimmer. Once you've performed a few jobs, however, you'll find this procedure a fast, accurate way to handle this window work.

PAPER HALFTONES
Using paper velox halftones on pasteups

In years past it was common procedure to make paper halftones or "velox prints" which were contacted from film halftones. These velox prints were then pasted down on the pasteup along with photo proof material, composition, etc. and the entire page shot as a single line negative. The halftone dots are already on the paper prints and are photographed on the film of the entire page.

What would create a reason to use these paper halftone prints? An example might be a catalog of wearing apparel where you have a multitude of halftone illustrations, many of them outline. Now, suppose you want to have tint areas running up next to the illustrations. It is easy to pasteup the paper halftones and make overlays to register. It makes this tonal achievement next to the halftone much easier and less expensive, and precise registration is assured.

What might be the disadvantage of this method? The paper halftone is made from the film halftone. The print is shot with the pasteup to become a third generation. Often a coarse screen is used such as 100-line or coarser. It takes care and skill to get the necessary exposure and obtain the best results.

The advent of the diffusion-transfer process has tended to replace the process of making velox prints from film, because of the quick direct method of the transfer halftone print.

Diffusion-transfer halftone prints

A fast method of getting a positive screened halftone print is by using a *diffusion-transfer process* in the camera room.

This diffusion process is often called PMT (Photo

85 LINE PMT   **100 LINE PMT**   **133 LINE PMT**

Mechanical Transfer), the trade name for the Kodak material.

A piece of PMT negative material is placed on the image plane of the camera back with a contact screen over it. The photo to be screened may be reduced or enlarged. It is placed in the copy board, exposed, and flashed.

This exposed paper negative material is then inserted in a diffusion-transfer processor with a positive paper

Flashing halftone after exposure.

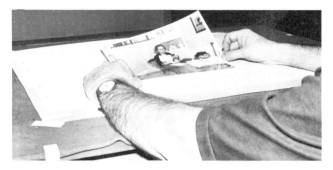

Photograph placed in camera copyboard.

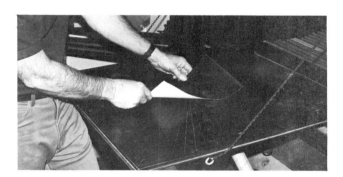

PMT negative material placed on vacuum back of camera.

Negative PMT placed in processor with receiver sheet.

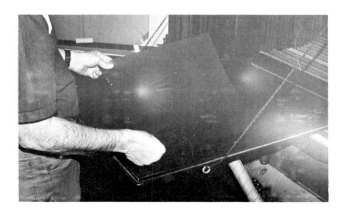

Halftone screen placed over PMT material.

74

The two papers emerge from the processor.

*After 30 seconds, papers peeled apart
and halftone is transferred to receiver sheet.*

receiver sheet. This processor has two slots in it and contains one chemical to process the halftone print. Into the processor the operator inserts the exposed paper negative next to a white receiver sheet. These two sheets feed through the motorized mono-bath processor and travel between rubber squeegee rollers. The two sheets emerge from the processor, the operator waits for 30 seconds, then peels apart the two sheets and the image that was exposed on the negative paper is transferred to the white receiver sheet. This right-reading positive print is semi-dry, ready to trim, wax, and apply to the base sheet.

When the positive print screened halftones are pasted up on an assembled pasteup, the entire job is camera-ready with the pre-screened halftones in position on the pasteup. Now, a single negative can be made of the entire page at one time to eliminate the need to strip in the halftones using film.

Selection of screens for PMT halftones

For general reproduction printing on metal offset plates for reproduction on sheet fed presses, the 100-line screen will produce good results easily. Using finer screens will require more precise control of light and development control of the line shot of the combination halftone and line copy. Halftones for photo-direct usage in quick printing shops should be made with an 85-line screen for best results.

Types of presses and the paper on which a job will be printed can also influence the screen usage.

Poor results of halftones can occur when improper exposures are used to produce PMT halftones. It is wise to learn correct exposures of halftones by keeping a notebook of exposure times along with samples of various photographs. Printers receive photos which may be of low or high contrast, and color prints of varying quality. Camera operators must learn to get the very best halftone possible from the photo submitted.

Advantages of PMT for halftones.

For regular publication work this process is fast and you have many advantages:

1. The PMT screened halftones are pasted up on the page with the copy so all can be shot as a line shot.

2. You can white-out unwanted areas on halftones with Graphic White to eliminate cutting a mask for regular film halftone work. The graphic white is applied directly on the screened print.

3. It is fast. It is quick and simple to make a halftone in a few minutes.

4. It is cheaper. You eliminate the need for a window, and processing of a film halftone negative and stripping of the film halftone into a window area.

5. Proofing of your printing job is simpler. You can use the photocopier to make a copy of the complete page with the prints in position. The customer can proof the copier reproduction for a final OK. No need to go to a negative and strip in the halftones and make a silverprint in order to get a customer's final OK.

The entire procedure of diffusion-transfer print production can be handled on vertical or horizontal cameras. Good maintenance of the processor is most important. Poor processor maintenance, worn out chemicals, improper exposure and storage methods can cause poor results.

How to produce an outline halftone.

*Using red or amber cut-mask film, an overlay is cut
to match the area which is to be outlined.
The coating on the film is peeled from the background area
so the amber patch is over the area to print.
The photo shows a piece of paper under a portion
of the overlay to illustrate how the overlay was cut.
Using this overlay mask, an outline halftone
can be produced on one piece of PMT paper or film.*

*Step 1 Tape photo on copyboard
so it does not move.*

*Step 2. Place a piece of white paper
under overlay mask.*

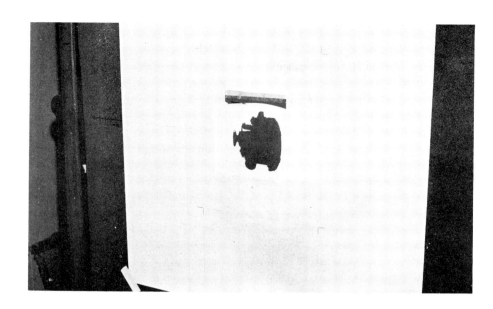

Step 3. Expose on PMT paper (line shot)
to knock out background.
(Remember, you are exposing the background!
Step 4. Lay screen on the PMT negative paper
(Vacuum must remain on during entire proces
so PMT material does not move.)
Step 5. Flip mask out of the way
of photo in copyboard.
Step 6. Expose photo in regular way and flash.

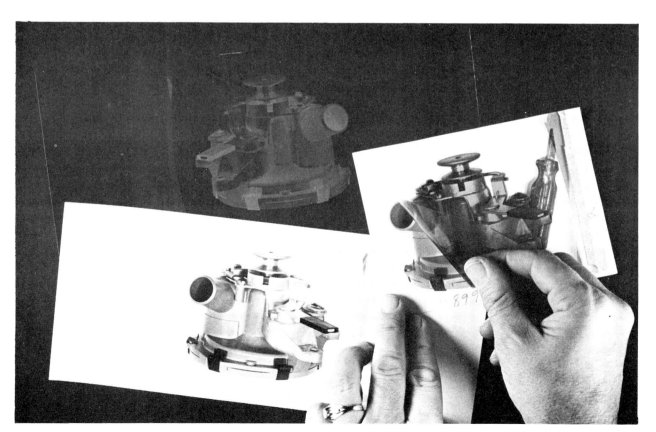

From the PMT negative paper the photo is transferred
in perfect outline form to the receiver paper.

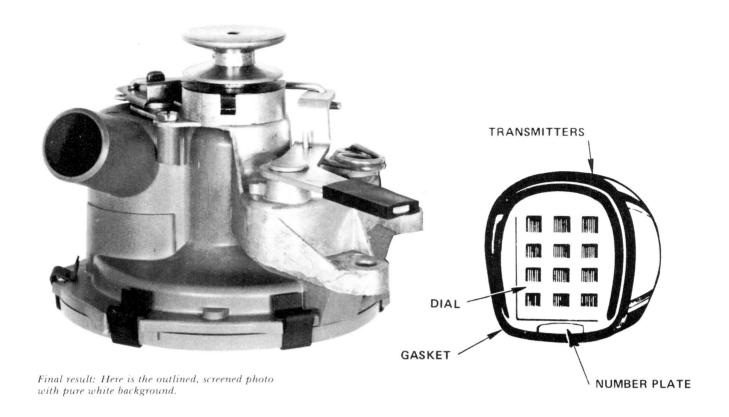

Final result: Here is the outlined, screened photo with pure white background.

CALL OUT PREPARATION

A "call out" is a term used in technical illustrating to call attention to a part or item in an illustration or photograph by indexing it. It is any letter, number, word or group of words used within an illustration or halftone as either identification or information.

Call outs should follow a clockwise order and be located conveniently to the associated items. When space is critical, "flagnotes" can be used to key with a number positioned near the identification point.

Lead lines should be used as necessary from a call out to the item being called out or identified. These lead lines should be short and should not cross other lead lines or exploded parts. If there are multiple lead lines, they should originate from the same point. If at all possible make it a rule that lead lines be straight without angles or bends. It's a good rule to always place an arrowhead tip at the end of the leader line so it just touches the item being identified.

When using call outs on line illustrations such as exploded views of parts and machinery, the entire line work is combined with the call out information using a single line negative for platemaking. However, when preparing a call out in combination with a photograph, the use of a plastic overlay is required to separate the line call out information from the halftone. This overlay prevents screening of type, lead lines and arrows and allows for corrections without disturbing the continuous tone print. Place register marks at margins of the base art or halftone to allow correct placement and registration of call outs, lead lines and arrows.

The halftone can be screened to whatever size required, then the call out overlay can be shot at the same camera setting. By overburning the line negative over the halftone in register, the line information will be combined with the halftone to produce solid line call outs in combination with the halftones.

GRAHAM PERFECT SQUARE CUTTING GUIDE

This device makes it quick and simple to cut 90 degrees on all four sides of a paper halftone print, window or negative.

Angle A is placed on the print to align with the side and bottom crop marks. The bottom and left sides are cut. Angle B is held firmly while angle A is moved to the right to make the right side cut, then A is moved to the top for the final cut. In a minute the four sides are cut 90 degrees. A scale printed in relative measure allows the user to measure the width and height of the cuts as it is used. This is an ideal device for anyone who must cut out large quantities of paper halftones to position on pasteups.

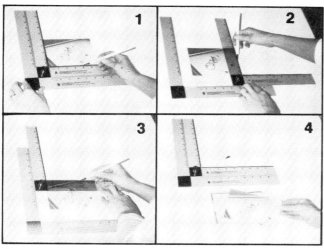

GRAHAM PERFECT SQUARE CUTTING GUIDE

1. Angles positioned to cut bottom and left side.
2. Angle A moved to right measure for right side cut.
3. Angle A moved to top for top cut.
4. Screened print has been cut 90 degrees on all four sides.

Note: The above montage was produced from a 100 line PMT halftone. Numbers were burnished on the screened print with dry transfer.

THE PHOTOMONTAGE

A photomontage is a combination of photos that blend into each other. There are several approaches to preparing camera-ready montages. First method: Cut and wax down the actual continuous tone photos to a base sheet. This grouping would then be screened at one time and stripped into a negative or exposed in register on an offset plate in combination with line copy.

Second method: Screen the individual photos on film. A skilled stripper would lay up the screened negatives on a clear base. He would be required to overlap the halftone negatives and cut through several film layers so that the halftones would fit and meet together according to a planned layout.

Third method: Screen the individual photos using diffusion transfer prints. These screened prints are waxed and positioned on a base sheet and the photomontage photographed along with line copy as a line shot. This method will prove easiest and very practical because the photos are screened individually to get the best screened halftone exposure for each particular photo, particularly when working with photos of assorted contrasts that must be combined together in the montage.

In using the first method, the assorted continuous tone photos must be shot in combination using what may be a compromise exposure to get the best result possible if there are assorted contrasts. Method two has the advantage of individually exposed negatives, but

does require time and skill to assemble the negatives together.

Captions on the montage.

In method one and three, the captions can be placed in position on an overlay to register in position on the photos. Care would be taken to be certain that the type does not appear on dark areas of the photo so type is readable. If type must print over dark areas, the stripper could prepare a film positive to lay over the final screened negative to reverse the type in the halftones. If in method one, you were to paste type on the continuous tone photos, the type strip would be screened. This screened type and paper background behind the type would not be as readable; therefore is not considered the best captioning technique. Flapping and double exposing the captions would be considered the best technique.

In method three, you could paste caption strips directly on the screened prints and there would be no screen in the type, because the entire assembly would be produced as a line shot. Your photos are already screened as PMT diffusion halftone prints. This method is therefore considered very versatile and less costly to prepare.

In method two, the captions should be pasted down on the base sheet in correct position according to a carefully planned layout.

Montage, 133 line film halftone.

14
Cutting Boards, Sharp Knives and Trimmers

CUTTING BOARDS
SHARP BLADES FOR HAND CUTTING
TRIMMERS

CUTTING BOARDS

Cutting photo proofs and composition output for splicing, correcting and trimming should be performed on a cutting board using sharp-bladed art knives. Trying to cut out little pieces, words and lines with scissors is slow, difficult and inaccurate.

The waxed proofs should be placed on a "cutting board" and cut with an art knife and straight edge. This cutting board can be made of a variety of materials. Many materials will work, but some have advantages over others.

Pressboard is handy, stiff material to have at your desk to slip under a sheet to cut and trim. Its surface is very slick and waxed proof copy will release from it rather well. This is the same material used for inexpensive notebook covers, and it's available in several weights. The heavier weight will last longer and you're not apt to cut through it.

Vinyl plastic is a softer plastic material. It's an excellent backer material. Sheets approximately .010 thickness make handy sheets on which to place assorted waxed strips and pieces.

Clear and translucent plastic sheets of the softer plastic variety are also available to use as cutting backers. These are conveniently used on light tables to provide good visibility along with a surface which allows cutting ease when overmounting and splicing.

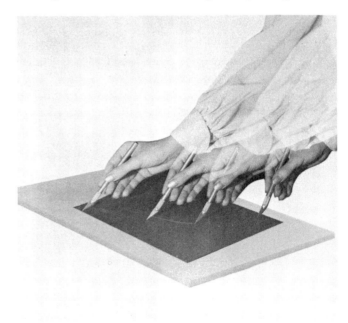

High-molecular plastic cutting board.

Linoleum or vinyl floor covering remnant material is an inexpensive cutting surface material. You can buy a piece of smooth linoleum and cut it into convenient-sized sheets or glue the pieces on squares of 3/8-in. plywood. Waxed material will release easily and the blades will last longer.

Aluminum sheet is a softer metal surface for cutting. An old aluminum offset printing plate for a duplicator-

A waxed proof on a sheet of pressboard.

size press is about the right size. The metal surface will score with usage, but the surface can periodically be burnished with a putty knife to dress the surface.

High molecular plastic material is sold under the trade name, Art Sharp Cutting Board. It is the best cutting surface available for trimming waxed proof copy. The board size is about 11″ x 18″ and 3/8-in. thick, has a polished surface which will not retain wax from proofs. Knife blade life is extended many times with this board. After the surface is full of marks it can be smoothed by scrubbing with an SOS soap pad and warm water, then dried. This action will tend to close the knife wounds. Using this high molecular plastic surface for cutting will tend to prolong the life of your blades and give consistently high quality trims. It is the most expensive cutting board, selling for around $20.00.

SHARP BLADES FOR HAND CUTTING

There are a variety of knife handles on the market which hold replaceable blades. The most popular knife is the X-acto knife with the No. 11 blade. This pointed

The art knife.

blade in a round handle is easily manipulated for close and intricate cutting between lines of type proof material and overlay masking films. Acquiring the finesse in handling this knife will prove a great asset to quickly cut accurately all of the cutting required in pasteup preparation. Some graphic artists use single edge razor blades, but some cutting operations are difficult to execute with the razor blade.

Knife blades can be sharpened on a small Arkansas stone or on No. 400 wet-or-dry grit paper. A few drops of water on the paper or stone will keep the surface clean to assist in producing a sharp edge on the blade very quickly.

Some shops feel that time should not be taken to sharpen blades and will discard dull blades.

TRIMMERS

A trimmer is a necessary device in any pasteup department for trimming excess paper from phototypeset strips or copy typed with strike-on machines.

The accurately trimmed strips are easier to work with when aligning the strips on the base sheet. Using scissors for this procedure is slower and the trims are not as even or straight. The proof material should be trimmed after correcting and splicing and before waxing.

In the newspaper field where photocomposition proofs need to be trimmed on either side of the column

Cutting on the cutting board.

The motorized trimmer, Trimkleen, trims output accurately and quickly.

edge, they need to use a piece of equipment that will trim these proofs quickly and accurately. Therefore, electrically operated devices are used to trim edges from long galley material from print-outs. For example, a device such as the TRIM-KLEEN will trim galley output so that all columns are trimmed exactly alike as close to the type as desired. This edge can be the guide for placement on the pre-printed base sheet for the newspaper or magazine page.

Another device which is hand-operated for trimming is the Genesis Trimmer with Edgelite. It is hand operated by cutting accurately along the edge of the output by moving a sharp wheel which cuts through the paper. The Edgelite accessory casts a light on the paper to show exactly where the blade will travel and cut. It is also possible to trim pieces or strips of copy after the material has been waxed, because the light will show through the proof paper to give identification for the cut. This trimmer is available in four different sizes, and can be used for nearly all pasteup trimming.

The *Safe-Trim* is a table top trimmer which will fast-trim film and paper. Paper is placed on trimmer surface and the type is sighted over the cutting bar, a push, and the blade cuts through paper exactly where positioned. This trimmer is available in two different widths, 34″ and 17″.

The Genesis Trimmer.

The Safe-Trim.

15
Correction Pasteup

HAND CORRECTIONS
Mortising
Over-mounting
TYPESETTING THE CORRECTIONS
CORRECTION STEPS
DEVICES FOR CORRECTIONS
DIFFUSION-TRANSFER PRINT OF
    CORRECTED PROOF COMPOSITION
ERROR-FREE COMPOSITION

HAND CORRECTIONS

Let us examine a procedure for making corrections from start to finish.

You have output of photo composition in a long strip, and you probably have a few bad lines of garbled composition which must be eliminated. You should first eliminate these bad lines of composition, so that you end up with continuous galleys in convenient strips, perhaps 14 inches long (longer if newspaper galleys). Before waxing the proofs, use the splicing method to eliminate these incorrect lines.

You now have some typographical errors within the text matter and corrected words, phrases or lines are generally overmounted on top of the incorrect material. These become hand corrections.

Waxed proof material is cut systematically with the art knife on a cutting board.

Mortising corrections

The technique of mortising a correction on an output galley, involves the actual replacement of a word or line by cutting out the incorrect line and replacing it with the correct line, inserting it so it is flush with the surface of the paper.

This technique must be used when correcting on film positives, and is considered by many to be good correction technique when correcting on paper as well.

Mortising, whether on paper or film, is accomplished by cutting through two layers of material. Using the light table and transparent cutting board, the corrected line is placed over an incorrect line. A knife cuts through both layers. The correct line replaces the incorrect. The galley is turned over and a strip of clear tape is affixed to the back to hold the correction.

There are several reasons to favor the mortise technique. Its use eliminates the possibility of a correction falling off the galley, or slipping at an angle. The second reason is that there is no opportunity for a shadow to cause a hairline to pick up on the negative to require careful opaquing between lines or near words.

Over-mounting

Today with highly efficient lighting systems on camera equipment we can make our corrections by mounting correct words or correct lines over incorrect words and lines. This technique is called over-mounting.

The technique is fast and can result in a clean correction when adhesives other than rubber cement are used. The best time to do correcting is while the strip of output material is in galley form. You are working with a thinner piece of photo or repro paper.

Now you can correct by affixing the correction on the incorrect words by viewing over a light source. By aligning with the aid of light you can quickly get the line positioned generally without need for a t-square by placing the correct line over the old line. The corrections must be made carefully. A grid under the type may be useful to aid in alignment and leading consistency.

TYPESETTING THE CORRECTIONS

A good example of how to save time in pasteup by virtue of good composition can be illustrated in the following example. A variety of words and lines are required for corrections and alterations. How would you set the composition in preparation for cutting and pasting?

Set the output, wax and cut

By setting the words in a continuous line, time is saved because there are fewer cuts to make with the knife blade. The procedure to follow would be to wax the typeset correction output and place this proof output on a cutting board. The knife cuts should be made in the order as numbered in the illustration. There are 16 cuts to make. Had the type been set with one word above the other there would have been a minimum of 26 cuts, and the objective is to keep the number of cuts to an absolute minimum.

Set type correction output in continous lines, then cut between the lines first horizontally to the bottom of the proof. Next make the small vertical cuts required.

CORRECTION STEPS

1. Set corrections
2. Wax
3. Hand cut

TYPESETTING CORRECTION OUTPUT

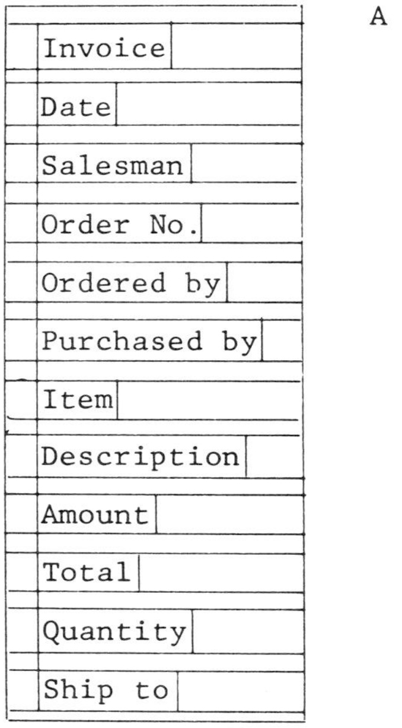

Incorrect method of setting typeset
proof correction output.
This proof requires 37 cuts
as shown by the ruled lines.

A

Invoice
Date
Salesman
Order No.
Ordered by
Purchased by
Item
Description
Amount
Total
Quantity
Ship to

The correct arrangement for
typesetting small pasteup corrections.

Invoice	Date	Salesman	Order No.	Ordered by	Purchased by
Item	Description	Amount	Total	Quantity	Ship to

The cutting should proceed as shown by the ruled lines
and in the order as numbered. Too much space between
lines would require double cutting as in illustration A.
Only 16 cuts are required to cut out the same words
shown in illustration A which would need 37 cuts.

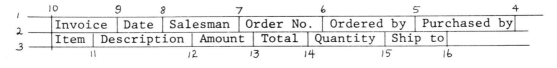

---

4. Splice

5. Position, square, burnish

Set corrections

Set the correction output as discussed previously.

Wax

Wax coat the correction output.

Hand cut

Place correction output on cutting board and cut as outlined previously.

Splice

When the output comes off the photo-composing machine or strike-on composer, there usually will be some lines which may need deleting due to mistakes. The time to cut out these bad lines is when the output is still in galley form and before waxing.

Tape the strip of proof output on the cutting board with white paper tape (see cutting board discussion). Cut out the bad line above and below using a sharp art knife. Now place a piece of paper tape under the section so that you have a sticky side uppermost with a portion exposed below the removed line. Next butt the next good line up flush with the previous good line so that you have a neat splice held together with the white pressure-sensitive tape. A good tape for this purpose is white paper tape, 3/4-in. wide.

Another technique is to tape the strip of composition

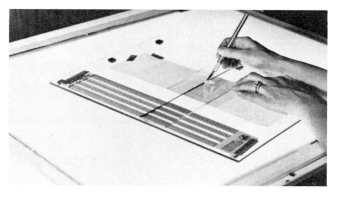

Cutting through a double layer of aligned composition output on a transparent cutting board on the light table.

Positioning the correct type in position.

Securing the composition insert with clear tape.

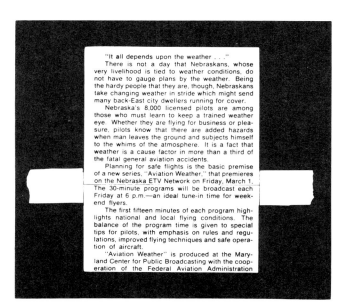

Bad lines are first eliminated from the output strips by the splicing method. White paper tape, sticky side up, connects sections and pieces into convenient galley lengths.

output face down on a clear cutting board on the light table. Then cut and insert added lines in position and tape together using clear or matte tape. A line gauge taped near the edge of the cutting board will aid to position inserted copy in proper leading sequence when using a t-square along the edge of the cutting board; or, a strip of composition or a positive film with matching leading marks may be taped near the edge. Leading marks can be typed on a strip of paper using the IBM composer and striking the hyphen key.

Position, square, burnish
Placement of bits and pieces

The small waxed type elements must be handled by picking them up and placing them in position on the incorrect element on the composition output.

Grids

Grids can be obtained in a variety of increments to simplify type line correction work. For instance, by using a positive grid with 10-point squares and placing a proof strip of 10-point typeset lines over this grid on a light source, the incorrect lines can be cut out and replaced. This replacement can be accomplished accurately by viewing these lines on the grid.

A variety of grids may be necessary to satisfy the variety of point type usage in typesetting and leading variations.

When cutting proofs over a grid you would not cut into the grid, but would place a clear acetate sheet over the grid so that you would not damage the grid.

The transparent cold type line gauge can also provide aid for correct type line alignment when making hand corrections.

Handling bits and pieces

Each element must be lifted up from a cutting board surface after final trimming with a sharp knife. The question is: how do you pick up those little pieces and handle them efficiently?

You may insert the art knife point under a correction piece and lift it from the surface with your finger on top. However, an excellent method of handling small elements is to use a good pointed tweezer. Strips of type, headings and words are easily lifted with tweezers. You have excellent control as the tweezer points grip the bit of proof. The points easily slip under the proof edge to pull up easily, without damage, and with complete control.

If you ever collected stamps you remember that you always picked up your stamps with "stamp tongs." These tongs have flat tips especially good for handling stamps. The pointed-tip tweezer is better for pasteup bits because you need the points to adjust the element into position using the closed tips.

Using tweezers will take some practice, particularly

if you have been using other tools. After a while you'll feel comfortable using them, and "get the hang of it" and will find it faster and easier.

Sharp, pointed tweezers make an excellent tool to pick up waxed elements from the cutting board for placement on the base sheet. With tweezers closed the sharp points can slide the element to adjust it for precise alignment.

The Pick-er-upper tool

Here is a highly recommended tool which will save many hours of correction time.

There are times when very small numbers, boxes, letters, etc. must be placed on a pasteup. A computer card often involves this type of requirement when small agate type bits must be positioned all over the card. With practice, a system can be developed using a pick-up tool made of a plastic handle with a metal edge strip.

Wax must be used with this method, because the wax on the underside of the proof paper will stick to the edge of a metal strip. Small pieces stick to the edge to be positioned on the pasteup. Merely poke down with knife tip and later burnish in position.

The procedure is as follows:

Put a coating of wax on the back of your proof, and place on a cutting board. Cut all elements with an art knife. Push the pick-er-upper against the bottom edge of the line of bits and pieces using a scraping motion, and the type will stick to the metal edge. You can now place the piece in position and push to stick down using knife tip.

You may be "all thumbs" when you try this, but with practice and time, you'll find that you'll develop the technique of handling small bits and strips. It is a very practical and fast technique, particularly for those who prepare computer cards and complicated form pasteup.

The Pick-er-upper tool allows for a quick and easy method to control waxed elements by picking them up and placing them on the pasteup. Push the metal blade against the waxed cut element. Pieces adhere to the edge securely.

The element attached to the blade's edge can be placed in almost exact position before pressing down with tip of knife or pointed tweezers.

Very little adjustment should be required after placement.

The Akukut

The Akukut is a device that holds a single-edge razor blade. It is so constructed to adjust the blade for cut depth of less than a thousandth of an inch. The blade is on the outside surface so that it is in contact with the straight edge used with it.

The Akukut can be used to trim galleys, cut out lines of type, and particularly cutting on pressure sensitive paper because the depth of cut can be adjusted to cut through the top layer of paper, and barely cut into the backing sheet.

This device sells for approximately $18.00.

The Akukut holds a single-edge razor blade, and can be controlled to precise depth of cut. This device is ideal for film cutting or cutting on self-adhesive paper attached to release papers.

Korektorule

The Korektorule is a series of eight, 10-inch long transparent scales which have accurately laid-out, engraved hairlines on the undersurface.

The hairline is aligned with the baseline of the type and an art knife or the Akukut is drawn along the straight edge. The cut falls automatically between the ascenders and descenders of adjacent type lines. For each type size, there are two hairlines. One is used to cut above the type line, the other to cut below the type line.

When cutting with this device, you can then butt your cut lines and retain proper leading in galleys or in made-up pages. The Korektorule eliminates need to eyeball proper cutting distances between lines. These rules are manufactured by Tobias Associates.

The Korektorule set will provide scales so that cutting with the Akukut will indicate exactly where to cut between lines.

The Akutrim Galley Trimmer

The Akutrim is a 24-inch long, pin-mounted, transparent straight-edge scale with a reference line engraved on the undersurface 1-1/2 points from the top long edge. A column of proof composition output is placed under the scale. The right hand edge of the copy is aligned to the reference line. The Akukut cutting device is run along the right hand edge to trim the copy.

This device will trim the sides of galley photo proofs so there will be exactly 1-1/2 picas of white space on either side. It is designed for copy widths of 10, 10-1/2, 11, and 12 pica columns.

The advantage to this unit is that with the 1-1/2 points on each side, the pasteup of the columns is fast. The waxed column can be placed even with a blue-line edge on a base sheet very quickly. This unit is manufactured by Tobias Associates.

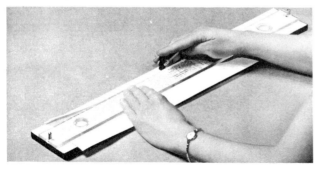

The Akutrim Galley Trimmer allows exact trims along the edges of galleys when used as a straight edge.

Trimak

This device is used to cut out one or more lines of type on film or paper.

It consists of a cutting-wheel device on a platform and is accurate in cutting precisely between lines. The second cut can be made be moving the film or paper so

that the following line can be cut by alignment with a base line.

An alternate technique for making the second cut uses the movable platform which can accurately advance the film or paper from five points up to 36 points. Any width material can be cut up to 10 inches. An adjustable side guide is provided to position the work square to the cutting edge. This unit is particularly good for mortising film positives.

Trimak is manufactured by Tobias Associates.

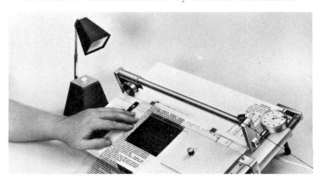

The Trimak is used for film makeup.
A cutting wheel device will cut accurately between lines.

DIFFUSION-TRANSFER PRINT OF CORRECTED PROOF COMPOSITION

At times the corrected output may be full of small paste-in corrections due to alterations, mistakes and machine errors. These galleys can be difficult to work with due to their "fragile" nature. It is best to take this overworked galley and shoot a Diffusion-Transfer print to use for the pasteup proof copy.

Some composition firms will follow this procedure for all their work, so the user will not get a pasted-up proof, but instead, receive a final error-free print copy.

This way more than one print can be made to provide extra copies when required.

ERROR-FREE COMPOSITION

While we have discussed a systematic method of making corrections which has taken for granted that a typeset proof is full of mistakes, we must give emphasis to an important point of keyboard operation.

When keyboarding for output, there is no substitute for error-free composition. This is the ultimate goal for those in our field of composition output preparation. To keyboard the typewritten material without errors is essential, so that we can eliminate the need for additional time-consuming splicing and hand correcting on the photo proof material.

The absolute first consideration in setting composition is to make it error-free. In time, speed will result along with the production of error-free proof output.

16

Graphic White, Graphic Black and Techniques

GRAPHIC WHITE

A graphic artist requires a good quality water-soluble opaque white "paint" in the desk ready for quick usage. A water-soluble white is desirable because it can be thinned with water if necessary and used in a drafting pen. Some typewriter correction fluids require fast drying solvents to thin down.

With the water-soluble white you can rule white lines on photos, or on black patch areas on the pasteup. You can then clean brushes in plain water.

Opaque white is needed primarily to "touch up" the pasteup as may be required. This might include covering up an accidental "blob" or to eliminate words or letters by painting over them using a small art brush.

Dirt and blemishes on the pasteup will pick up on film and cause extra opaquing work by the stripper. The Graphic White can be used to touch up these blemishes so the pasteup is clean. On the other hand, don't overdo this white-out work and spend a lot of time covering every little edge. Cover the obvious photographable blemishes that appear. By looking at the negatives of your pasteups you'll become familiar with what does pick up and what doesn't. You should keep your pasteups very clean while in preparation to avoid time-consuming touch up. There is no substitute for good clean pasteups.

Graphic White may be used to paint out an unwanted area directly on a photo before a film halftone is shot, if you wish to use this method for some photos. The stripper can get good definition to opaque the outline halftone. This procedure is sometimes followed on simple outline work, instead of cutting an overlay mask to eliminate a background photo-mechanically (see overlay section). Whiting out with Graphic White is easy to use on PMT halftone prints when outlining with an artbrush.

GRAPHIC BLACK

Graphic Black is important for the production of black areas on pasteups. Those times when it is easier to "paint" an area on a pasteup rather than place the red masking film on the base sheet and cut out with a knife.

When black is required, it is often desirable to use a "Graphic Black" tempera. It produces a smooth dull-finish opaque application on base sheets and frosted polyester drafting film.

India ink can be used to black areas but may require several applications of the ink to get a solid even black area.

GRAPHIC WHITE USED IN A MECHANICAL DRAFTING PEN

A white rule can be run down the edge of horizontal rules which have been ruled in black ink and extended beyond the final stopping point. This white rule cuts off the stopping point cleanly. This is probably the best method of cutting off the rules, but requires the skill and knack of using the white in the ruling pen. The proper consistency is important so the white will flow properly and still cover to provide a dense white-out.

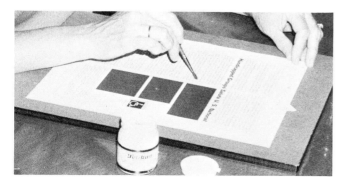

Touching up blemishes on the pasteup can save negative opaquing.

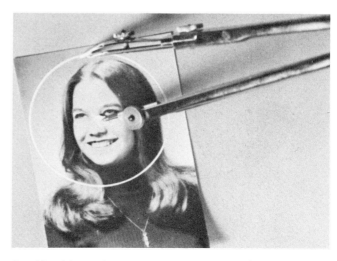

Graphic white can be used in a mechanical drawing pen.

Graphic White can be used in the mechanical drawing compass. Suppose you want to produce a circular halftone. By drawing a white circle on a PMT print you can create a circular PMT halftone. Don't poke the pin of the compass into the PMT directly; instead, place a tiny piece of card stock in the center (hold with wax) and place the pin into the cardboard. Thus you will not damage the dots in the PMT.

BRUSHING TECHNIQUE

It is important that you use the correct technique when painting with Graphic White or Graphic Black.

The correct method is to place the brush *flat*, and let the flat tip draw along the edge of the subject. By putting the brush down *flat*, you can maintain control of the brush tip to make your outlining perfect, even though your hand may be a bit unsteady. A little practice using some old newspaper photo reproductions will give you a chance to learn to outline carefully and obtain precise results.

Some photos look better when they are outlined, particularly if there is a confusing background that conflicts with the main point of interest in the picture. Therefore, learning to use Graphic White skillfully is very important.

The circle gives definition to paint around the edges with graphic white.

Painting around a PMT halftone with graphic white to produce an outline halftone.
(See the overlay mask technique in the halftone section.)

17
Overlays, Tints and Tones

BENDAY SHADING FILM

Benday shading film provides a quick, simple method of placing a tone or shade on an area of an illustration or pasteup.

Benday is screened tone percentages printed on pressure sensitive plastic sheets with a release paper backing.

The advantage of using shading film is that it produces tonal values inexpensively. A map of the United States indicating various degrees of shading to identify areas, is economically prepared as a camera-ready pasteup for production as a line shot. There is a limitation of 85-line screen as the finest screen generally available.

For best results this film must be applied over a smooth, clean surface. Any uneven surface will create objectionable marks on the negative where edges may show up on film. The shading film is applied directly to the pasteup surface, and the entire page is photographed as a line shot.

Furthermore, the customer can see the shading on the pasteup and will know exactly where the shading is to appear and exactly how it will look.

If the surface of a pasteup is bumpy with overlapping bits and pieces, you can make a PMT print of the page to obtain a print in one flat surface. On this print you can then burnish the film benday to lie flat and reproduce satisfactorily.

Applying Benday Shading Film.

Benday shading film applied to line illustration, 85-line, 20 percent.

Applying the Benday

You can have problems with poor application of this shading film.

Do not just plop the piece of benday on the surface of the area to be covered. There are a few important procedures for the application of the film to the surface of the pasteup.

1. Be certain the surface where the benday is to be applied is free of dust and specks.

2. With your art knife, cut out an area of benday from the large sheet you have purchased. This piece should be larger than the area to be covered. Pull it from the surface of the release paper to which it is affixed.

3. Carefully allow one corner of this piece to touch the area on your pasteup. Let the Benday gradually touch the surface as you lightly rub the material with your fingers starting with the corner.

By using this gradual application method, you eliminate the opportunity for air bubbles to form under

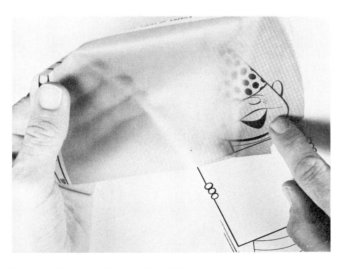

Start application of benday by rubbing at one corner.

After cutting out the area, burnish with bone or roller.

the surface. If by chance an air bubble does occur you can stick a pin in the bubble so the air can escape, then press down the bubble without pulling up the entire sheet and starting over again with your application.

Once the benday is down over the required area, a light burnishing is all that's required to make it stay in position.

WHAT IS AN OVERLAY?

An overlay is a transparent sheet placed over a base pasteup so that additional mechanical art for color, line or halftone material is already separated for the camera.

For example, a base pasteup may be exposed on film, plus an additional negative of the overlay. A plate is made from each negative, and when the job is printed on the press with the proper inks, you have a two-color printing job from the mechanically color-separated pasteup.

WHAT THE OVERLAY CAN DO FOR YOU

Let us examine what an overlay can do, and begin by stating that an overlay can do anything you want it to do. A broad statement, but, a well-cut overlay, combined with knowledgeable camera-stripping, can produce a multitude of final results.

AN OVERLAY FOR TINTS

An overlay with a solid patch over an area of a pasteup can produce a tone area in the patch on the overlay. Merely mark on the flap what percentage of tone you require, and the stripper can position a screened film tint in this area and expose on the plate to result in a tonal effect as you request. The patch on the overlay produces a "window" on the negative. A piece of screened tint film can be laid on this window at the time of exposure on the plate.

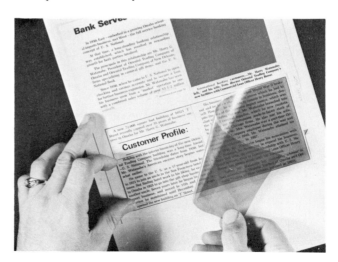

Amber film overlay to produce tint area over pasteup section.

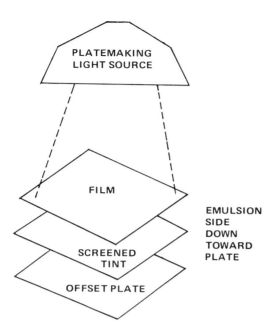

Exposure to make plate using screened tint.

FOR A REVERSE

The overlay, when cut to cover an area of type on the base pasteup, can help create a reverse of this particular area. The camera operator makes a negative of the base type, makes a contact positive, places this positive in the overlay negative window to expose on the plate. This method is not used as much today because reverses can be produced by the diffusion-transfer method.

FOR A SECOND COLOR

What is cut on the flap can be printed in a second color in register with the base pasteup. Place all the elements to appear in the second color on the flap if possible and if practical.

IF A JOB PRINTS IN TWO COLORS PLUS TINTS IN THE COLOR

It may be necessary to make two overlays. First prepare the base pasteup. Make a flap for the solid color. Make a second flap for the tint areas. This can simplify the production of the job as the stripper can position the tint over the negative resulting from the tint flap overlay and double expose on the plate along with the solid color flap negative.

OVERLAYS AND REGISTER MARKS

When the camera operator photographs an overlay he must also photograph some marks on the base which can be used to position the overlay negative in registration with the base.

For example, he might photograph the trim marks on the base while he is making his negative of the overlay. He will place a piece of white paper under the overlay patches when he exposes the overlay, and he should not cover any marks which will be convenient to use for negative registration purposes.

You can place three register marks on the base outside the work, positioned on each side and one at the bottom —as a triangle.

If register marks are placed inside the work, it is *possible* that they *could* get printed by failure to opaque out on the negatives.

POLYESTER AND ACETATE FILM

It is generally recommended to use polyester films for overlay preparation because of its stable base. This is the type of film that is nearly impossible to tear. Several brands of this type of film include Mylar, Estar and Cronar. It does not stretch or shrink, and when punched for pin register work, perfect registration is assured. While acetate films can also be used, more care must be exercised in their use.

Three films for general use in preparation

1. Clear inking polyester.
2. Frosted or matte one-side polyester.
3. Frosted or matte two-side polyester.

Clear Inking polyester, three or four mil.

This is clear film which has been treated to accept ink ruled lines. Both sides are treated; therefore, it can be ruled on either side or on both sides. It's useful for general overlay preparation.

Frosted one-side polyester, three mil.

The frosted surface provides a mild "tooth" on its

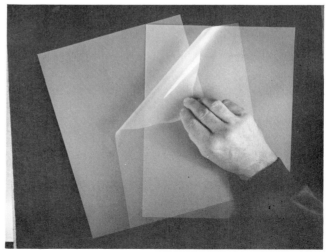

Frosted-one-side overlay film.

surface. You can draw non-reproducible guidelines on the frosted film in non-photo blue or faint gray for guidelining and layout. The matte surface holds quality dense black line definition.

Frosted two-side polyester film, three mil.

Both sides of this transluscent film are frosted to accept sharp ink ruled lines. You may therefore ink rule horizontal lines on one side and verticals on the opposite side so all rules are independent of each other to allow removal of lines for correcting and altering. This technique offers many advantages in the production of forms.

A form may be guidelined on the film surface with faint rules, then ink ruled with horizontals on the front and verticals on the back. Any unsatisfactory rules may be removed with liquid eraser fluid. Future revisions of rules can be accomplished by erasing only those lines altered and drawing revised rules. The type matter can be affixed directly on the film surface, or the type can be on the base sheet with the double matte overlay in register to the base. When the latter method is used, it will be necessary to shoot two negatives, one of the base and one of the overlay. These two negatives are exposed on a plate in register. This plate will then have a combination of the type and rules.

When preparing the overlay on the two-sided polyester, it is important to accurately guideline the form on the film prior to ink ruling. Once guidelines are complete, the lines are inked in one direction on the front. The film is next turned over to rule lines in the opposite direction. These opposite rules are placed in exact position by viewing the guidelines through the translucent film. When film is turned over, you will be viewing the form as a "mirror image"; therefore, it is

Vertical lines ruled on frosted film overlay.

important to follow precisely those visible guidelines which were not inked on the front side. When the second side ruling is complete, the film is returned to its front side image and the rules on the back will appear to the human eye to have been drawn on one side, and the camera will photograph the rules to perfection.

This two-sided ruling method can prove itself as indispensable for any complicated ruling job or any ruling work which will require future revision.

OVERLAY RULING TIPS

When using frosted film, it is often a problem to get the ink to stick consistently when ruling lines or applying ink for other purposes. The film can pick up a bit of oil from one's fingers so the ink will not take to this particular spot.

Clean the film surface with rubber cement thinner or alcohol. Use a tissue and rub over the film to prepare for use.

To erase ink from film, you can apply a commercially available product called "liquid erasing fluid." This liquid will remove ink quite satisfactorily, and when the liquid is dry, you can rule over the area again. An abrasive should not be used as the surface can become rough causing a surface which is difficult to accept sharp rules. In an emergency, household window cleaners may be found useful to remove ink from film. For example, *Windex* has proved a satisfactory ink removal agent. Small cotton swabs, such as Q-tips are handy to dip in solvents to rub on film to remove lines.

RULING ON POLYESTER OVERLAY FILM

There are several advantages to ink ruling lines on frosted polyester film.
1. The overlay film can be printed as an overlay on a pasteup and rules drawn in the exact position required.
2. Ink is easily removed in the event of an error, by using liquid eraser.

The frosted film has a mild tooth surface to aid in the adhesion of the ink when ruling with a technical pen. The film is available in rolls or sheets in a .003 or .004 thickness for practical overlay usage.

When ruling on the polyester, you should dowel-pin the overlay and tape down the corners temporarily to insure that the film will lie flat over the base. There is a tendency for the corners to curl up a bit and this could cause ruling inaccuracies.

Trim marks on the base pasteup can be photographed with the base negative, then with the overlay. The same marks will appear on both negatives and can be used to line up the negatives on the plate in relative registration. There must be marks that can be used for registration purposes which can be photographed with the overlay and also with the base.

Register marks can be added if required. They should be placed outside of the printing area, yet in a position so they will pick up on the negative.

The camera operator will first shoot a negative of the base with the flap turned up and out of the way (or removed from the dowels). Then he will place a piece of white paper over the base and allow the overlay to lie on the white paper. The camera will then see only the rules and/or other patches and type which may be included on the overlay.

The negative that results from the overlay can be "double-burned" on the offset plate to combine with the images on the base.

The overlay may have been prepared for use as a second color.

OVERLAYS AND DOWEL-PINS

It is convenient and practical to two-hole punch the base pasteup and then punch the overlay.

Place dowel pins into the base holes, place the overlay film on the dowel pins for preparation. You can then remove the overlay as necessary, then reposition it in register.

Dowel-pinning overlays will tie-in with the pasteup punch system for signature work as described in another chapter of this book.

Plastic or metal dowels about .060 in thickness are practical for pasteup pin register work.

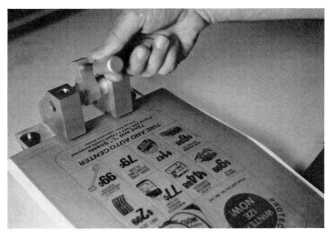

The overlay material can be punched with the base sheet along the bottom edge.

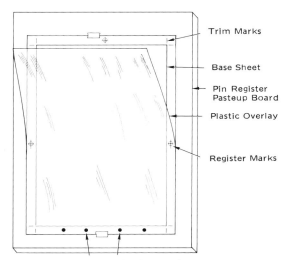

- Trim Marks
- Base Sheet
- Pin Register Pasteup Board
- Plastic Overlay
- Register Marks

Punched overlay and base sheet secured on pegs.

Red Blockout Film

This film is a transparent, self-adhesive, ruby-red, matte finish, thin, plastic film. It is sometimes referred to by various brand names such as Formopaque or Red Zipatone.

It photographs the same as black.

It is a versatile film with dozens of uses, and ideal for pasteup work to use as a substitute for blacking-in larger areas. This film can be placed directly on the pasteup, then cut to any contour with an art knife or swivel knife. Since it is transparent you can follow the light guidelines on the base while cutting.

Because the red material is transparent, you can see where to cut directly on the guidelines, and the edges will be sharp. The excess film can easily be pulled from the surface of the pasteup as the adhesive is removable. This product is used for windows by many lithographers.

Sometimes you might have a large pasteup with a small patch area on the overlay. Rather than use a large

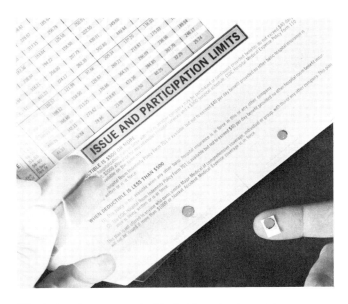

Plastic dowels are convenient to hold overlay in register, yet overlay can be removed and replaced to register properly.

sheet of peel coat material, and practically peel off 90 percent of the film coating, you can use a sheet of clear or frosted polyester and then apply the small patch using the red self-adhesive film.

Red masking film, pressure-sensitive, used on a pasteup as a substitute for blacking area with ink.

Amber and ruby peel coat film

This product is a clear acetate film base which has a red or amber film coating on its surface.

Place a sheet of this film over the pasteup, and cut through the ruby or amber film coating around the area you want to photo on the overlay. Peel off the area you *don't want* to pick up on camera. You get a good sharp edge when cutting overlays on this film.

Sometimes the film is cut for direct exposure on an offset plate. In this procedure, the cutting film becomes the same as an offset negative, and must be cut to be used as a negative for exposure on the plate. Why use amber or ruby? The amber color is a bit easier to see through, especially when cutting marks over photographs for the preparation of outline photographs.

It's a good idea to have both amber and red on hand because you can use a sheet of each when you have a job requiring two overlays. The contrast between the two overlays will help keep the two visibly separated. Furthermore, use red film when the overlay will be

Peeling off overlay from cut-mask film.

exposed directly to film or plate. Because some light sources have a yellow cast, there could be some light transmission if the amber is used. The red film will assure complete blockout of light. The amber will prove completely satisfactory for exposure through the camera lens.

This film is highly recommended because it produces a very high quality overlay, and is easy to use. Be careful not to cut completely through the film. You must learn to cut only through the film surface, then peel off the excess to leave the coating in place where it must be photographed.

This film is ideal for tint and color overlays, outlining over photos and cutting masks for contact printing.

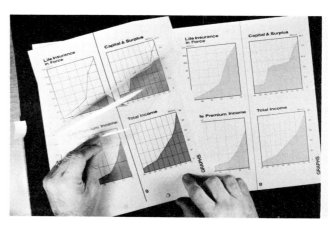

Amber peel-coat film used to produce second color on graphs at right.

OVERLAP OVERLAY PATCHES SLIGHTLY

When two colors join each other on a printing job, it is necessary that the colors slightly overlap. This is known as "lap register" and will aid the press operator to register the two colors.

How much should this overlap be? Cut the overlay so the red film will overlap into the edge of the base color about the width of a line . . . about one point.

Practice makes perfect . . . or nearly so

The first time you cut an overlay it is difficult.

You may cut beyond the line and expose some "white." Some of the edges might be a bit rough, and you've cut too deep.

Upon examination of this first attempt, you may find that you must do it all over again. The importance of precision cutting cannot be overemphasized.

With practice and as you continue to cut overlays, you will get them done easier and faster, and the work is exact. Practice pays off to make you more efficient at cutting overlays.

WHEN <u>NOT</u> TO OVERLAY

Let's say that you have a page which has a tint area and some of the words contained in the text on the base are to print in color.

It is obvious that to attempt to attain precise alignment of words if placed on the overlay would be very time-consuming.

For this situation, leave the words on the base and indicate on a tissue sheet which words print in color. It is not difficult to combine these words with the overlay and expose on the plate.

A few minutes of opaquing or covering with orange paper on the negative is quick and easy for the stripper. The alignment will be absolutely perfect.

It is a good policy to always indicate the color separation on a tissue overlay on top of a pasteup if a comprehensive layout is not available.

If this pasteup were produced in two colors,
there is no need for an overlay . . . it is a simple separation.

FRISKET MATERIAL AND ITS USE

Frisket is a material that is applied to parts of a surface so that a pigment can be applied to the parts not protected by the frisket. Therefore, frisket is in reality a stencil.

A commonly used frisket material is "frisket paper" which is sold in rolls or sheets. The word "paper" is a misnomer because it is actually very thin film held on a sheet of release paper with an adhesive.

In use, the frisket film is peeled from the release paper, then applied to the artwork or photograph. A portion is then cut with a frisket knife and removed. The open area, after careful cleaning, is then ready for application of pigment, generally with an airbrush. Once the pigment is dry, the remaining frisket is removed and discarded.

A few of the common problems in using frisket material include:

1. The possibility of the pigment seeping under the edges of frisket. Be certain that the edges are adhered sufficiently.

2. The frisket adhesive may weaken to cause bubbles or cracks particularly if the artwork is stored for a long period of time in a changing temperature environment.

3. Frisket may pull off the surface of the area to which it is adhered. Don't leave the frisket material on the art for any longer than absolutely necessary. Frisket should not be applied and left over night. The longer the frisket remains on the art, the bond increases to cause damage to the art when removal is attempted.

Frisket film will accept strike-on composition using carbon ribbon. This copy typed on frisket can be cut and applied to film positives for contacting.

SPREADS AND CHOKES

If you wanted to print color inside of an open outline letter, you could cut an overlay on peel coat film which would serve as a photographable overlay to produce a negative which would produce a plate that would print the color on the inside portion of the letter.

Let's look for an easier perfect method of producing color inside the outline letter.

A contact positive can produce a film which will allow
a second color to print inside the outline letters.

A simple contact negative procedure can produce a film that can be used to expose on a plate. This contact positive can be made with a slight overlap of the color to provide lap register. This is accomplished by making what is called a *spread*.

You must indicate on a tissue hinged over the pasteup just what you want in color. Color pencil the area which is to print in color on the inside of the open area of the lettering. The camera operator should then understand that it is necessary to make a spread.

The spread is made by placing a clear sheet of film between the original negative and the new film. The light will spread as it passes through the negative from the light source to create a contact film positive which is then used to produce a plate for the color plate. This contact film work is done in a vacuum frame with a contact light source.

There may be instances when you want to produce the *opposite* of a spread, and this would be a *choke* or sometimes referred to as a "skinny." To produce the choke, a positive must be contacted, and from this positive a choke is made by contacting with unexposed film and a clear film spacer. The image will therefore shrink slightly.

In summary: Spreads are produced from film negatives and chokes from film positives.

A SIMPLE PRINCIPLE OF PHOTOGRAPHY FOR OFFSET FILM

Remember, we are photographing the background and not the text. The image put on paper, literally, is not seen by the camera. It is the white space, the non-printing area, which creates the exposure on the film.

133 LINE SCREEN TINTS
(Placed On Windows)

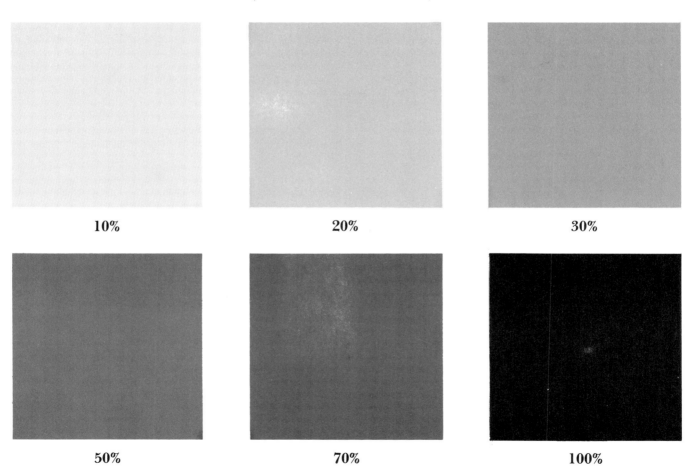

10%	20%	30%
50%	70%	100%

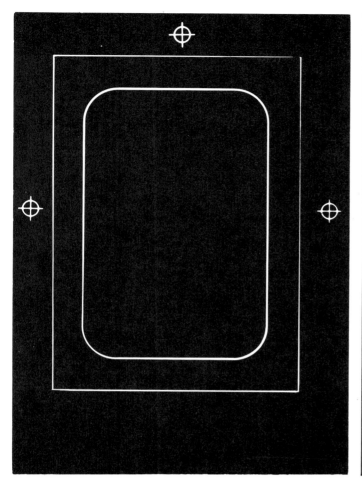

From this negative a contact positive is produced.

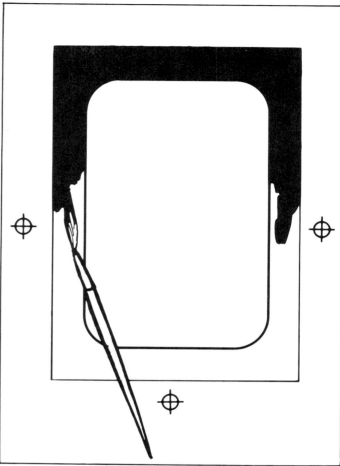

The positive must be opaqued and the remaining inside portion will expose on the plate.

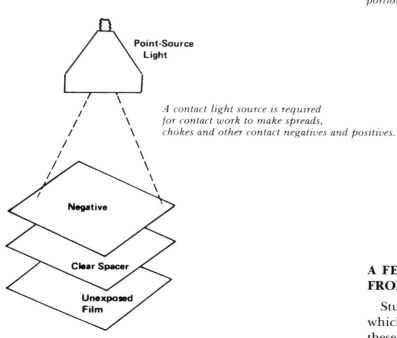

Point-Source Light

A contact light source is required for contact work to make spreads, chokes and other contact negatives and positives.

Negative

Clear Spacer

Unexposed Film

A FEW REPRODUCTION POSSIBILITIES FROM A SIMPLE PIECE OF LINE ART PASTEUP

Study the following examples of printing possibilities which can be achieved from one simple pasteup. Apply these same techniques to any printing job you may produce.

ORIGINAL PASTEUP

**50% TINT ON INSIDE PORTION
OF THE CONTACT POSITIVE.**

Step 1. Shoot negative of original.

Step 2. Make contact positive from negative.

Step 3. Place 50% screened tint film cut to cover inside border area only.

Step 4. Expose positive-tint on offset plate.

Step 5. Print from plate.

**PLATE MADE FROM CONTACT POSITIVE
OF NEGATIVE OF ORIGINAL PASTEUP**

Step 1. Shoot negative of original

Step 2. Make contact positive from negative.

Step 3. Expose positive on offset plate.

Step 4. Print from plate.

SIMPLE SEPARATION WITH TINT

Step 1. Shoot two negatives of the pasteup.

Step 2. Place tint, 50%, over circle area on negative for black.

Step 3. Make plates for black and red printers.

Step 4. Print plates.

Other examples of reproductions in two color using the negatives, positives and a combination of the negative and positive.

18
Line Prints and Proofing

LINE PRINTS
Requirements for line prints
The photocopier
Contact line prints from line negatives
Diffusion-transfer prints
Other print production methods
PASTEUP PROOFING
The photocopier
The silverprint
Plastic proofs
Diazo proofing

LINE PRINTS

A line print is a photographable reproduction of any line art or copy. This print may be required because a reduction of line art is needed to affix to a pasteup. Generally a line print is used as a camera-ready element. For instance, you may need four line prints to position together so the job will be imposed four-up. It doesn't take long to realize the continual need for line prints when preparing pasteups. A source or equipment to make prints is essential for anyone preparing pasteups. Let us examine a few methods of making prints, pointing out their advantages and disadvantages.

Requirements for line prints

1. Good *quality,* dense black print with even, black solids and dots faithfully reproduced which can be used as a camera-ready element.

2. Ability to *reduce or enlarge* to produce a print of the size required. Many cameras will reduce up to five times,

and enlarge up to twice size. The camera can be set to focus sharply to expose to photo-sensitive material within the range of the camera's reduction and enlargement capabilities.

Note:

Sometimes it is necessary to make a line print and reduce it more than the camera's range for a one-shot reduction. In this instance it is possible to reduce in two stages: 1. Reduce the copy and produce a print. 2. Place this print in the copyboard and reduce again to the final required size and produce a line print. The same plan can be used to produce enlargements. Be aware, however, that these double enlargements can produce fuzzy images unless the original is extremely sharp.

The photocopier

While electrostatic and other office copiers are producing better quality all the time, they generally do not make duplicates that would be considered satisfactory for placement on a camera-ready pasteup. Furthermore, most models do not reduce or enlarge to give us the versatility to make prints to our size requirements should the quality be highly acceptable. We will admit that the photocopier has got us out of a jam in pasteup preparation such as the time we made a black copy from a form printed in light green ink. This black copier-print was then worked over and used to shoot in the film process camera.

Contact line prints from line negatives

If you have a film negative and want a print of its image, it is a simple procedure to make a contact print from this negative. This is accomplished by using a contact frame with a light source. The negative and paper are placed together in the frame so the light will expose through the clear part of the negative and expose the print paper. The paper is processed with developer and fixer to produce a faithful reproduction of the negative.

When a line print is required of an art element, a "line shot" can be made to produce a film negative of the required size. After the negative dries, it may be contacted to the print paper to make a line print for use on the pasteup.

Line art same size and reduced size.

This process has been the method used by lithographers for many years; however, the diffusion-transfer process has come into use to produce a one-step positive print.

Diffusion-transfer prints

Our need for line prints can be satisfied by a convenient, fast and inexpensive process called the Diffusion-Transfer Process or by Kodak's trade name PMT.

We do need an offset camera, darkroom and processor to make these prints. If you do not have your own darkroom-camera set up, you can have an outside trade shop make these prints for you. Making these prints is accomplished without the need for a film negative.

With this process, you place a sheet of photo-sensitive black negative paper on the camera-back. The original line art is placed in the copyboard. An exposure is made through the lens. Now a sheet of white receiver paper is placed over the exposed black negative paper and these two sheets are placed into a motor-driven automatic diffusion-transfer processor which contains a chemical

The effect of enlargement on dots.

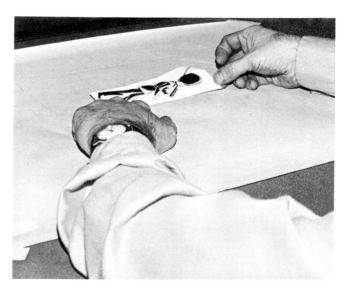

Line art placed in copyboard.

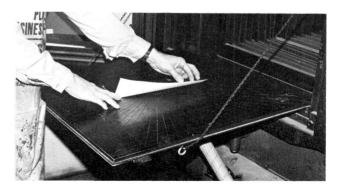

PMT negative paper on vacuum back of camera.

103

After exposure, negative paper placed with receiver sheet into processor.

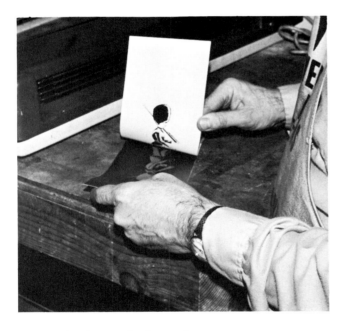

After waiting 30 seconds, the two sheets are peeled apart and the print is ready for pasteup.

activator. A chemical reaction takes place during the process when intimate contact is made between the negative paper and the receiver paper. After waiting 30 seconds, these two sheets are peeled apart and a right-reading image is tranferred to the receiver paper to form a line print which will dry in moments and be ready to wax down on a pasteup. This process takes place in a darkroom.

The advantage of the diffusion-transfer process is that you get a quality print quickly and inexpensively.

It is important to get acquainted with this process and to study the techniques of print production using it. This is a highly recommended method of producing prints for pasteups. Newspapers preparing food ads will often make a print of the ad pasteup, then use this print to burnish-down Benday in areas required. This final print and Benday combination is then used as the final completed pasteup. The print produces a smooth surface to accommodate the Benday smoothly.

Other print production methods

There are other devices on the market to produce line prints for pasteup. A variety of "stat cameras" are available which make prints directly on positive print paper. Those who have need for a special production print device can investigate this equipment in order to have on hand a specialized piece of equipment that will produce positive prints.

PASTEUP PROOFING

After a pasteup is completed, a proof is usually necessary and preferred as a means of checking and correcting. This will avoid excessive handling of the original pasteup and enables you to keep the pasteup in the department so it will remain clean and undamaged.

The photocopier is our "proof press."

A window-type photocopier makes an excellent proofing unit. The pasteup is placed in the copier window and one or several copies may be reproduced.

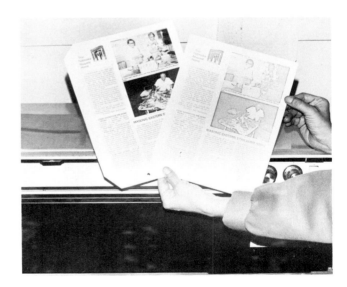

A photocopier provides proofs to show for customer approval. The photocopy on the right was produced from the pasteup with PMT screened prints in position.

Today, with photocomposition and strike-on methods so popular, it is almost a necessity for a printing preparatory area to have a window-type photocopier to produce galley proofs of composition output, dummies and pages.

To give the customer a finished pasteup for proofing purposes can invite problems. Dust, fingermarks, smearing and possible damage to the pasteup surface are a few of the disasters that can come about. It is better to give the customer a copy of the pasteup which he can check and approve.

Read the *Basic Steps of Pasteup Preparation* which indicates the steps where the photocopier must be used to prepare pasteups efficiently and to allow checking.

The silverprint

Sometimes called a Van Dyke or Brown Print (and some Blue Line paper is used). Its production requires a negative. This negative is exposed to the silverprint paper, then processed by development to provide a print for final checking of the printing job.

Silverprint paper can be multiple-exposed in varying degrees of density to differentiate between colors to offer a check on the correctness of color separation.

It is better to get approval before the expense of a negative is incurred. If corrections are required, a new negative or stripping may be necessary. It is therefore cheaper to use the copier to obtain approvals whenever possible. When film halftones are stripped in on the negative, it is necessary to contact a silverprint to see the photos in position and check for cropping, quality, etc.

Plastic proofs

Proofs can be made from a negative by contacting the negative onto a sheet of plastic which has a color coating

Checking a blue-line print before sending out for customer approval.

on it of the same color as the ink which will be used in the press to print the job.

This material is often referred to as "color key." It produces a very high quality proof to show a customer for approval. The colors can be laid over each other to view the multiple colors as they will appear on the final printing. Color-key is used extensively for proofing color process work, and the press operator will refer to these color-key proofs when printing the job and thereby check his ink density and color.

The color key is more expensive than the silverprint, but may be desirable on very critical printing jobs to provide a precise final check before printing. They are easy to make as the material is exposed to the negative, and then a solution applied that washes off the color to allow the image to remain in view when placed on a sheet of white paper (or on colored paper of the same stock on which the job will be printed.)

A color-key proof is made up of plastic sheets with the pigment on the surface. Here four layers make up a color process proof of a photograph.

Diazo proofing

This method is used by some newspapers to produce proofs of large ads when they might require a dozen copies to submit to the advertiser.

Using this system, the pasteup is placed in a vacuum frame with a sheet of special thin photosensitive paper on top of the pasteup. The exposure is made and the sensitized paper is fed through a processor to produce a positive image which is then contacted through a sheet of diazo paper, run through a processor to render a proof image quickly. These final contacts can be made quickly and inexpensively to produce proofs of large pages.

19
Offset Presses, Gripper and Bleed

OFFSET PRESS
Sheet fed
Web fed
The importance of gripper
Bleed

OFFSET PRESSES

Sheet Fed

Offset presses are built in different sizes. The most common being the duplicator-type which accommodates a sheet 10″ x 14″ or 11″ x 17″. Other popular sizes are 14″ x 20″, 18″ x 25″, 23″ x 29″, 23″ x 35″, 25″ x 38″, 35″ x 45″ and on up to presses more than 70 inches wide. Sheets of paper are fed rapidly into the press cylinders a sheet at a time.

Web-Fed Presses

A web press is one that prints from a roll or a "web" of paper. This equipment is used to print newspapers, magazines and books, because as the paper travels through the cylinders to get its impressions, the paper feeds into a folding attachment so the folding is performed while printing. Web presses can be equipped with sheeters so the paper will bypass the folder and be sheeted at a fixed cut-off dimension.

The importance of gripper

All sheet-fed offset presses have grippers or little metal fingers which grip the paper to pull it through the press cylinders while printing.

A printed image cannot be printed along this "gripper" edge of the paper. If a job is to be printed on 8-1/2″ x 11″ paper you would have to avoid any printing along the gripper. If you wanted to print at the gripper edge you would have to print the job on larger paper, and then trim it back on the cutting machine after the sheets are printed.

The amount of gripper for the press will vary, depending on the specifications of the particular offset press. Gripper margins will usually require 1/4-, 5/16- or 3/8-in. Be sure to allow this margin free and clear of any printing when on actual size paper.

What would you do if the customer wants his letterheads printed on 8-1/2″ x 11″ paper and the design bleeds all four sides?

1. If OK with customer, you could reduce the size of the letterhead photographically to 8-1/8″ x 10-1/2″ and use 8-1/2″ x 11″ paper to run the job.

2. Print on oversize paper such as 9″ x 12″.

Some offset presses grip the sheet on the "wide side" of the sheet. An 18″ x 24″ Heidelberg offset press would grip the sheet on the 24″ edge. If the press were to print an 11″ x 17″ sheet, it would grip along the 17″ side.

On the other hand, the small duplicator-type offset presses will grip on the narrow edge. A 10″ x 14″ multilith will grip the 10″ edge. If the press prints an 8-1/2″ x 11″ sheet the gripper edge would be along the 8-1/2″ edge.

You should become familiar with the press specifications for gripper that would pertain to your pasteup preparation for this equipment. Before doing a pasteup you should know what size press sheet will be used for a

A space along the edge of the press sheet
must be left clear of any printing
to allow for gripper margin on the press.
A space of 1/4-in. to 3/8-in. will be required
depending on the press manufacturer's specifications.

job. Then you can determine whether you can bleed or run printing close to the gripper edge of the sheet. Printing on an oversize sheet will of course, give you all the area you need to bleed off the trim size and still allow sufficient gripper margin.

BLEED

Bleeding or allowing halftones or tints to run to the very edge of the paper, can result in attractive layout. Very often you can make photos larger by utilizing the margins of a job by allowing the photos to bleed off the page. Sometimes price is a consideration that will prevent the use of bleed. The larger paper size required will increase the price of the job by virtue of the larger paper size.

When you bleed you must remember that larger paper is necessary so that you have gripper edge for the press operator, and still print beyond the trim size of the page.

For example, if a job is 8-1/2″ x 11″ and it bleeds all four sides (no matter how narrow the bleed may be . . . it's still bleed), you'll need to print the job on 9-1/2″ x 12-1/2″ paper so that there will be sufficient gripper and trim area. The 9-1/2″ x 12-1/2″ can be cut from 25″ x 38″ paper size. If the job prints on a duplicator press, the gripper edge would be along the 9-1/2″ edge. After the job is printed, the sheets can be trimmed to the finished size in the paper cutter and the edges will be clean and neat.

It is not a good policy to print bleed jobs that bleed, let's say, along the bottom, by using paper right to finished size. Why? Because the ink can pile up a bit along the bleed edge due to the excess ink on the plate that builds up on the blanket of the press.

If you are preparing pasteups it's a good idea to find out if a bleed design is OK before you go ahead and paste up. Budget requirements may make this necessary. Some publications, for instance, do not allow bleed due to press design or higher cost.

Allow 1/8-in. extension beyond the trim size of the job for bleed. If you have a window on the job for a halftone, let it extend 1/8-in. past the trim size. Keep in mind that this 1/8-in. will trim off the edge, so you must watch your photo cropping so that you are not going to cut off something that should show up in the picture that will be placed in the window. Let the trim-off be some tonal unimportant area that is not vital to the appearance of the photo.

Always bear in mind where the trim edge is located. There is a tendency for newcomers to pasteup to want to run type to the very edge of a sheet, without thinking of exactly where the trim is going to be. You must get used to working with the larger sheet and recognizing the trim edge and visualize how it will look after it's trimmed. To get visualization, you can put strips of black paper along the edges of the trim marks, to get a look at the definition of the trim edges.

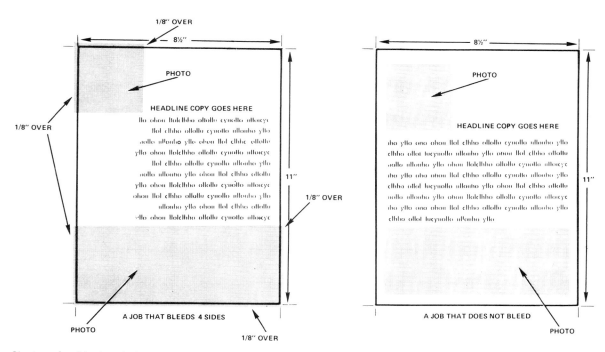

If a page has bleed on it, be sure to extend photos, tints, etc. 1/8-in. beyond the trim size of the job.
Bleed jobs must be printed on larger paper to accommodate the bleed.

20

Imposition

Work-and-turn
Work-and-tumble
Work-and-twist
Work-and-back
Multi-page jobs
Pasteup Punch System
Step and Repeat

IMPOSITION

It is helpful and almost necessary that those preparing pasteups understand "Imposition" . . . that is, the positioning of multiple pages in proper relationship with each other so the pages will follow each other in proper sequence after the printed sheet is folded.

It is best to consult with someone in the bindery department to determine the correct imposition for the equipment on hand to produce a particular job.

Why is it necessary for one doing pasteup to become familiar with imposition?

There are several reasons, and the main one is that you can simplify the job as it goes through the different steps of production. You can help a job get printed at lower cost by understanding imposition requirements. How you impose a job on a pasteup can save camera work, stripping, make-ready on the press and time in the bindery.

The terms that should become familiar to you are: *Work-and-Turn, Work-and-Tumble, Work-and-Twist,* and *Work-and-Back.*

The reason we print work-and-turn and work-and-tumble, is because we can print from *one press plate* when a job prints on both sides. The press operator must print on large enough paper to accommodate the front and back image. This is a logical economical approach to two-sided printing.

Let's examine each of these terms to learn simple set-ups for the various arrangements.

Work-and-Turn

Sheets of paper are run through the press. After the stack is printed it is turned over to print on the back blank side.

The sheets are turned from left to right, using the *same* gripper edge on the paper. When these sheets are run through the press after the turn, the front of the job will print on the back, and the back on the front.

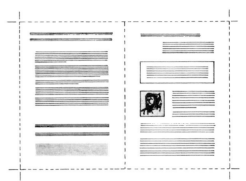

Work-and-turn, no bleed, chop cut.

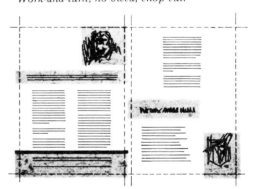

Work-and-turn, bleed, gutter required.

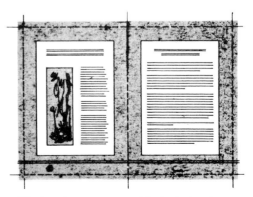

Work-and-turn, constant bleed, chop cut.

It is usually the best practice to have the pasteups ready to shoot by the camera all set up for work-and-turn (or any other set-up for that matter). This way, the camera operator can shoot the entire pasteup as one shot. This procedure saves strip-up of the single page negatives. It is therefore important to understand what to do, so the pasteup will be correct for plate preparation.

If you paste up a job which is work-and-turn and does *not* bleed, you must not leave a gutter in the middle of the sheet. Why? Because the one who trims the job at the paper cutter will be forced to make an extra cut to trim out the excess. This takes more time.

A job set up to work-and-turn that has no bleed, should be set up for a "chop-cut" so that *only one cut* will be required in the bindery.

Now there *could* be a reason why you would set up a bleed job without a gutter. And here is where common sense judgement can enter into the preparation of a job for the camera.

Suppose you have a job which has a solid or tint bleed on all four sides of both sides of the sheet! Why put in a gutter for this because the bleed is continuing from one to the other. Here a chop cut would be the way to set it up, and you have helped save time in the bindery!

Work-and-Tumble

We are printing a sheet of paper with the front and the back of the job on the same plate. After one side of the stack of paper is printed, the sheets are turned over from *gripper* to *back* and run through the press again. This press sheet yields two printed pieces when cut in half.

When setting up for work-and-tumble, you must be certain that there is ample gripper at *both ends* of the sheet. The paper is run through the press, then the stack is rolled to grip at the opposite end of the sheet.

For example, suppose you are setting up a jumbo mailing card which is 5-1/2″ x 8-1/2″, printed two sides. You are going to print on a sheet 8-3/4″ x 11-1/2″.

The job does not bleed, therefore, as in the previous example shown in the work-and-turn, we do not need a gutter. A chop-cut can be made in the bindery. There is adequate gripper margin at both ends of the sheet.

You might ask the question, "Why not work-and-turn this job instead of work-and-tumble?" The answer lies in the accommodation of the press equipment and the nature of the job. The jumbo postcard illustrated could be printed on a duplicator offset press. The press would not be wide enough to feed the paper stock into the machine the 11-1/2″ way. Generally, press operators do prefer work-and-turn over work-and-tumble due to the advantage of maintaining the same gripper edge on the sheet.

Suppose we have the jumbo mailing card, 5-1/2″ x 8-1/2″, printed two sides, to bleed on all four sides.

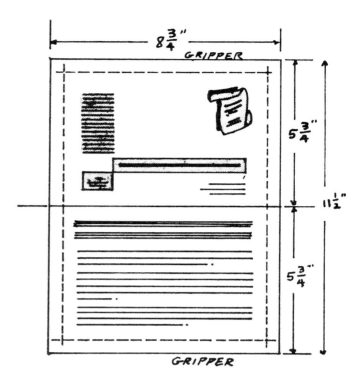

Work-and-tumble, no bleed.

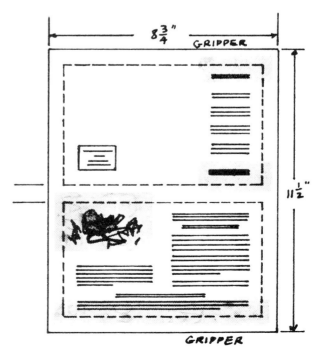

Work-and-tumble, bleed.

The previously illustrated press sheet, 8-3/4″ x 11-1/2″, is too small for the bleed job because there is *not* adequate gripper for work-and-tumble. The solution: Use a larger press sheet such as 9-1/2″ x 12-1/2″. The larger paper will add more to the cost of the job, and must be so figured. It is therefore more expensive to bleed than not to bleed. As you can note, we need *larger paper plus* extra trimming of the stock after printing to trim out the gutter.

Let's apply our common sense approach to keeping the cost down and producing the jumbo card. Why not undersize the card a bit so that it can bleed and get printed on the 8-3/4″ x 11-1/2″ stock? We could make our pasteup for a card 8-1/4″ x 5-1/4″ and have adequate room for bleed plus gripper margins at each end of the sheet. Undersizing a printing job slightly often can make it possible to use fewer pounds of paper on a job, and still satisfy the requirements of the print job.

Work-and-tumble jobs of this nature should be pasted up on one base sheet, head-to-head, with trim marks, ready for the camera.

Work-and-Twist

One image is put on the plate and a double sheet is run. After one side is printed, the sheet is twisted to print the other half with the same image. This procedure was widely used during the prominence of letterpress printing when making duplicate letterpress printing plates was very costly. Stepping and repeating an image on an offset plate has made this work-and-twist procedure obsolete. However, keep it in mind because there are times when it can be very handy.

Work-and-Back

This is exactly the same as work-and-turn except that you must change plates when printing the second side of the sheet. When you require the two plates for the two-sided job, you call it work-and-back.

In any of the pasteups for signature work, be sure to include trim marks outside of the work which can be exposed on the plate to print on the press. These marks are necessary for positioning the negative on the plate, positioning on the paper, folding and trimming.

One-up image on double sheet for work-and-twist.

Multi-page jobs

Pasteups of pages should be arranged in their proper position so that they can be photographed by the camera as a single unit. When these units are printed, the resulting sheet forms a "signature." This signature is a folded printed sheet which forms a section of a printed piece or book.

These signatures may be printed work-and-turn, -tumble or -back, depending on the page size, press size and folding and stitching capabilities.

Let's be very basic in our discussion and examination of the signature. This basic understanding can be projected to preparation for larger sheets and utilize the same basic principle.

Here is an eight-page booklet with a page-size 4" x 5". It can be printed on a sheet of paper 8-1/2" x 11". Two plates can be used and the job is "work-and-back." Note that there is gutter space in the middle of the sheet. Why? Because you need to trim the job after it is folded into a signature by trimming off the folded edge. Four pages are printed-up on each side of the sheet. Remember that a page is counted *one side for each page.* Confusion can result on this point very easily. So often, people will refer to a single sheet of paper as a page when actually it is two pages if it prints on the front and back—one page on one side and another page on the back of the sheet. Always remember that book pages are numbered on both sides of the leaves.

A folding dummy should be made up using the same paper stock on which the job will be printed. This will tell you the thickness and bulk of the signature, particularly important when a number of signatures are nested together. This folding dummy can be notched as shown in the example which will indicate to you, after it is opened up, the page heading direction. The pages are head-to-head and must be placed exactly according to the dummy plan. Check and double check here when making up books. It is easy to make a mistake that can be very costly.

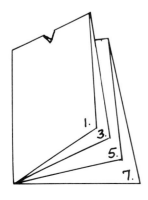

A folding dummy of a signature, 8-page, work-and-back.

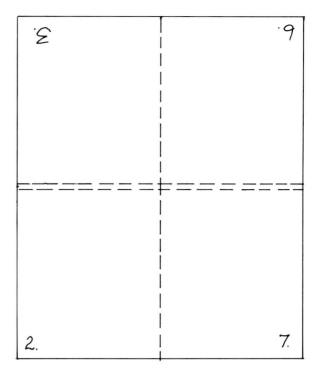

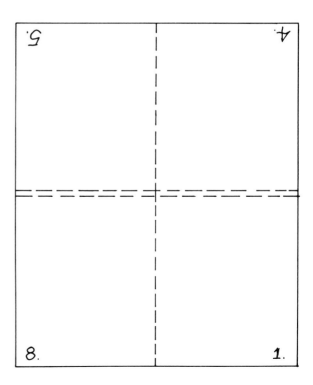

An 8-page, work-and-back signature.

WORK-AND-BACK

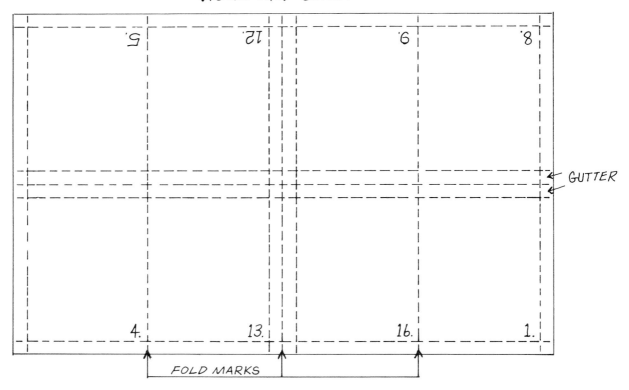

A 16-page booklet set up for work-and-back.

When you have pages which contain copy that runs sideways, such as in statistical and tabular work which may lend itself to this arrangement, be certain that the pages read down from top to bottom as you look at the pages as a spread. The illustration will clarify this point, and this type of imposition can get mixed up without careful checking.

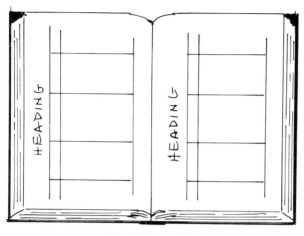

RIGHT WAY

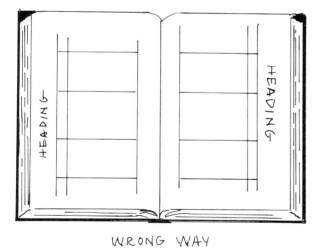

WRONG WAY

The right and wrong way to face pages in a book.

Signatures can be work-and-turn, -tumble or -back.

We can take our same little eight-page booklet job and convert it to a work-and-turn sheet. It would be printed on a sheet 11″ x 17″. The advantage here is that one plate is used for the job requiring only one make-ready on the press. When the sheet is turned for back-up, page four will back-up page three, etc.

Your assembled pasteup of the pages on the base sheet, is called a *flat*.

If we tumble the signature.

Using our same eight-page booklet, we could print it work-and-tumble.

Note that there is a change in the page locations on the imposition. When we print on the 17″ x 11″ sheet and tumble the job, our final signature strip will fold from a sheet 17″ x 5-1/2″. What might cause us to want to use this tumble set-up for our job? This might be done because of the folding equipment available. The work-and-turn set-up will require the necessity for a right-hand fold, while the work-and-tumble can be folded with two parallel folds from the 17″ x 5-1/2″ strip.

Getting the feel of the signature.

When you must prepare a booklet in signature form on your pasteup, first make up a dummy, by folding up a sheet of paper as it will be folded on the folding machine. Use the same paper stock on which the job will be printed. You want the knowledge of the bulk of the particular paper stock that will be used. This will become apparent when you must make a booklet which has sufficient pages to require the insertion of one or more signatures nested together.

After these signatures are nested together they may be stapled at the backbone or fold. Allowances must be made when positioning the pages on the flat for the push-out or "creep". This is discussed under the *Pin Register Imposition System.*

A great deal of care must be taken to produce an accurate, straight pasteup and using the punch system is an ideal method to obtain accuracy in the imposition of the pages on the flat.

You will need to draw up your flats which you will use to impose the pages for the planned signature imposition. To prepare accurate flats, a large grid is placed on the light table, and a sheet of light card stock taped to the grid. Non reproducible guide lines can now be drawn with precise squareness following the grid lines. All trim marks and center marks are ruled on the flat using a fine point pen with black ink.

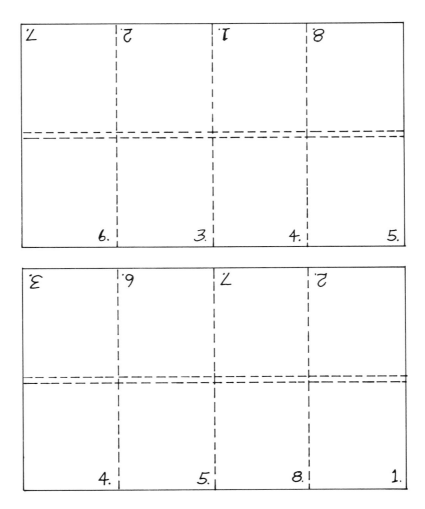

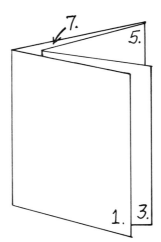

The work-and-tumble signature and folding dummy.

PIN REGISTER IMPOSITION SYSTEM

Here is a system to greatly simplify the pasteup preparation of pages for booklets and publications which are made up of signatures. It is called the PIN REGISTER IMPOSITION SYSTEM. This system eliminates the need for the stripper to lay-up pages according to a signature paging arrangement, because all of the pasteups are punched to register with punched signature flats. Only one prepared flat is required whether a booklet is four pages or hundreds. And the flats can be used over and over.

Requirements

1. A fixed punch with a center mark or line.
   a. This can be a standard stationery punch which punches two 2-3/4″ on center holes, 1/4″ diameter.
   b. However, a recommended 4-hole punch which punches two 2-3/4″ on center and two 7″ on center holes will provide better stability to secure pages to flats.

2. A pin copy board or flat made on durable white card stock. This flat is punched to register with punched individual page pasteups when they are placed on the flat.

3. Register pins or dowels to fit 1/4″ holes.

4. Base sheets on which to prepare pasteups. These should be a card with extra margin at the bottom to allow for punching space. Pages may be prepared singly or two-across. It is recommended that the pages be pasted two-across as you would view them in a book. In other words, paste page two and three at the same time . . . two on the left and three on the right. Then you would prepare pages four and five, six and seven, etc. When the pages are complete you merely need to cut them apart so that you end up with individual cards which are the individual pages to apply on a flat to photograph as they will print on the press. Pasting two-across is the logical approach to the preparation of the multiple page books (with some exceptions.)

THE BASE SHEET

It is preferable to use pre-printed base sheets to accommodate the two-across preparation.

If you do not wish to use a pre-printed base sheet, cut the card stock for double width but add 3/4″ additional margin at the bottom of the sheet. If your page size is 8-1/2 x 11, cut your base sheet to 17″ wide and 11-3/4″ high. You may wish to add an extra 1/8″ or 1/4″ at edge for bleed if required for a specific job. The pre-printed base sheets illustrated will accommodate bleeds.

After the pasteups are completed and have been

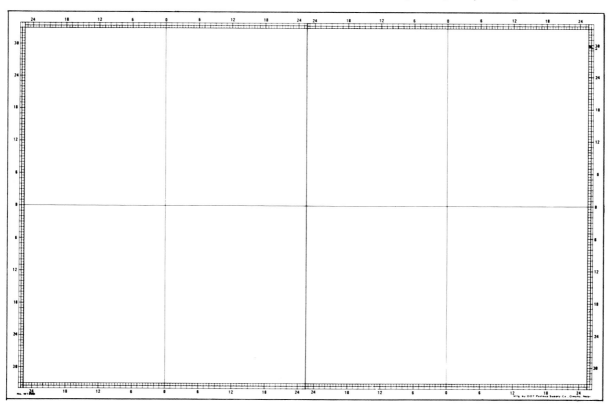

Base sheet for two-across page size: 8-1/2″x11″

approved by the customer, you are ready to cut them in half for individual punching on center at the bottom of each page.

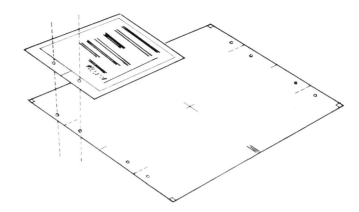

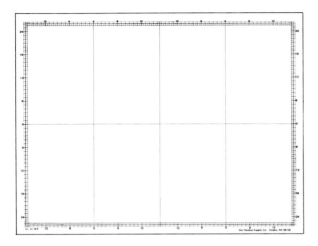

Base sheet for two-across page size: 5-1/2"x8-1/2"

DOWEL OR REGISTER PIN

Dowels

You will need a supply of plastic or metal dowels, 1/4-in. in diameter and about .060 thickness. They can be removed and used over and over on a variety of flats which you might prepare.

Pasteup preparation for two-across.

Using the pins or dowels

Using the 2-hole punch, holes are punched on center at the bottom of each page area on the base flat. These holes will line up exactly with those on the individual pages. These holes on the flat are in permanent fixed position. Any adjustments for creep are made on the individual pages after they are pasted up.

The dowels are pushed up through the holes in the base flat. They will form a post extending above each hole. Put a strip of pressure sensitive tape on the underside of the dowel base to secure the dowel on the underside of the flat. You can leave these dowels permanently installed on the flat for continual usage. The pasteups of the pages, when punched at the bottom on center, will position correctly when placed on these posts according to the dummy you have made up for your particular book.

Therefore, with only one base flat, punched pages, and the dummy, the camera operator need only place the pages on the posts according to the dummy, and

Pages cut apart after preparation.

expose the negatives. These negatives will have the multiple pages correctly imposed.

It should be noted that these base flats can be used to position sheets, even though they are not for signatures. If you have a lot of flat work to print 4-up for instance, the base flat can be used to accept the punched base pages to save time in the stripping room.

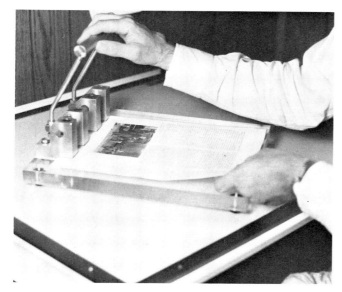

Individual pages punched for imposition.

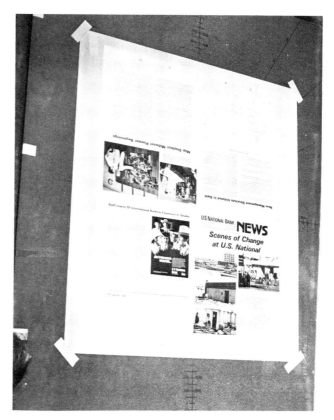

Flat in copy board of Camera.

Placing pages on the pin copy flat.

Positioning eight pages on a pin copy flat for 5-1/2"x8-1/2" page size.

NOTE: If you have a booklet containing several signatures, you will want to adjust the punching for **creep**. This creep results because when signatures are inserted, the inside signature will have **more** outside trim due to the thickness of the spine on a saddle-stitched book.

Therefore, you adjust the punching slightly to the right or left of center to allow for the extra trim. The best way to determine the amount of creep is to make up a dummy booklet using the same weight paper stock the booklet will print on. Then tap a straight pin to make a pinhole through this dummy on the outside edge equal to the distance of the trim.

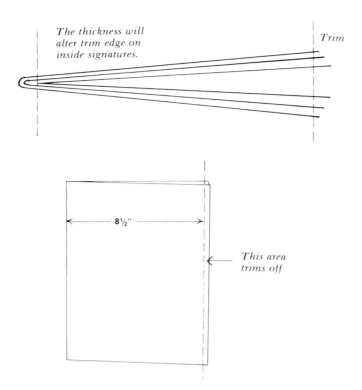

The thickness will alter trim edge on inside signatures.

Trim

This area trims off

8½"

When you open up the dummy after you have accurately tapped the pinholes, you can measure the distance from the fold to the pinhole. This distance can be used to accurately determine the amount of creep on the inside signatures.

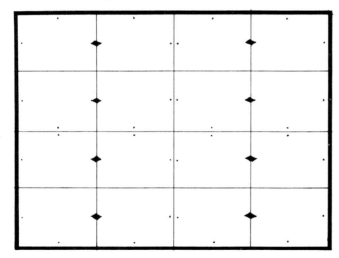

A 96-page, saddle-stitched catalog made up of six 16-page signatures, will trim at the center spread about 3/16-in. narrower than the outside cover page when using 50-lb. paper. Therefore, you will need to make a revised center line to use in place of the one you marked on your base sheet. Use this revised line as the center when punching the 2-holes. Use the Graham Color-Coded Centering Rule to quickly locate the center of the page after the creep has been determined.

COMMON PIN COPY FLATS

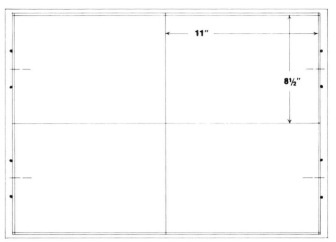

8-page signature flat or 4-page work & turn without bleed

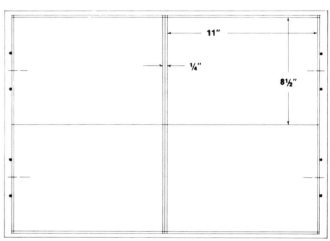

8-page signature flat or 4-page work & turn with bleed

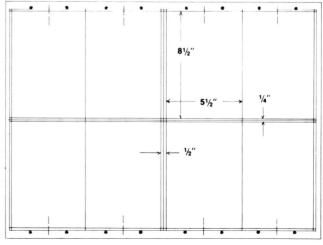

16-page signature flat or 8-page work & turn with or without bleed

A punch with clear acrylic base and center line designed for pin register imposition.

A grid is placed on the punch bed if needed to align page copy parallel to punches. Punch may be placed on light table for illumination of grid and copy.

Step-and-repeat

Sometimes it is important to print a job more than one-up on a sheet of paper. The quantity ordered by the customer may be large, and it is economically advisable to prepare a plate with multiple images on it. What does this mean to us in pasteup?

If the local library orders 100,000 bookmarks 1-1/4" x 5-1/2" from your shop, you'll want to print them more than one-up. In this instance, you can print seven across and two down on a sheet 8-3/4" x 11-1/4" or "14-up." Divide 14 into 100,000 and you get 7,143. This would be a sensible press run for such a print job. After

the printing, the sheets can be cut apart in the paper cutter, banded into packets of 500 for convenient delivery to the customer. To prepare this job in pasteup, you would make one single pasteup of one bookmark. The photo department would then make a negative and 14 duplicate negatives and strip all together to make the plate. Some shops may have step-and-repeat equipment that could be used to expose multiple images on the plate using the one single negative. Sounds like a lot of work? Try this:

From your one pasteup, make 14 diffusion-transfer prints and paste them all up on one base sheet. The camera operator can shoot the single pasteup with the images all in place using one negative of the conglomerate. This has the following advantages:

1. The prints are quick and inexpensive.

2. There is no need to strip or step.

There may be a reason, however, why you may not be able to set up a job using the print-pasteup procedure suggested.

1. The job contains various screened tints that should be stripped in the negative.

2. Benday is used and does not reproduce as faithfully on the prints as on to film and then to plate.

3. Multi-color overlay work.

First, do what you can in pasteup to make your multiple assembled pasteup complete, if the job will allow it. A common-sense approach in evaluating the job at the time of preparation is essential in order to make the final decision.

16-up bookmarks on 8-3/4" x 11-1/4" sheet, no bleed.

21

Updating Directories

The Composlide
Visible Strip and Visible Strip Panels

UPDATING DIRECTORIES

Updating directories, classified pages, price catalogs, specification books and manuals is accomplished for volume users with computers and sophisticated typesetting equipment.

A lot of jobs need to get revised periodically where the investment in computer equipment cannot be justified. Therefore, let's discuss an idea for a simple, practical and inexpensive system to handle this work.

An 8,000 circulation evening paper in Georgia uses this system for its classified pages. The system lends itself to many varieties of material in need of constant revision and periodic reproduction.

You set your classified material in galleys, one ad after the other. These galleys are delivered to the office where they are organized into classifications.

These output photo proofs are not waxed, but merely cut apart and placed under the proper headings on 1/8- or 1/4-in. white plastic sheets like trays with 1/8-in. beveled plastic guide strips fastened to the surface of the boards. The galleys are trimmed so that two or three picas of white paper remain at right and left margins. Then the individual ads are cut apart. This is best

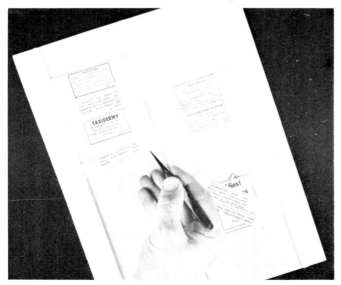

A plastic tray made to hold lines and pieces of output and classify for shooting on PMT paper.

done with a wheel-type trimmer.

There is no effort to make the ads even along the bottom, because your main purpose is merely to get the pieces into the proper order. This can be an office assembly job, removing old material, and adding in the new and keeping what is reusable. Alignment is controlled by the plastic strips and the trimmed cut edges above and below each ad.

When the deadline arrives, you make a peel-apart diffusion-transfer print which comes out in one organized piece. Now you can wax this print and handle the organized material as a unit by burnishing down the print copy in larger pieces.

The boards can be most any convenient size to accommodate the particular type of work and column widths you desire. Make up one board first, to experiment shooting the plastic board with the copy in position.

You may need to make some adjustments in your lighting or strips so that shadows do not show up. Experiments have shown that backlighting has not been necessary to eliminate shadows; however, tests have not been made with all types of darkroom cameras, nor all types of light sources.

The Composlide

The Composlide consists of a mount-up plate which is precision-grooved. The individual ads are slid into these grooves and held in place by marginal retaining T strips. The ad pieces can be removed and adjusted as required, and new pieces may be added.

With the Composlide system, the assembled pieces on the base plate are photographed as a unit in a standard camera, preferably with back light. The diffusing quality of the Composlide plate prevents shadowing along the retainers. A small amount of back lighting will eliminate the need for opaquing on the negative produced directly.

This unit is manufactured by Tobias Associates, 50 Industrial Drive, Ivyland, Pa. 18974.

The Composlide.

Visible Strips and Visible Strip Panels

Applications: Address lists, customer lists, location reference, mailing lists, telephone numbers, inventory lists . . . and many more.

Visible typing strips are made from resilient veneer surfaced with bond paper and backed with two backing sheets. Sheets have been die cut as the strips are 1/6", 1/3" or 1/2". Sheet is placed in the typewriter, any number of strips typed, then removed from outer backing sheet. Changes in any part are made quickly. Flex out old strip and insert new strip. Proper sequence is maintained by moving strips up or down in visible strip panels.

To use the directory system:

1. Type listing on visible strip.

2. Separate strip or strips from backing sheet and insert in panel.

3. Reproduce panel or panels in photocopier or from offset plate.

Visible strip panels are made so that typed strips fit snugly side to side under narrow plastic edges.

Ring binders are available to contain visible strip panels. These strips and panels are manufactured by Ring King Visibles, 215 W. Second St., Muscatine, Iowa 52761.

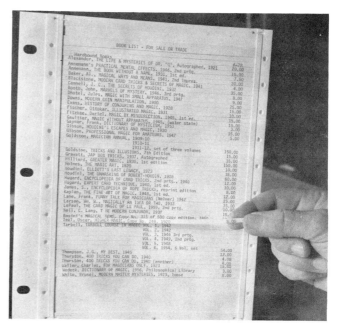

Typed visible strips may be removed and replaced with updated strips.

Panels may be organized in ring binders.

22
Newspaper Pasteup

General procedure
Display advertising
Full page assembly

NEWSPAPER PASTEUP

Procedures of pasteup can vary according to the specialization involved. For instance, a different procedure is used in pasteup for the newspaper field as compared to preparation for forms or labels. The newspaper will take a number of shortcuts in the interest of speed.

Hot metal slug lines can be "leaded" after the metal type has been placed in the chase. It is simple to insert slugs between lines to adjust the columns to come out even at the bottom of a page. When pasting up photocomposition output, it becomes impractical to cut between lines and paragraphs for perfect alignment. It is acceptable to allow a small amount of white space to appear at the end of a column resulting in a variation in the alignment at the bottoms of the columns.

General procedure

Pasting up the daily newspaper requires individual responsibility to meet absolute deadlines. Those who work in newspaper preparatory departments do have an advantage of repeating the same job every day, unlike the varieties of pasteup required by the job printer.

Work tables, boards and equipment can be designed and located to specifically accomplish page makeup. Newspaper pasteup requires an area large enough to allow full freedom of movement and best locations of the various work stations. Those pasting up must move about gathering elements here and there and are often half sitting and half standing while they make up the page.

All straight matter output and headlines are set, corrected and trimmed in the composing room. These galleys are waxed, placed on cutting board backers and then distributed to the pasteup personnel.

Pages are pasted up on grid base sheets which are delivered to the camera as they are filled up according to a planned schedule. The grid lines on these base sheets are printed in light non-reproducing blue ink.

The columns are placed in position on the grid sheets without using a t-square. In order to get all type squarely in position, it is important to trim the galleys accurately, usually exactly 1/2- or 1/4-pica from the edges of the columns. Motorized trimming devices are used to speed up the trimming operation and assure accuracy.

Display advertising

The pasteup continuity for the display advertising matter in the paper is handled *separately* from the straight output.

The procedure will often follow this outline:

1. Ad plan

A blue-penciled plan is prepared on planning paper with clip art waxed down in position so type output can be set to fit the areas marked.

2. Mark

Ad copy is marked to specify type style, leading, etc.

3. Set composition output

4. Wax

5. Apply/Square/Burnish

The ads are pasted up on the grid base sheets, often directly on a blue-penciled ad plan sheet which contained the clip art. Those keyboarding must be careful to keep this plan clean and flat when this procedure is used. The ad is filed for later placement on the full size grid page.

6. Photocopy

Photocopies are produced for approval by the advertiser. A copier which accommodates a full-size page is necessary to produce photocopies which can be proofread.

Full-page assembly

The ads are placed in the newspaper according to a plan of layout prepared on sheets of planning paper printed on 8-1/2" x 11" sheets. The same horizontal and vertical rules that are printed on the base sheets are reduced and printed on the planning paper.

It is convenient to plan the position of the ads on these smaller sheets rather than pencil the plan on full-size newspaper page sheets. From this full-page layout plan, the ads are assembled into position on the base pasteup and the type composition output is then placed in the areas filling in around the ads.

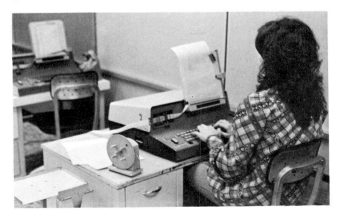

Producing a perforated tape by keyboarding.

By viewing lines on the video screen,
the composition can be positioned and sized according to the layout.

Proofreading by reading the copy on a video screen.
Corrections can be made at this time to produce
a tape that has been corrected.

Classified advertising is optically scanned
for production of the output
without need to type a second time.

This Fototronic unit produces the output for the newspaper
by using the perforated tape.

A wheel-type trimmer to
trim type output of galleys.

A waxer and Nikor trimmer.

Display advertising pasteup.

Classified advertising pasteup.

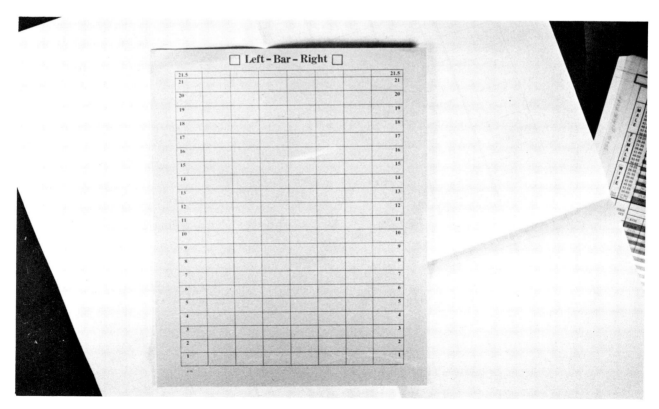

*This layout sheet is used to indicate placement
of all display advertising on the newspaper pages.*

*A large photocopier is used to produce proofs
of display advertising.*

*This carousel contains bins where individual pages
are kept after they are camera-ready.*

*A second carousel unit has space
at the top so that pages
may be placed there for final checking.*

*Note:
*All photos in this section
from the Omaha World Herald,
Omaha, Nebraska.
Daily circulation: 240,000.*

23

Four-Color Process Pasteup

Reflective
Materials
The transparency method

FOUR-COLOR PROCESS PASTEUP

Perhaps the occasion has come up when there is a need to reproduce a page with four or five pictures in full color along with type.

How does this job get camera-ready?

Reflective

Why not paste all the color snapshots down on a base sheet in position so the entire page can be color separated in one piece?

The page can be prepared in this manner; however, there are a few cautions that must be observed.

First, let's take a look at the advantages of the procedure, that is, pasting all the pictures on a sheet for a combined color separation which will include all pictures, type proofs, and color art.

The color separation is made of an entire page which is less expensive than separating each picture and tediously stripping up the individual screened negatives for four-color printing. If there are five color photos to print on one page, and each picture is color separated individually, there are 20 strip-ins on the base negatives.

If color prints are made to actual reproduction size and pasted up on a sheet in position, all photos are printed from one color separation.

It is cheaper to have color prints made to size by the photo lab, rather than enlarged or reduced to fit on a page through color separation. A photo lab can make the pictures to finished size and the separations made as a unit.

When color separating the photos why not paste down some different color patches, paint some color with a brush or even paste down a piece of yarn, wallpaper, carpeting . . . anything with color on it?

This can be done, but be careful. There are a few basic rules to remember:

1. Use the very whitest card stock for the base sheet.
2. Paste all color photos and other pieces on the base sheet.
3. Paste type proof copy on an overlay so it can be shot separately and double-burned on the black plate.
4. If the pasteup is clean and free from any dirt, dust, specks or blemishes, the separations can be prepared without the necessity for a multiple contact negative to use to get the dots out of the pure white background area.

By use of four-color process color pasteup there is a full latitude of versatility for placement of color on the base sheet.

Four-color pasteup is an excellent substitute for a job that would normally require layers of overlays and tedious stripups of film tints, etc. The set of color separations eliminates the need for flapping.

For example, a road map with its multiplicity of colored highway lines, emblems, and shields, could be pasted up using color tapes. When complete, the color pasteup is as though it were a "painting" in full color. The map can be color separated for plates to print in the colors pasted on the base sheet.

The pasteup must be extremely clean. Light sketchy lines must not appear on this pasteup. Base sheets with printed blue guidelines or grids cannot be used. A color separation of the entire pasteup will pick up literally everything.

Materials for four-color pasteup

1. Color tapes. These tapes are in various colors which can be positioned on a pasteup to reproduce. They are excellent for charts, graphs, maps, borders, rulings, etc.

2. Colored inks. Colored inks can be used in your Rapidograph pen to rule lines for reproduction in the color of ink that is in the pen.

3. Color Aid. Sheets of colored paper are available in attractive flat colors. These are ideal for pasting down for separation work. Handle them carefully and when one color patch is next to another, carefully butt the two pieces side by side. Do not stain or scratch the surface.

4. Bourges transparent color film sheets with low-tack adhesive backing are positioned on base sheet and cut to an exact outline with an art knife, and excess film is peeled away. These Bourges color sheets are available in 100%, 50%, 30% and 10% values. These percentage values are continous tones.

Careful planning using a comprehensive layout is

required for process pasteup preparation. A color element on the base sheet is intended to remain in position and not get shifted or altered.

This pasteup preparation is for reflective color separations. The separations can be produced directly from the pasteup through the lens of a camera, or by making a color transparency and separating it. Generally, this latter method is used because contact separation methods can be used without need for camera-time. If quality color photos on the page have about the same contrasts and densities, the results are excellent using this reflective pasteup method.

The transparency method

Today there are methods of producing duplicate transparencies with amazing fidelity to the original. It is this technique that makes it possible to use transparencies provided to us in any size, and know that duplicates can be produced to the finished size for use on our job.

Suppose there are five pictures to print on a sheet.

Windows are placed on the pasteup the same as for black and white.

Duplicate transparencies are made to the exact size of the final reproduction (window size). These transparencies are then positioned in the window of a negative shot of the base pasteup. The entire page is then separated as a unit from these duplicate transparencies in the windows. Eliminated is the need to strip four screened negatives for each transparency, because the entire page is in one piece and will register as a unit. Five photos in color would involve 20 strip-ins while the one-set method would involve no stripping. It would only require placement of the transparencies in the windows.

Making the duplicate transparencies would involve more cost than the color prints for reflective. work. Each job must be evaluated on the basis of what is available and on the final results. Experienced color separation technicians can improve on the quality of a color picture by individual screening when the quality is extremely critical.

24
Layout and Clip Art

LAYOUT FILE
ART AND PRINTING TECHNIQUE FILE
CLIP ART FILE

LAYOUT

Anyone working in pasteup should be able to prepare a neat pasteup from a manuscript. That is, a professional layout which is acceptable.

To help you prepare pasteups, you must establish a file of ideas which can help you.

Whenever you run across a printed piece that you like, file it in your file under the appropriate heading. This source file will prove a valuable reference and will give you an idea that you can adapt to a printing job you have to prepare.

Naturally, you'll want to add other special headings in addition to those suggested so that you can be helpful for certain clients, departments or types of printing.

Don't save and file everything you come across. Select those printed pieces or pages that you can visualize adapting to another use. Or you may want to file unusual ideas that might be shown to clients as a suggestion for adaptation to a particular printing job. Often a rough layout is prepared in advance to submit to a client, by using the file as a reference.

The thumbnail layouts provide a guide for production of the final pages.

LAYOUT IDEA FILE HEADINGS by Walter B. Graham			
Layout ideas should be placed in file folders under these headings.			
ANNOUNCEMENTS	CATALOGS	FORMS	LETTERHEADS
ANNUAL REPORTS	CATALOG SHEETS	FUND RAISING—General	MENUS
BOOKLETS	CHARTS AND GRAPHS	GOODWILL BUILDERS	MISCELLANEOUS
BROADSIDES	CHRISTMAS IDEAS	HOUSE ORGANS	NOVELTY PIECES
BROCHURES	COVERS	INVITATIONS	PERMITS
BULLETIN HEADS	DIRECT MAIL IDEAS	JACKETS	POSTERS
BUSINESS CARDS	ENVELOPES	JUMBO CARDS	ROSTERS
BUSINESS REPLY CARDS	FOLDERS	LABELS	SPECIALTIES—Die Cut

There are many sources of ideas for layouts. Probably one of the best is to be found in the annual reports published by corporations. The annual reports are usually well done as they represent a company, and are given special attention to layout and typography. Obtain any annual reports you can, examine them and save portions or file them for layout ideas for the future.

ART AND PRINTING TECHNIQUE FILE

Another file that can prove most helpful is the *Art and Printing Technique File.* Under these headings you can place printed sheets or pieces that appropriately illustrate a particular rendition or printing treatment.

For example, when you note a particular halftone screen that is different from a dot pattern, you can file it under the "halftone screen" heading. Perhaps a job will present itself that can utilize this screen to enhance its appearance.

ART AND PRINTING TECHNIQUE
FILE HEADINGS

Benday
Color Combinations
Crayon
Duotones
Halftone Screens
Pen and Ink
Pencil
Scratchboard
Wash

CLIP ART

Clip art for use in pasteup is available from a number of firms who produce this material for sale in book form or through a monthly service by subscription.

This clip art only has value if you can quickly locate those elements you require for a particular pasteup.

You need to file the material under heading appropriate to the particular piece of clip art.

In the following heading list are suggested clip art headings to place on file folder tabs. Letter the headings on legal-size folders so that you'll have ample room for the art elements.

When you receive those books of clip art, cut them up and file the material under the proper heading. Some heading topics overlap. Familiarity and use of the file will help you locate any element you require quickly and easily.

CLIP ART FILE HEADINGS

AGRICULTURE	FLOWERS	MUSIC	PEOPLE—Men—Sleeping
ANIMALS	FOOD	NAUTICAL	PEOPLE—Women—Elderly
ANIMALS—Farm	FOOD—Beverage	OBJECTS	PEOPLE—Women—Fashions
APPLIANCES	FOREIGN	OCCUPATIONS—Announcer	PEOPLE—Women—General
ARROWS	GOOD LUCK CHARMS	OCCUPATIONS—Appliance Repair	PEOPLE—Women—Housewives
BIRDS	GOVERNMENT	OCCUPATIONS—Artist	PEOPLE—Women—Pointing
BORDERS	GROUPS	OCCUPATIONS—Carpenter	PEOPLE—Women—Reading
BUGS & INSECTS	HANDS	OCCUPATIONS—Chef—Cook	PEOPLE—Women—Sleeping
BUILDING MATERIALS	HEALTH—Sanitation	OCCUPATIONS—Clerk	POSTCARD
BUILDINGS—Business	HISTORICAL	OCCUPATIONS—Dairy	ROMANCE—Wedding
BUILDINGS—Homes	HOBBIES—Miscellaneous	OCCUPATIONS—Delivery	SAFETY
BUSINESS—Banking, Credit	HOBBIES—Photography	OCCUPATIONS—Detective	SCIENCE
BUSINESS—Moving	HOBBIES—Sports	OCCUPATIONS—Doctor	SCHOOL—Cheerleaders—Graduation
BUSINESS—Office	HOLIDAYS—Christmas	OCCUPATIONS—Fireman	RELIGION
BUSINESS—Printing	HOLIDAYS—Easter	OCCUPATIONS—General	SEASON—Summer
BUSINESS—Real Estate	HOLIDAYS—Fourth of July	OCCUPATIONS—Mechanics	SEASON—Spring
BUSINESS—Retail Sales	HOLIDAYS—Holloween-Columbus	OCCUPATIONS—Musicians	SEASON—Fall
CALENDARS	HOLIDAYS—Labor Day	OCCUPATIONS—Nurse	SEASON—Winter
CAMPING	HOLIDAYS—Lincoln—Washington	OCCUPATIONS—Office	SCENERY
CARNIVALS—FAIRS	HOLIDAYS—Memorial Day	OCCUPATIONS—Painters	SIGNS
CARTOONS	HOLIDAYS—Mothers, Fathers Day	OCCUPATIONS—Policemen	SITUATIONS
CIRCUS—Animals—Acts	HOLIDAYS—New Years	OCCUPATIONS—Postman	SPACE
CLEANLINESS	HOLIDAYS—Thanksgiving	OCCUPATIONS—Salesman	SPORTS—Basketball—Baseball
COMMUNICATIONS—Mail	HOLIDAYS—Valentine—St. Patrick	OCCUPATIONS—School Teacher	SPORTS—Fishing & Hunting
COMMUNICATIONS—Newspaper	HOLIDAYS—Veterans Day	OCCUPATIONS—Secretary	SPORTS—General
COMMUNICATIONS—Radio-TV	HOTELS	OCCUPATIONS—Service Station	SPORTS—Golf
COMMUNICATIONS—Telephone	HOUSEHOLD FOODS & EQUIP	OCCUPATIONS—Social Worker	SPORTS—Rodeo—Horse Rider
CONVENTIONS	IDEAS	OCCUPATIONS—Workman	SPORTS—Swimming
CONSTRUCTION—Homes—Repair	INDUSTRIAL	PANELS	SPORTS—Winter
COUPONS	INSURANCE	PARKS	STARS—Boxes
CRIME	INVITATIONS	PEOPLE—Children—Babies	SYMBOLS
DESIGNS	KEYS AND LOCKS	PEOPLE—Couples	TIME
EMBLEMS	LAYOUT MATERIAL	PEOPLE—Crowds	TOOLS
ENTERTAINMENT	LETTERING—Assorted Words	PEOPLE—Gay 90's	TRANSPORTATION—Auto—Bus
EYES—Nose—Ears	LETTERHEAD	PEOPLE—Men—Elderly	TRANSPORTATION—Planes
FAIRY TALES	MAGIC	PEOPLE—Men—Expressions	TRANSPORTATION—Railroad
FAMILY	MAPS	PEOPLE—Men—Fashions	TRANSPORTATION—Ships—Truck
FEATURE PAGE	MEDICAL	PEOPLE—Men—General	TREES
FEET	MILITARY	PEOPLE—Men—Pointing	VACATIONS
FISH	MISCELLANEOUS	PEOPLE—Men—Reading	WEATHER
FLAGS	MONEY	PEOPLE—Men—Salesman	WESTERN

25

Six hundred Classified Job Printing Ideas for Graphic Artists

Announcements
Booklets
Broadsides
Bulletins
Business Cards
Mailing Cards
Catalogs
Envelopes
Folders
Handbills
House Magazines
Labels and Stamps
Letterheads and Four-page Letters
Magazines
Manuals and Handbooks
Maps and Charts
Menus and Programs
Newsprint Specialties
Novelties and Die-cuts
Office Forms
Portfolios
Posters
Packaging Materials
Reports
Self-Mailers
Specialties
Window, Wall, and Point-of Purchase Displays

SIX-HUNDRED CLASSIFIED JOB PRINTING IDEAS

This section of Job Printing Layout Ideas is meant to give you suggestions for the preparation of printed material. You will find that you can adapt many of these suggested layouts to your own use.

A virtue of any pasteupper is to be idea-minded. To be able to come up with an attractive printing job for your client is important. It will pay you to become familiar with a variety of styles of printing, shapes, sizes, type faces and some basic advertising knowledge to help you tell a story simply and logically in a proper printed presentation.

This job printing section will provide you with some basic ideas for printed pieces that will help you get started as an "idea-minded" graphic artist.

Suggestions on how to use the ideas contained in this section

1. Study the various classifications and ideas contained in this section.

2. Make rough dummies based on the ideas and layouts when you are required to plan a job of printing. You can use the grid planning paper suggested in this book.

3. Accumulate additional printed idea samples to place in your file as suggested in the chapter discussing the layout and clip art file.

4. Gather ideas that show art technique reproduced in printed pieces. These might include pencil, crayon, pen-and-ink, scratchboard, wash, Benday and shading film, various line halftone screened photo reproductions.

5. Gather specimens of color combinations.

ANNOUNCEMENTS

These varied layout styles for announcements indicate areas for headlines, sub-heads, illustrations, trade marks, text type and signature cut or name line with address, phone, etc.

Some are conventional in style, others relatively more novel or individual. All are drawn in proportion to the suggested size. Any of the styles can be adapted to announcements as small as government postal cards (3-1/2" x 5-1/2"). Others may be single, shortfold, or longfold cards—or French fold, folding to about 4" x 5", 5" x 7", 6" x 9", with envelopes to match. Others are standard 8-1/2" x 11" letterheads used for announcement purposes, laid out so that folds will not go through type matter or illustrations.

15 Basic Styles of Announcements: With envelopes to match, except post cards

1. Right edge of each line makes arrow shape pointing to a trade mark, photo, or sketch of product, person or event.

2. Horizontal announcement card.

3. An idea for a postcard style card.

4. Background can be produced by using Benday, solid or tint. Print in black or color.

5. Upper right type mass is flush left and with uneven lines at right edge; vice versa for type mass at the lower left corner.

6. Lines uneven at left and right. Large decorative initial letter for first word, rest of word in caps or small caps. Rest of copy upper and lower case.

7. This layout is suitable for vertical use on a post card, or it may be adapted to other sizes and shapes of announcements. Rather lengthy copy is made more readable by placing top paragraph at upper right,

and bottom paragraph at lower left, with trademark and illustration filling up the spaces. Additional details can be carried below the logo.

8. Sketch or photo of a building, product, or person, etc., bleeds off upper left.

9. Semi-circular photo or sketch at top and type line at bottom, making racetrack shape.

10. For vertical use on a post card. Or, it may be adapted to other sizes and shapes of announcement cards

or folders. Background can bleed off all four edges, or else come to within a pica or so of the edges. Background can be tone in black or color, or a solid color or a reproduction of an ornate design in line.

11. Headline at angle to which text conforms.

12. Beveled panel effect with rules.

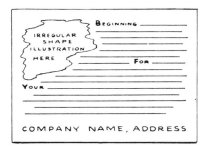

13. Text type flows around line illustration of irregular shape.

Words at start of key sentences start in a bold gothic type, with balance of each such word in small caps of the body type. No indentions.

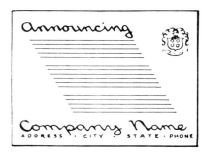

14. Type lines of equal length are made to form a parallelogram, sloping from left to right. The company name, address, etc., are set in display type for bottom base.

15. Letterhead folded for 6-3/4″ envelope. Can use type or pictures.

16. Letterhead folded for Baronial envelope. Can vary type area.

17. Letterhead folded for No. 10 envelope. Note centered lines.

BOOKLETS

Only careful analysis of all the sales, design, and cost factors involved in each job will determine the exact size and shape of a booklet; whether to use one, two, three or more columns; whether to bind on the long or short side, and what kind of binding method to use; how to treat the cover; whether to use colored or white papers for text pages and cover; whether to use a second color of ink for headlines, tint backgrounds, spot drawings; whether to use a non-rectangular shape; whether to use as a self-mailer or in an envelope, and so on.

Our purpose here is to indicate just a few of the major types of booklet layouts which may help your planning. Sometimes the best style of layout for the job at hand can be approached by first eliminating unsuitable styles, then modifying or combining several suitable styles until a good solution is reached.

Listed in the table below are untrimmed booklet page sizes, all of which cut without waste from standard book paper sizes listed. They are listed in the order of the shorter dimension. The number of pages which cut from a sheet is in parenthesis.

25 × 38			32 × 44			35 × 45		
2-3/8	×	3-1/8	(256)	2-2/3	×	7-1/3	(144)	2- 3/16	×	5-5/8	(256)
3-1/8	×	4-3/4	(128)	2-3/4	×	4	(256)	2-13/16	×	4-3/8	(256)
3-1/8	×	6-1/3	(96)	3-2/3	×	4	(192)	2-11/12	×	4-1/2	(240)
3-1/8	×	7-3/5	(80)	3-2/3	×	5-1/3	(144)	2-11/12	×	7-1/2	(144)
3-1/8	×	9-1/2	(64)	3-2/3	×	8	(96)	3-3/4	×	5-5/6	(144)
3-1/6	×	4-1/6	(144)	4	×	4-2/5	(160)	3-3/4	×	8-3/4	(96)

25 × 38			32 × 44			35 × 45		
3-1/6	× 6-1/4	(96)	4	× 5-1/2	(128)	4-3/8	× 4-1/2	(160)
3-4/5	× 6-1/4	(80)	4	× 7-1/3	(96)	4-3/8	× 5-5/8	(128)
4-1/6	× 6-1/3	(72)	4	× 8-4/5	(80)	4-3/8	× 7-1/2	(96)
4-3/4	× 6-1/4	(64)	4-2/5	× 5-1/3	(120)	4-3/8	× 9	(80)
4-3/4	× 8-1/3	(48)	4-2/5	× 8	(80)	4-1/2	× 5-5/6	(120)
5	× 9-1/2	(40)	5-1/3	× 5-1/2	(96)	4-1/2	× 8-3/4	(80)
6-1/4	× 6-1/3	(48)	5-1/3	× 7-1/3	(72)	5-5/8	× 5-5/6	(96)
6-1/4	× 7-3/5	(40)	5-1/2	× 6-2/5	(80)	5-5/8	× 7	(80)
6-1/4	× 9-1/2	(33)	5-1/2	× 8	(64)	5-5/8	× 8-3/4	(64)
6-1/4	× 8-1/3	(36)	7-1/3	× 8	(48)	5-5/6	× 7-1/2	(72)
7-3/5	× 12-1/2	(20)	7-1/3	× 10-2/3	(36)	7-1/2	× 8-3/4	(48)
8-1/3	× 9-1/2	(24)	8	× 8-4/5	(40)	8-3/4	× 9	(40)
9-1/2	× 12-1/2	(16)	8	× 11	(32)	8-3/4	× 11-1/4	(32)

Some page sizes lend themselves equally well for binding on the long or short side of the page by saddle or side-wire stitching based on running 4-8-12-16 or more pages. Others are sizes adapted for binding along just the short side; still others just along the long side of the page, unless a flat style of binding is used, in which case any size can be bound along either edge.

Economy in folding and gathering must be considered.

There are many other possible sizes which cut without waste.

Check mailing envelope size as well as method of running and determine binding edge before deciding on page size and standard paper size to use.

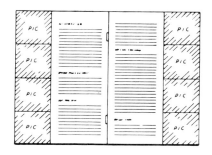

1. Double spread with photos or drawings in vertical panels bleeding off left edge of left pages, off right edge of right pages—also at top and bottom of each page. There may be one tall, narrow picture per page, or two tall pictures, or three reproduced from the usual 8″ x 10″ vertical photo size, or four about square, or five or more horizontal pictures. Some pages may combine reproductions of different heights but the same width.

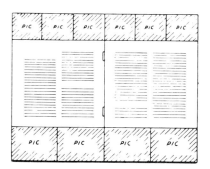

2. Double spread with photos or drawings in horizontal panels

bleeding off top and bottom of each page, as well as both sides. This layout shows how eight pictures can be used on a two-page spread. Text is placed in two columns per page.

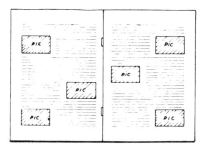

3. Double spread with pictures spotted flush left and flush right, the text can often be read more easily if the eye is relieved by this alternating arrangement. Also, each individual picture stands out to maximum advantage. Text can be related to each nearby picture area. The layout is very flexible, and can accommodate one, two, three or more picture areas per page. In this layout the photos or sketches should be small.

4. Booklets may be die-cut to circular shape.

5. Type and illustrations printed on an angle across a square, then folded.

6. When perspective is wanted on cover of small booklet for building, etc.

7. Here a square booklet has been round-cornered at the four corners.

8. Octagonal shape for this small booklet, trimmed after stitching.

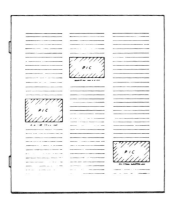

9. For the lengthy booklet where extensive text matter can be relieved by small photos or sketches, consider this three column set-up, with one, two, or three illustrations per page.

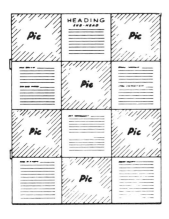

10. Here six photos or sketches are laid out in 3 x 4 checkerboard squares.

11. Extra readability can be gained by printing the main story in large type in a wider column width than a subordinate topic—or group of short paragraphs—set in smaller type.

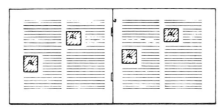

12. A square shape (here using two columns) is relief from usual rectangle.

13. Here a miniature booklet (e.g., 2-3/8″ x 4″) uses one bleed illustration.

14. Where dark halftones are to be used, consider bleeding one off bottom of each page.

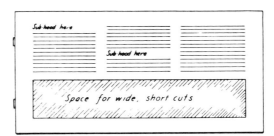

15. Sometimes pictures in a booklet must be long and narrow. If horizontal, as for long, low factory buildings, or landscapes in a real estate promotion, bind at narrow edge with three columns for type. If vertical, as for tall buildings, bind long way, use one type column.

16. This layout can be enlarged to 3-7/8″ x 8-3/4″ for use in a No. 10 envelope. Here type runs around small photos or sketches.

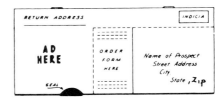

17. The booklet as a self-mailer— e.g., 4-1/4″ x 8-1/2″ size, with seal over bottom edge. Addressed on outside back cover (of a paper of government post card thickness) with perforations for detaching as a busi-

ness reply card (indicia on reverse side). Order form must not come closer than 3-1/2″ from right edge. Max. width 5-9/16″, height 3-9/16″.

18. This booklet has trim size of 3-1/2″ x 5-1/2″. One side of each post card weight sheet uses picture of a product with short description beneath, sales copy at upper right, order form at lower right. Reverse side of each sheet bears business reply card indicia. In this way separate orders can be mailed in at different times by different departments or to various advertisers in same booklet.

BROADSIDES

Broadsides offer advertisers great advantages by providing a variety of layout areas from small to large in the successive spreads. They arouse a special curiosity as each spread is opened. They also have the advantage of a very large center spread which lends itself as a poster for display purposes. They depend for results on size and smash effect. Text is usually short. Most type, lettering, drawings and photos are large.

Broadsides may be sent as self-mailers—sealed with a gummed sticker at the bottom of the address area—or put in a suitable envelope, either alone, with a covering letter, or with other enclosures.

Broadsides usually have 4, 6, 8, 12, 16, 24 or 32 pages. Size is usually at least 11″ x 17″ and not over 24″ x 38″. Possible combinations of from two to four or five right-angle and parallel folds are numerous. Your choice will depend on the sequence of area sizes and shapes desired in relation to practical use of your folding machine.

An organization publicizing a membership drive or sponsored event can supply several copies of a broadside to each of its members so they can give them to friends for centerspread posting in offices, stores, factories.

Forty broadside sizes which are cut from standard papers are shown in the chart. The number in parenthesis is the number cutting from a sheet without waste.

The other chart lists ten broadsides, using varying folding styles. The diagrams show how each opens out in sequence from mailing sizes to inner spread. Each opened area should be treated as a separate unit, yet as one which flows smoothly from preceding to following spreads.

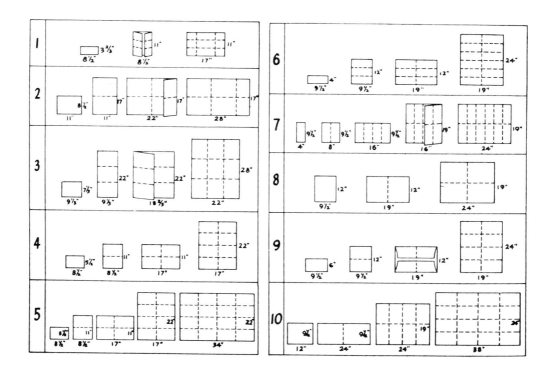

40 Broadside Sizes (before trim) from Standard Papers

BOND			BOOK				COVER	
22 × 34	28 × 34	24 × 38	25 × 38	28 × 44	32 × 44	35 × 45	23 × 35	26 × 40
11 × 17 (4)	11 1/3 × 28 (3)	12 × 19 (4)	12 1/2 × 19 (4)	14 × 22 (4)	11 × 16 (8)	11 1/4 × 17 1/2 (8)	11 1/2 × 17 1/2 (4)	13 × 20 (4)
11 1/3 × 22 (3)	14 × 17 (4)	12 2/3 × 24 (3)	12 2/3 × 25 (3)	14 2/3 × 28 (3)	14 2/3 × 16 (6)	15 × 17 1/2 (6)	11 2/3 × 23 (3)	13 1/3 × 26 (3)
17 × 22 (2)	17 × 28 (2)	19 × 24 (2)	19 × 25 (2)	22 × 28 (2)	14 2/3 × 32 (3)	15 × 35 (3)	17 1/2 × 23 (2)	20 × 26 (2)
22 × 34 (1)	28 × 34 (1)	24 × 38 (1)	25 × 38 (1)	28 × 44 (1)	16 × 22 (4)	17 1/2 × 22 1/2 (4)	23 × 35 (1)	26 × 40 (1)
					22 × 32 (2)	22 1/2 × 35 (2)		
					32 × 44 (1)	35 × 45 (1)		

10 Examples of Broadside Styles

STYLE NO.	UNTRIMMED SIZE: FLAT	FINAL FOLDED SIZE	BOND PAPER	BOOK PAPER	COVER PAPER	COPIES/ SHEET	TOTAL FOLDS	NO. OF SURFACES	SECTIONS IN CENTER
1	11 × 17	3 2/3 × 8 1/2	22 × 34	22 1/2 × 35	23 × 35	4	4	3	9
2	17 × 28	8 1/2 × 11	28 × 34			2	3	4	6
3	22 × 28	7 1/3 × 9 1/3		28 × 44		2	4	4	9
4	17 × 22	5 1/2 × 8 1/2	22 × 34	22 1/2 × 35	23 × 35	2	3	4	8
5	22 × 34	5 2/3 × 8 1/2	"	"	"	1	4	5	16
6	19 × 24	4 × 9 1/2	24 × 38	25 × 38	26 × 40	2	4	4	12
7	19 × 24	4 × 9 1/2	"	"	"	2	4	5	12
8	19 × 24	9 1/2 × 12	"	"	"	2	2	3	4
9	19 × 24	6 × 9 1/2	"	"	"	2	4	4	8
10	24 × 38	9 1/2 × 12	"	"	"	1	3	4	8

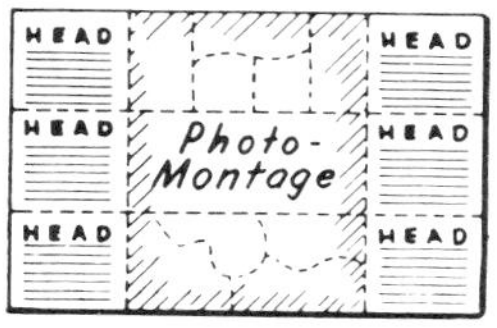

1. Two side wings of broadside's center spread are used for text, mid-section for photo-montage.

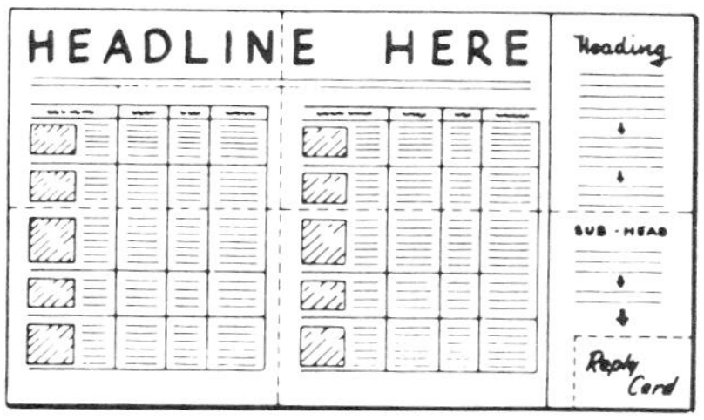

2. Six areas in center spread. Two smaller ones for text and detachable reply card. Chart has photos of products in left column, four columns for text.

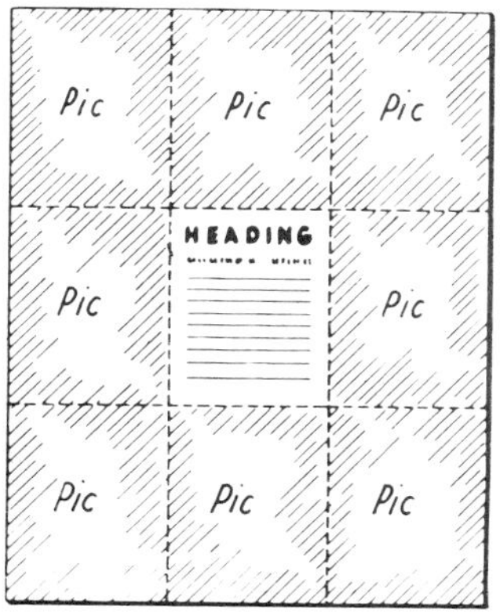

3. Folds make nine areas in this center spread. The eight outer areas are used for bleed photos (or a series of drawings) with strategic center area for text.

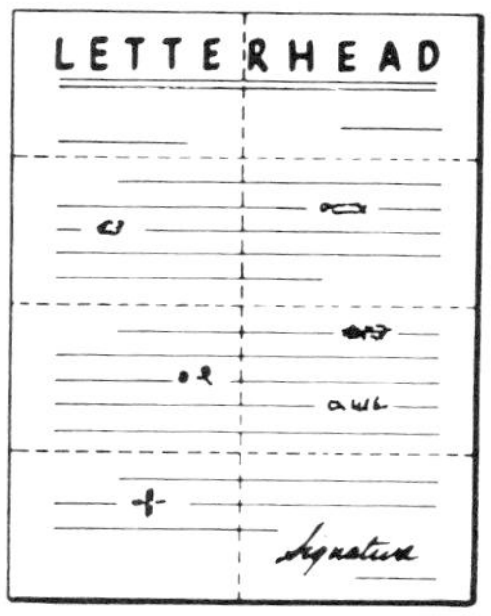

4. Important news on products or company policy can go in animated letter (e.g., 17″ x 22″).

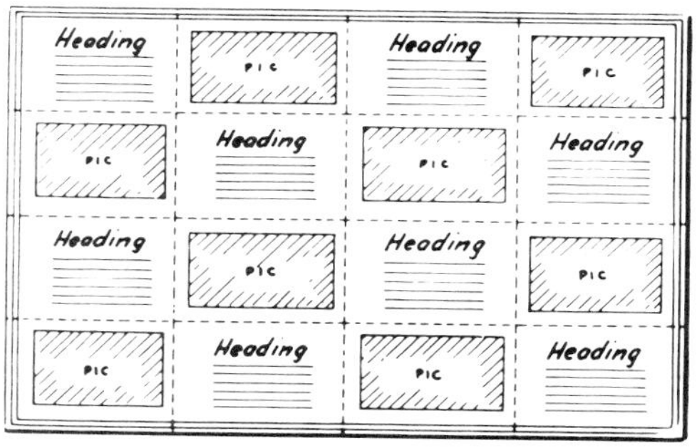

5. A checkerboard layout is good to secure individual attention for each of the eight photos or drawings used here and for the eight descriptive copy areas alongside them. A decorative border bleeding off the four sides provides frame effect. Three folds in each direction make sixteen equal rectangular areas for the material. Illusion of a checkerboard is even more realistic if square areas are used instead of rectangles.

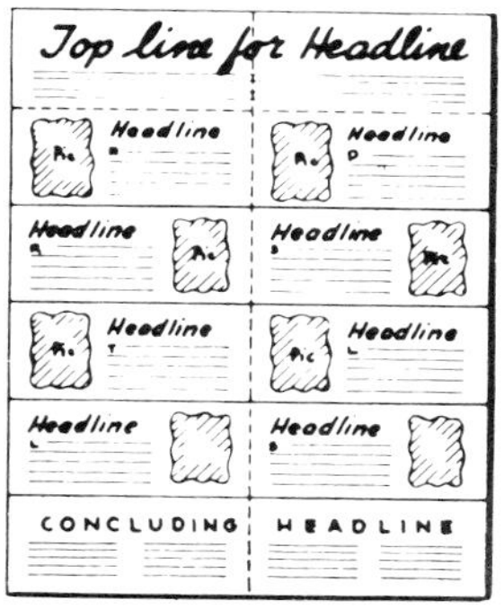

6. Attention-getting, pictures first at the left, then at the right of the text.

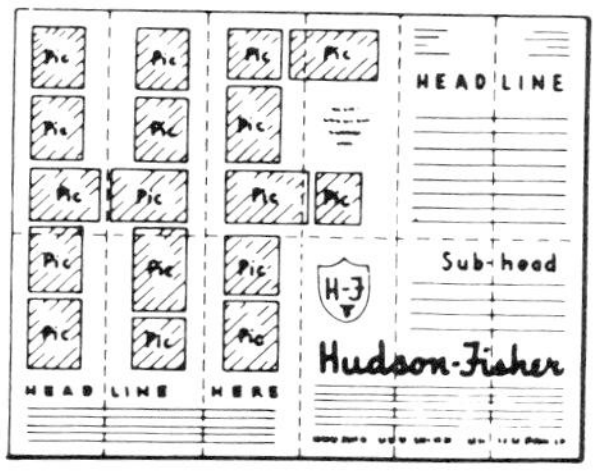

7. Often the advertiser's initials in block letter form are good for photo-montage use.

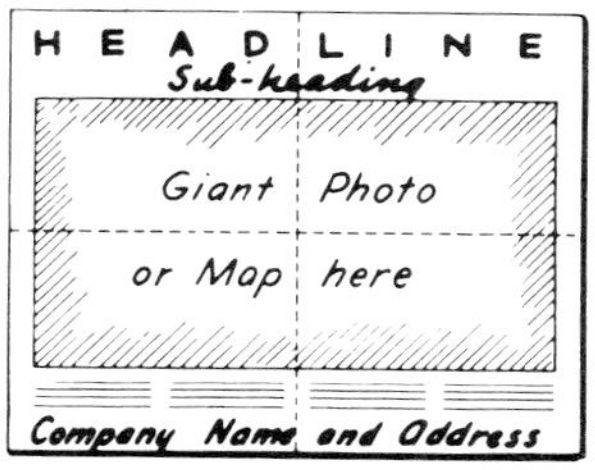

8. For minimum folding through large picture consider French-fold (e.g., 17″ x 22″ to 8-1/2″ x 11″).

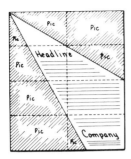

9. Searchlight beam area cuts dramatically across montage.

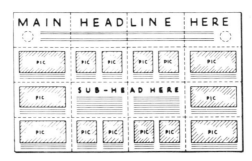

10. Folds make sixteen equal area rectangles, good for "picture magazine" layout technique, with large photos, each with a short caption in big type, set flush left and right beneath. Here six of the pictures are large and horizontal, eight are smaller and vertical. Descriptive text on a series of products gets high readership by being interspersed between the large pictures.

BULLETINS

One of the best ways to start layout ideas flowing when you face any particular design problem is to look simultaneously at various possible alternatives. By rapid trial of each idea for the given need, you are able to select quickly, several possible layout styles to accomplish your purposes. Then, by further study and refinement, one of these styles can be adapted fully to your requirements.

Manufacturers, wholesalers, retailers, clubs, organizations, and so on, issue promotional bulletins to their staffs, customers, prospects, members, etc. They also issue news releases to the media.

Those preparing pasteups are often called upon to suggest ideas for bulletins and releases.

12 of many possible styles

EXAMPLE	Description	SIZE UNTRIMMED	CUTS NO OUT	Standard Sheet
1, 10, 11, 12	Single letter sheet	8½ × 11	4	17 × 22
2	Half letter sheet	5½ × 8½	8	
3	" longfold	8½ × 11	4	
4	" shortfold	5½ × 17	4	
5	Bottom flap	8½ × 14	4	17 × 28
6	Monarch size	7¼ × 10½	9	22 × 34
7	Legal, longfold	14 × 17	4	17 × 28
8	Side flap	11 × 11½	6	22 × 34
9	Legal size	8½ × 14	4	17 × 28
13	Top flap	8½ × 14	4	-
14	Shortfold letter	8½ × 22	2	17 × 22
15	Longfold letter	11 × 17	2	"

1. Single-space narrow items for variety.

2. Short bulletin form, 5-1/2" x

8-1/2" with top head bleeding-off.

3. Short items only. Printed 8-1/2" x 11" folds to 5-1/2" x 8-1/4". Indent alternate items.

4. Bulletin printed 11" x 17" work-

and-turn, cut to 5-1/2" x 17", folded to 5-1/2" x 8-1/2". Folds twice to fit a No. 6-3/4 envelope.

5. Release 8-1/2" x 14" with flap 3" deep for basic data about concern.

6. Six items in a sales bulletin each illustrated with a chart, sketch or photo, alternately left and right.

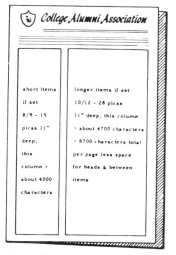

7. Bulletin (14″ x 17″) folds to 8-1/2″ x 14″.

8. Size flat 11″ x 11-1/3″. Side flap 2-5/6″ wide folds over left edge; area for release is standard 8-1/2″ x 11″ size. Same background data on the society—history, purposes, officers, on the flap of each release. Can use both sides.

9. Bulletin, 8-1/2″ x 14″ with detachable reply.

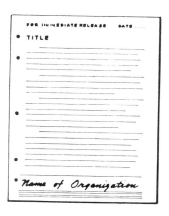

10. Five-hole punch, two or three ring file.

11. Two-fold self-mailer for release.

12. Short news items to narrow column.

13. Bulletin has three-inch top flap.

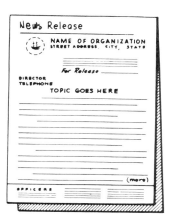

14. Release folds to 8-1/2″ x 11″.

15. Short items in center column.

BUSINESS CARDS

Here are a number of basic formats which may provide ideas for either conservative or novelty fashion.

There are folded cards, some with bleed, borders and novelty shapes, and some which require die-cutting.

The standard size for a business card is 3-1/2″ x 2″, but cards can vary in size.

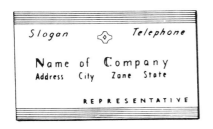

1. Separate color tint bleeds at top and bottom or rules can be used in same color as rest of card.

2. Separate color tint bleeds at left and right edges. Or, use rule borders in same color as text.

3. Three-dimensional effect

through use of frame-style border with shadow, from rules or special drawing.

4. Photo of sales representative often desirable for remembrance value. Here halftone bleeds off upper left corner.

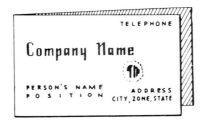

5. Dynamic symmetry in this layout, featuring trademark in off-center position. Shortfold, more copy inside.

6. Reverse line cut of company name in black or separate color. Small trade mark is centered above it.

7. Sometimes nature of the company or its main product makes it appropriate to use a decorative border.

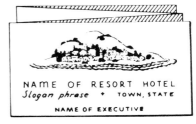

8. Accordion-folded along short

edge of card. Printed both sides for 7-page story following business card on top.

9. Sometimes a company can feature an old-time woodcut or drawing in its own industrial field or firm's history.

10. Many companies produce or sell products which make effective overall backgrounds, with white card at angle.

11. Accordion folded on long edge of card. Printed on both sides for 7-page story besides business card on top.

12. An early woodcut can be used effectively to bleed off two sides.

13. A texture pattern makes effective background to bleed top and bottom of card, in black or color.

14. Sometimes printing type and illustrations at an angle across the card can make it more memorable, less ordinary.

15. Two cards angle-trimmed on the cutter after printing. Card on right silhouettes top of a building.

16. Top or side of card may be die-cut to conform to trademark, giant letter or other illustration.

17. Twelve-month calendar printed on large size business card. Longfold reversed to stand up on prospect's desk.

18. Unusual vertical card gets attention. Halftone of building tract bleeds at top.

19. Large vertical card has name area at top for price quotations, personal messages.

20. Vertical layout, die-cut figure illustration (e.g., trade mark) to tie-in with product.

21. Note pad of white or colored bond paper attached by padding to projecting card.

22. Longfold card can gain extra attention value by being angle-trimmed, round-cornered or die-cut before or after folding.

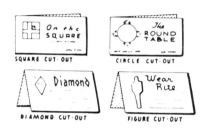

23. Folded cards, top surface features cutout area of special shapes. Drawing or short text copy shows from under surface.

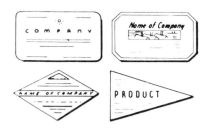

24. Cards can be round-cornered, corner-trimmed, cut to diamond, pennant or other special shapes.

25. Cards may be die-cut to circular shape.

26. A firm can make its card the cover of miniature mechanical-bound booklet.

27. Business reply card (3-1/2" x 5-1/2" when detached on perforation) continues as business card cover of booklet.

MAILING CARDS

Here are ideas for a variety of mailing cards, single or folded cards for bulk mailing, and business reply cards. Some of the layouts are for horizontal cards, some for vertical. Some use one column, others two or three. Some have space for illustrations, others are all type. Some are conventional in format, others less usual in style. It is important to keep the design and typography quite simple. You may look over these styles and select the one you wish to follow using the copy you have been provided. It is simple to modify any of the designs.

Sizes. A government postal card measures 5-1/2" x 3-1/4". Cards may be printed and the postage affixed for mailing. Other convenient and standard sizes for mailing cards are: 4" x 6", 3-1/2" x 8-1/2" (fits No. 10 envelope and prints 3-up on 8-1/2" x 11"), 8-1/2" x 8-1/2", 6" x 9", 8-1/2" x 11", and 9" x 12".

These cards are convenient when customers wish to mail out information and save the cost of an envelope. They are used for advertising, notices, direct mail campaigns, etc.

1. Type lines are set flush left, uneven right margin, c.l.c. Key words in boldface.

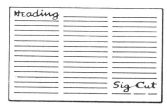

2. For long copy. Three columns, lines run parallel to length of card. Head and sig. line in bold or in color.

3. Lines of equal length, but alternately indented first flush left, then flush right, makes striking effect.

4. Company letterhead (reduced) at top. Message: typewriter composition.

5. Border tape used to make decorative border at left and right of vertical card. Trademark or small logo centered at the top.

6. Here nine lines of the message radiate in sunburst effect.

7. Heading in reverse, bleeds at top of card. Two columns are used for the text matter.

8. The headline is placed at an angle with type lines which follow conforming to it. Secures attention.

9. Photo or sketch of product bleeds off left edge. One column for text items, separated by dots.

10. Heading in reverse, bleeds at top of card. Text lines are of uneven length, and are centered.

11. Photo of product bleeds at upper left, descriptive copy below. Wider measure at right.

12. Two-column set-up, with lines parallel to length of card. Head and subhead are centered.

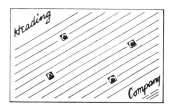

13. Text is set so lines will fit card when pasted up at angle.

14. Checkerboard effect, using three square photos with text in the three other spaces.

15. Three sketches or photos staggered with the text. Sig. line in bold for balance.

16. Tall picture at the upper left corner of a vertical card layout, description below.

17. Business reply card on self mailer card should be set at right-angle to it.

18. Dramatic effect in use of repro of actual news clipping, or set part of ad in this style.

19. Bottom part of mailing card used for detachable coupon.

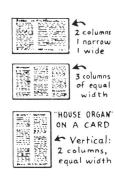

20. Postal cards can hold 300-400 words set in 8-point type, solid.

21. Omnibus style card. The heading is printed with photo.

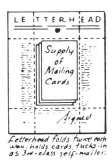

22. Organization's form letter has cards on coming event. Members mail to own friends.

23. Double post card with return portion. Be sure that business reply indicia prints on the inside of the card according to postal regulations.

24. All-purpose reply card enclosed with business letters. Person addressed simply fills in, expedites answer.

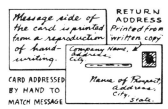

25. Added attention value is sometimes secured by reproducing the message from handwritten copy.

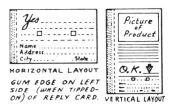

26. Reply card gummed at edge, perforated for detaching when mounted on catalog, letter, etc. Gets attention.

Additional Layout Ideas

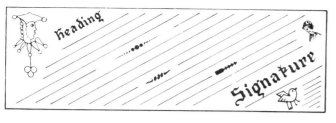

CATALOGS

Many factors must be considered when designing a catalog: nature of the product, types of users, ways in which catalog is used, cost per copy in various editions, etc.

If a certain size and style has been put out consistently in the past, this pattern and the company may be so closely associated in the minds of the recipients that it would be a mistake to change, even though certain improvements could be made. The company would risk loss of identity. Changes might be made if improvements in readability, reference value, impressiveness of illustrations and economy can be achieved.

A catalog is any kind of company or product reference list on goods, or services, or both. There may or may not be detailed descriptions, prices, illustrations, cover and separate envelope.

1. Large space for two important company products, six smaller spaces for lesser ones; table, diagram.

3. Some catalogs need pictures of scores of varied sizes, shapes, with columns subdivided accordingly.

5. (A) Back cover projects as file tab; (B) Opens for file, closes for pocket.

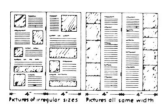

2. Catalogs, 4″ x 9″ for No. 10 envelope may alternate informal style with a more formal as on the right.

4. Two type columns spaced to allow illustrations to overlay, with space for sketches in the center.

6. Photos or drawings in squares, text adjoining.

4-page catalog
bulletin-style

7. Short items in "bulletins" at various angles. Color or tone background.

8. Self-mailer catalog-folder as display for dealer's walls, windows.

9. Three columns on left page, photos column width; two-column, right page photos narrower than column, staggered.

10. Catalog 4" x 18" folds to 4" x 9" to fit No. 10 envelope. Four possible layouts shown.

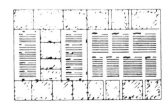

11. Photos in "I"-shape at left, captions at sides. Right: Text conforms to margins of photos.

3 x 5 inch file card made for each item

PRODUCT & Company Name

12. When many items are added or modified each year, with rapid changes desired, consider 3" x 5" card file.

13. Some types of catalogs are best with only one or two large pictures per page; informal bleed layout.

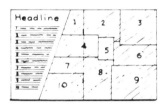

14. Some catalog spreads may use montage effect, bleed three sides, type margin at an angle, to conform.

15. Here nearly as much space is used for drawings to dramatize or show how to use the products.

16. Uniform size items in catalog may be treated in geometric style pattern; name of each on the band.

17. Catalog pages are stepped to show each division.

18. Center type, photos silhouetted, texture background.

19. Eighteen pictures frame double-spread, text in center.

20. Cover styles.

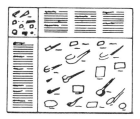

21. Photos of many small items are in two bleed panels.

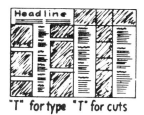

22. T-shape can be used either for type areas, or for cuts.

23. Lines in color or halftone separate the eight picture areas on this spread. Text: uneven right edge.

24. Eight of hundreds of possible geometrical shapes for grouping small catalog items; eye-catching patterns.

25. A company may issue gummed stamps every few weeks for new items; show where to mount in album.

26. Creating right atmosphere for favorable attention to the catalog by the prospect starts with the envelope.

ENVELOPES

When printing ready-made envelopes on a duplicator offset press, it must be remembered that gripper margin must be allowed. It would be impossible to print a ready-made envelope and bleed all four sides. Gripper is necessary. If an envelope must bleed, it must be printed on flat paper before it is made into an envelope. Printing a ready-made envelope with a large tint area printed on it can cause some printing quality problems. Envelopes are made up of several uneven thicknesses, and sometimes the pressure will cause a tint area to print poorly, depending on the location and size of the area.

Popular envelope sizes

No. 6-3/4 size: 3-5/8″ x 6-1/2″

No. 8 Monarch size: 3-7/8″ x 7-1/2″

No. 9 size: 3-7/8″ x 8-7/8″

No. 10 size: 4-1/8″ x 9-1/2″

No. 5-1/2 Baronial size: 4-3/8″ x 5-5/8″

1. Type lines form triangle, also flush left. Position type to allow 3/8-in. for grippers and 3/8-in. above the type.

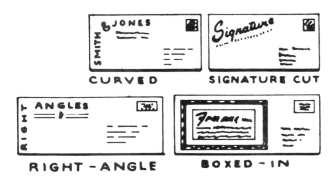

2. Main line curved around upper left corner; signature logo at angle.

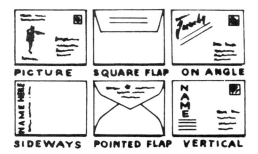

3. Layout ideas on baronial envelope.

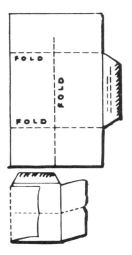

4. Order blank envelopes.

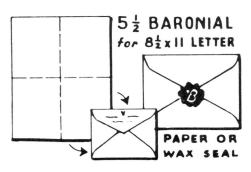

5. No. 5-1/2 baronial envelopes accommodate 8-1/2″ x 11″ sheet folded French-fold style.

FOLDERS

Folders, as presented here, would include envelope enclosures. See the section on self-mailers for additional ideas. Folders can be distributed on desks and counters, at meetings and exhibits, by salesmen or by wholesale and retail dealers, enclosures, package inserts, statement stuffers, etc.

Tables show the more common page sizes for folders to fit four widely used envelopes.

Paper sizes commonly used for folders:

BOND: 17″ x 22″, 17″ x 28″
BOOK: 17-1/2″ x 22-1/2″, 23″ x 35″, 25″ x 38″
COVER: 20″ x 26″, 23″ x 35″, 26″ x 40″

20 SIZES OF FOLDERS:

2, 4, 6, and 8 pages-parallel folds, also 8 pages
French fold - to fit four popular envelopes

Envelope No.		#6¾	Monarch	#10	#5½ Baronial
″ Size		3⅝ × 6¼	3⅞ × 7½	4⅛ × 9½	4¼ × 5⅝
1 sheet = 2 pp.	no folds	3¼ × 6¼	3¾ × 7¼	4 × 9½	4¼ × 5⅝
″	WORK + TURN	7 × 6¼	7½ × 7½	8 × 9½	8¼ × 5⅝
2 sheets = 4 pp.	one fold	7 × 6¼	7½ × 7¼	8 × 9⅝	8½ × 5⅝
″	WORK + TURN	7 × 12½	7½ × 14½	9⅛ × 16	8½ × 10¼
3 sheets = 6 pp.	2 parallel folds	10¼ × 6¼	11¼ × 7¼	12 × 9⅝	12¼ × 5⅝
″	WORK + TURN	10½ × 12½	11¼ × 14¼	12 × 18¼	12¼ × 10½
4 sheets = 8 pp.	3 parallel folds	14 × 6¼	15 × 7¼	16 × 9⅝	17 × 5⅝
″	French fold	7 × 12½	7½ × 14½	8 × 18¼	8¼ × 10½
″	W. + B. + TURN	14 × 12½	15 × 14¼	16 × 18¼	17 × 10½

Maximum Number Lower Case Characters Per Page

IF TYPE PAGE:	2¼ × 5¼	3 × 6	3½ × 8	3½ × 4½
SQ. IN. OF TYPE	14.8	18	26	15
8 - point	2575	3132	4524	2610
9 - ″	2072	2520	3640	2100
10 - ″	1716	2088	3016	1740
12 - ″	1184	1440	2080	1200

* Median of 61 commonly used machine-set text type faces

Deduct for: headings, sub-heads, pictures, extra space between paragraphs, short lines, etc.

	8-pt.	9-pt.	10-pt.	12-pt.
For 1-pt. leading, multiply above figures x	.89	.90	.90	.92
For 2-pt. ″ ″ ″ ″ x	.80	.81	.83	.84

FIFTEEN MACHINE FOLDING STYLES FOR FOLDERS:

4 Page Folds   **6** Page Folds   **8** Page   **8** Page   **8** Page   **10** Page   **12** Page

REGULAR IMP. ACCORDION   OVER‹OVER REG.   MAP   ACCORDION   RIGHT-ANGLE OR "FRENCH"   REG. ACCORDION   LETTER FOLD   ACCORDION

THIRTY-SIX POSSIBLE PAGE LAYOUT STYLES FOR FOLDERS:

V = VERTICAL H = HORIZONTAL	*All* TYPE		2/3 TYPE		1/2 TYPE		1/3 TYPE	
V for #5½ Baronial envelope	One column	Off-center	Top picture	Letterhead	Diagonal	Circle cut	Bleed Photos	One Picture
V for #6¾ & Monarch envelopes	Staggered	Centered	Bottom photo	Animated	Ornate	Checkered	Border	Cuts side
V for #10 envelope	Irregular	Light & Bold	Center photo	At angle	Centered	Informal	At angle	Captioned
H for #5½ Baronial envelope	Run-around initial		Illustration & 1 column		Illustration below		Large bleed photo	
H for #6¾ & Monarch envelopes	2 columns, sub-heads		2 columns & photo		cuts in checker-form		Text – centered	
H for #10 envelope	3 columns		Illustration centered		Alternating		Text at bottom	

1. A common enclosure is the four- or six-page folder of post card thickness.

2. Business reply label of 3" x 5" on gummed stock, used in lieu of reply envelope.

Picture of Product split by 'gate' fold

3. Gate-style folder is effective if you suggest to the prospect that you're taking him behind the scenes.

Photo on fold-over flap

4. Here, a fold-over flap halfway down or less, toward bottom of folder, features pictures of product.

COMBINATION – RUN......
3 four page folders run work & turn

5. To lower costs, small folders should be run work-and-turn, in combination with others in a series.

Tip-on Gadgets

6. "Gadgets" made of paper, cloth, plastic, metals, and other materials, can be tipped-on to tie-in with cover slogan or head.

7. Die-cut folder of the "pop-up" or "pop-down" variety is scored for folding and opening as shown in the sketch.

8. High attention value can be secured by attaching a sample of the product, or something related to its use, in transparent bag.

9. Two parallel cutting rules form a slot through which a small folded message or sample is inserted on folder page.

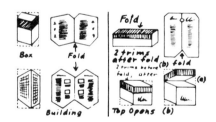

10. Novelty "box" folders can be used in advertising many products. Sketches show covers and center spreads, also which trims to make before and after folding.

11. Folders of four, six or eight pages can have added eye-catching appeal by corner trims or round cornering, made after folding, as suggested in four styles here.

12. Here are only nine styles among thousands of ways to achieve extra attention for folders and enclosures by means of special die-cut outlines, inner and outer.

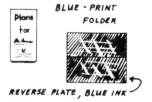

13. For effect of architect's or engineer's blue-print, suitable for many products, use reverse plate line drawing, blue ink.

14. If a great many gift ideas are included in a folder, consider using printed perforations between them for shopper to detach.

15. Often the front page of a folder can assume the form of a miniature letter or wire; or folder can contain montage of news clip.

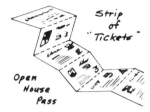

16. A manufacturer or retailer may use a folder to announce an "open house." Each "ticket" describes separate features.

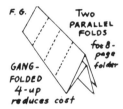

17. Economize by "gang folding" in runs of a series of folders or several "up," same folder.

18. Folder in shape of small letter with flap at lower left corner to show "before" and "after."

19. Instead of usual shape enclosure, use message on narrow strip or photos-captions, film style.

20. Miniature French-fold enclosures on bond can be printed in only one impression.

21. Make folder do triple duty as order blank and reply envelope also; strip-gum edge, score for folds.

HANDBILLS

Handbills usually involve printing on one side of the paper only, and in black or one color of ink only. Also, the paper used is usually cheaper, lighter weight and cut to small size. Bold headlines, large text type, and flashy appearance are other characteristics.

The name "handbill" usually signifies a small printed sheet handed out indiscriminately to passers-by on the street, or to visitors in a store, booth, sale, exhibit, etc.

Handbill sizes range in sizes from 3″ x 5″ to 4″ x 6″, 4″ x 8″, 5″ x 7″, 5-1/2″ x 7-1/2″, 8-1/2″ x 11″ and larger.

The handbill can be used as an envelope enclosure, catalog and package insert; mounted on bulletin boards, walls, trucks, windows, etc. Consider work-and-turn printing to use both sides of an opaque paper, featuring a different appeal, product or event on the other side. If then used as a poster also, take two copies for each location so as to display both sides.

1. Typical one-column set-up for a handbill. Two bold top headlines. Some copy set in narrower measure.

3. One column for text at top set alongside seal or trademark. Centered lines, then two columns.

5. A cartoon from a local newspaper can often be reprinted on a handbill for a meeting.

2. Two photos used near center of handbill. Some copy at bottom in narrow measure.

4. Ornate certificate-style border bleeds off four edges, preferably in second color.

6. A graph or pictorial chart is often very good for handbill use to show statistics at a glance.

7. Three-column set-up with featured copy set in box in the middle column for extra attention.

8. First word of type line in bold block letters. Copy starts in large type, one column; then smaller in two.

9. This handbill features six photos each with short caption to tell the advertising message, magazine style.

10. Two horizontal handbill layouts. Top: curved headline; three columns. Bottom: heading at angle.

11. The four corners of a handbill can be trimmed off to make a special shape, as shown. Color bleeds.

12. When a story involving a number of steps must be told in small space, consider comic strip style.

13. An ad or an invitation in a handbill can be reproduced from typewriting or handwriting.

14. Handbill can be die-cut to circular shape, as here for novelty approach.

15. Fire sale subject of this handbill is illustrated by flames in red, at bottom edge.

16. For dramatic effect, this reverse appearance is good. Make your pasteup in normal manner, cameraman can make contact positive to expose on plate to achieve the reverse.

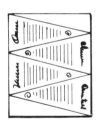

17. Handbill in pennant shape gets extra attention. Here four units are combined.

18. Large photo bleeds off the top of this handbill to dramatize subject of the advertisement.

19. A store wishing to feature its building and street location can use a photo with trimmed copy.

20. Handbill of triangular shape gets extra notice. Here two units are combined on a sheet.

21. Bleed photos are used around the four sides of this handbill to provide frame effect for text.

22. Tone backgrounds are at angle on two sides making novel center panel slant to right.

23. Red and blue can be used to good effect on white stock. Here they form red-white-and-blue lines.

24. Offer to deliver part of the run of handbills flat for handing out, the rest folded to use as inserts.

HOUSE MAGAZINES

The company magazine can take many different forms. It is a mistake to think that a company magazine must be large, elaborate and costly.

Each house organ should have its own distinctive individuality, not to be confused with any other publication, or company. This personality is a compound of the content, writing style, illustrations, size, shape, kind and color of paper, format, text type and heading styles, design elements, ink color combinations, humor, the "common touch" and so on. Unless it is inviting to the eye, the best text copy may go unread.

1. At left, three columns, equal width. Pictures across one, two or all three. Right, four narrow columns, short items. Two, center, merged for feature.

2. At left, one narrow column in center of page for short items, broader columns at left and right edges. At right, one wide column in the center.

3. Postcard weight cover stock, short house organs. Vertical on 4″ x 6″ card, two columns. Horizontal on 4″ x 8″.

12- page -- accordian

4. The length of copy of a 12-page booklet fits this accordion-fold house magazine. Saves cost of stitching, yet it is easy to hold and read.

5. Six-page, postcard weight stock, two parallel folds, third-class bulk mail. Three pages text, two for reply card.

6. A simple house organ, pocket size, can use a four-, six- or eight-page folder. Photos can use two-page spread.

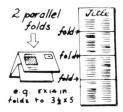

7. Long, narrow paper, e.g. 5″ x 14″, folds first to 5″ x 7″, then to 3-1/2″ x 5″. Display ad in center spread if desired.

8. Narrow booklet, saddle-stitched long edge. Fits No. 10 envelope.

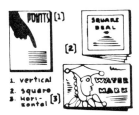

9. Basic shapes for booklets or folders as house organs: vertical, square, horizontal. Check on availability of envelopes.

10. Self-mailer folder with two parallel folds. Recipient opens first to letter. Following pages used for text and illustrations.

11. Long, single mailing card, e.g., 4″ x 9″, post card weight stock. Business reply card can be printed along with text copy.

12. Two columns of unequal width. Narrow column at left is best for short items. Note light, bold type.

13. House organ for agents, dealers, salesmen, purchasing agents, etc.; fits two- or three-ring binder.

14. Four pages, with one fold one way, two folds other way. Left hand page of center spread might be display ad.

15. French-folder has large photo on cover next to address area. Current display ad for inside spread.

16. Self-mailer booklet address on back cover. Recipient's name and address are on detachable reply.

17. Single-fold, light cardboard or cover stock, postcard weight. Cover for address, and photo or drawing. About 2-1/4 pages for text, plus reply card.

18. When important articles are to appear month-by-month in serial form, consider French-folder which opens to file folder with tab projecting along one edge.

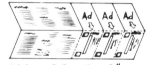

19. Three non-competing advertisers, appealing to same customer list, can share production and mailing costs using large folder of postcard weight stock.

20. Sketch shows zig-zag cutting die shape used, e.g., on 7-1/3" x 17" bond paper. Makes two letters with projecting section for 3-page house organ.

21. Magazine style layout for double spread, titles at angle to which text and pictures conform: Many variations possible.

22. Left page has seven square photos, eight text areas, checkerboard pattern. Right, picture and caption, or comic strip style.

23. Gate-style fold opens to center spread for wall display use by agents or dealers. Can show company's current display ads.

24. Twelve-page folder, three parallel folds. Text can run parallel or at right angles to folds, or both. Very flexible.

25. Newspaper style layout; four, or eight pages, or more. Five columns. Here the last two columns are merged for feature.

26. Miniature house organ booklet, e.g. 2-3/4" x 3-1/2"; insert in two diagonal slots in sales letter, or make it a part of regular monthly statement.

27. Two folds each way in covering letter hold small house organ.

28. Back cover of a postcard-weight stock makes reply card on this booklet. Print perforation.

29. Horizontal page, saddle stitch short way. Front cover each month set from brief text, in caps, in layout and type style to suggest telegram, for important message.

Address: top, over

30. Bulletin style, two parallel folds, self-mailer. Address on back of top section. Use short paragraphs.

31. Upper right corner, inner spread, cut away to reveal name and address also on reply card.

32. Center spread of booklet as double-size insert. Opens out for 4-page-size display ad, special map or other display.

33. Booklet folds once after stitching, parallel to binding. Seal over edge. Allows large page, fits pocket.

FRENCH-FOLD

34. Short copy. Distribute by hand this size, e.g., 11″ x 14″, folds 5-1/2″ x 7″.

LABELS AND STAMPS

Labels and stamps, shown here as both, are printed on gummed paper or pressure sensitive paper.

Some printers specialize in this field to print orders in combination runs for selling economically to purchasers.

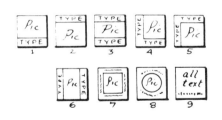

1. Nine of many possible layout styles for stamps: (1) type on bottom; (2) on top; (3) top and bottom; (4) side, bottom; (5) side, top; (6) two sides; (7) all around; (8) circle; (9) type.

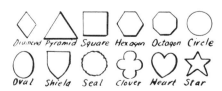

2. Five of the 12 special shapes for stamps shown can be made on the paper cutter. The other seven need

die-cutting. A non-rectangular shape often commands more attention than rectangular for stamps attached to letters and packages.

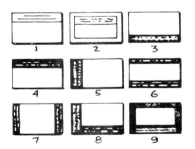

3. Nine of many possible layout styles for labels: (1) type on top; (2) border used four sides; (3) type on bottom; (4) reverse, bleed at top; (5) bleed at sides; (6) bleed top and bottom; (7) bleed two sides; (8) bleed side, bottom, and (9) bleed on all four sides.

4. Round-cornering often adds interest to a label, with border and type conforming to shape. Two trims silhouettes top of factory or building picture featured on label.

5. Often a photo of the owner of a

business or of a sales representative gives personal "warmth" to a stamp for attaching to memos, letters, packages, envelopes, literature.

6. By adding three printed perforations, labels can be used in any of five ways: first class, first class insured, parcel post, parcel post insured, or plain. Make your own variations. Tear off one, two or all three perforated edges.

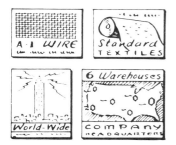

7. Stamps can picture a product tied-in with its trademark, as in the two top examples above; or they can feature world-wide distribution or locations of warehouses for use on letters, envelopes, packages.

8. A retailer, wholesaler or manufacturer, to encourage visitors and buyers, can feature his location in a city or rural area by use of sketch map on poster stamp showing location, highways, streets.

Multi-colored LABEL mounted on mailing card

9. Users of postal cards and third-class mail can attach a pressure-sensitive or gummed label to the message side of the card to get extra attention and add color.

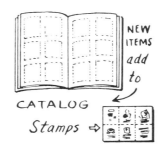

10. New items can be illustrated on stamps and mailed to customers to fill in areas of a catalog.

11. Perhaps inquiries sent to a company by distributors or customers can be answered by a particular one of many short paragraphs, prepared to go on labels 2" x 2-1/4" gang-printed on one sheet.

12. Here are 25 stamps on a small unit 4" x 5" printed on gummed paper.

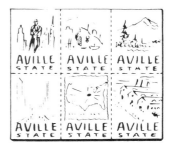

13. Stamps can be used to advertise the commercial advantages, scenery, climate, sports, festivals, etc., of a city.

TIP-ON ANNOUNCER

14. A two-color effect can be secured in an announcement or mailing card by mounting a label on card stock of a different color. Here a reverse plate in blue ink on white gummed stock, makes "blueprint."

LETTERHEADS AND FOUR-PAGE LETTERS

Here is a check list of various styles. Detail is held to the minimum. These are essentially "idea-starters."

The letterheads are a few of hundreds of possible styles of treatment of letterhead copy, with and without logos and illustrations. They suggest only the main elements of each layout scheme.

To produce a multi-color effect with one press impression, you can use halftone screen tints such as 30% or 20% plus the solid color. Color harmony is bound to result.

Instead of using the same paper for the entire press run, greater flexibility can be secured by splitting the run among various papers—e.g., rag bond, sulphite and perhaps a color and onion skin—to serve many types of uses and recipients, but all from the same makeready and press run.

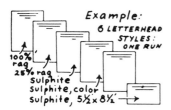

1. The same letterhead can be printed in the same press run on five or more kinds of paper for greater range of uses. To those shown can be added onion skin.

2. Often five, six or more, forms can be combined on a 17" x 22" bond sheet for economy.

FOUR-PAGE, ILLUSTRATED

3. Most four-page letters are 17" x 11" but shortfold style is often better for office, ad uses.

4. Two-tone or duplex paper is effective for 4-page letters; top sheet folds to show color.

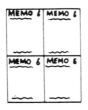

5. Here four personalized memo sheets, 4-1/4" x 5-1/2" for office members, run 4-up on 8-1/2" x 11".

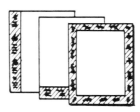

6. Tint area runs down the left edge, across bottom, and around the four sides of these three letters, either to bleed or not.

7. Lists of names of officers and/or committees can go: (A) left edge, (B) at bottom, (C) around three edges of letterhead.

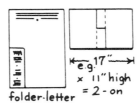

folder-letter   e.g. 17" x 11" high = 2-on

8. Copy about product or service printed from type on projecting flap, folds flush with letter. 7-1/2" x 11" letter, 2" flap, 2-up 11" x 17".

9. "Phantom" effect of a company building or factory centered. Halftone black or color.

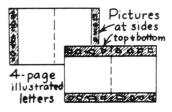

4-page illustrated letters

10. Four-page illustrated letters may use bleed illustrations or tint blocks (or non-bleed) at left and right edges, or top and bottom of the center spread area.

Circle   Square   Diamond   Octagon

11. Novelty letters of circular, square, diamond or octagon shape, create extra attention value.

12. Excerpts from letters of recommendation on product or service, on 4-1/4" x 5-1/2" sheet.

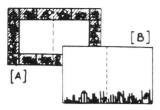

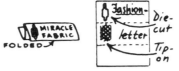

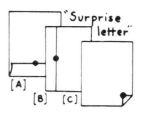

13. (A) Photos bleed at all four edges of this center spread. (B) Silhouette view of city skyline, or of real estate development, along bottom edge, center spread.

14. Here a swatch of material shows through a figure cut-out of top of letter, as folded.

15. Part of a sales message can be withheld from main letter, put underneath the "surprise flap" which reader finds after breaking seal.

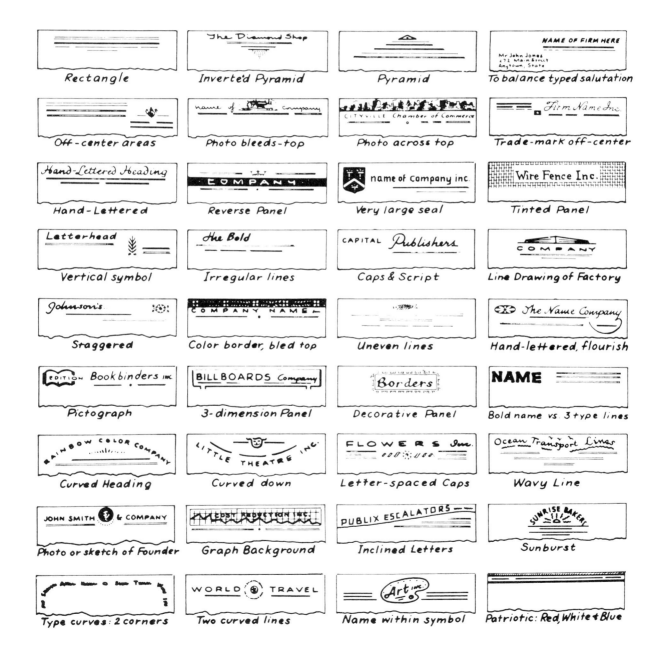

Rectangle | Inverted Pyramid | Pyramid | To balance typed salutation

Off-center areas | Photo bleeds-top | Photo across top | Trade-mark off-center

Hand-Lettered | Reverse Panel | Very large seal | Tinted Panel

Vertical symbol | Irregular lines | Caps & Script | Line Drawing of Factory

Staggered | Color border, bled top | Uneven lines | Hand-lettered, flourish

Pictograph | 3-dimension Panel | Decorative Panel | Bold name vs. 3 type lines

Curved Heading | Curved down | Letter-spaced Caps | Wavy Line

Photo or sketch of Founder | Graph Background | Inclined Letters | Sunburst

Type curves: 2 corners | Two curved lines | Name within symbol | Patriotic: Red, White & Blue

16. Picture or sketch appear on fold-over top, side, or bottom flap, text below.

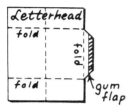

17. An order blank envelope printed with letterhead combine functions of letter and envelope.

18. An 8-1/2" x 11" letter, when French-folded to 4-1/4" x 5-1/2" fits a Baronial envelope, either as single letter sheet, or treated as four-page letter.

19. Back of single or four-page letter can be used for institutional ad, history of the firm, etc.

20. Letter has "gate-fold" (11" x 17" flat, each gate 4-1/4" x 11") with pictures; letter inside.

21. Two lines are cut at 45-degree angle at lower corner of letter to hold coupon, tickets, etc.

MAGAZINES

Here are illustrations to help visualize a few of the thousands of page layout possibilities. The layouts illustrate two column, three column and double spreads to show some of the many ways to integrate opposite pages.

It is a good exercise to review many layout alternatives, such as those sketched here at one time. Ideas, then, are often suggested for a particular page that would not be thought of otherwise. The rough sketches serve as a partial check-list of ways to secure variety in page lay-out. A sameness of format, page after page, is a sure way to produce monotony.

A few sizes of book paper with untrimmed page sizes, and number of pages per sheet (in parentheses), from each are:

25 x 38
4-3/4" x 6-1/4" .... (64)
6-1/4" x 9-1/2" .... (32)
9-1/2" x 12-1/2" .... (16)

35 x 45
4-3/8" x 5-5/8" .... (128)
5-5/8" x 8-3/4" .... (64)
8-3/4" x 11-1/4" .... (32)

Cut bled at bottom

Center cut bled at top

Two bled cuts at corners

Four cuts bled left

Ten cuts and text

Three cuts three stories

Narrow & wide column

Text set to run around irregular cuts

Uneven right edges; & thumbnail sketches

Title line runs at angle across spread

Decorative border bleeds on spread

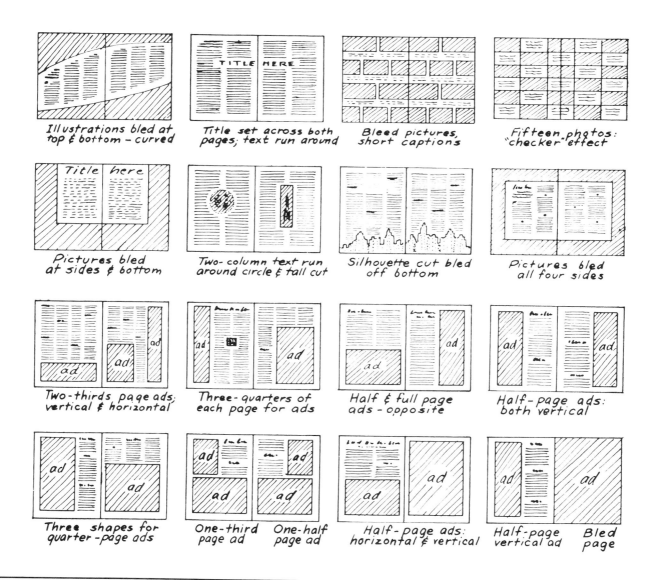

Illustrations bled at top & bottom – curved	Title set across both pages; text run around	Bleed pictures, short captions	Fifteen photos: "checker" effect
Pictures bled at sides & bottom	Two-column text run around circle & tall cut	Silhouette cut bled off bottom	Pictures bled all four sides
Two-thirds page ads; vertical & horizontal	Three-quarters of each page for ads	Half & full page ads – opposite	Half-page ads: both vertical
Three shapes for quarter-page ads	One-third page ad · One-half page ad	Half-page ads: horizontal & vertical	Half-page vertical ad · Bled page

MANUALS AND HANDBOOKS

"Manuals and Handbooks" as used here, refers to the various kinds of informational pieces put out by manufacturers, wholesalers, retailers, publishers, institutions and others. They are used to explain a somewhat complicated product or service so that it can be understood thoroughly by plant employees, salesmen, branch office staffs, stockholders, prospective investors, wholesalers, jobbers, retailers, customers and the general public.

Sometimes one booklet will be issued for use by all these groups. Or a separate publication may be issued to serve the special interests of each. It may describe a process or it may tell how to assemble, operate and service a particular device. It may be put for salesmen to show how to handle objections and difficulties, analyze competitive devices and stress sales points. It may be an employee manual outlining the company policy. It could be a style manual for those who handle correspondence to give the best way to cope with sales, service and collection problems.

These are usually printed in booklet form in a convenient size, such as 3-3/8" x 5-1/8", 4" x 6-1/8" or 5-1/2" x 7-1/4". There are many advantages for creativity in the presentation of this material. The layouts here suggest in very simple sketch form, some variations in page layout, picture use heading and indexing treatment, which may add to their readability.

1. Most products can be explained as shown with arrows from text to features described. Key parts of photo may be in second color, or darker with "phantom" of non-featured parts.

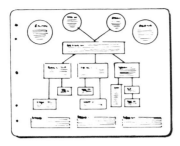

2. Flow diagrams are often the best way to explain the sequence of steps in a complicated process, or the handling of an order which passes through many departments.

3. (A) Steps in a process can be set up to suggest an actual flight of stairs; or as (B) segments of a circle, reading "clockwise", or (C) as a film strip using picture and caption style of treatment.

4. Small booklet attached to products on display helps sell them in absence of salesman; explains details of use, servicing.

	RIVAL A	RIVAL B	Our ITEM
M'F'R.→			
Design			
Material			
Patented features			
Cost			

5. Sales people can be educated on the merits of company's product compared with rival firms' pro-

ducts "A", "B", etc., if data on each are organized under main heading and printed in chart form.

6. Upper left: sub-title in bold type or color with text set to run around each one. Upper right: right margin irregular, alternating paragraphs in light and bold, or roman and italic or black and color. Below: sub-titles in outer margins.

7. "Thumbnail" sketches can attract readers to solid text areas which might otherwise be ignored. Run-arounds provide a welcome relief for the eye. At right is shown two-column layout, each right edge uneven, for informal effect.

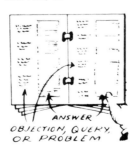

8. Small and large sales and service offices handling correspondence can make good use of a manual which indexes all kinds of questions and difficulties in left column, with "ideal" answer at right.

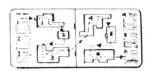

9. For visitors to a plant, this keepsake booklet has pictures of each stage in the operation and/or important machines and buildings. Descriptive paragraphs appear with each sketch or photo.

10. Company handbook features pictures of management personnel, history of firm and photos of various departments or activities across this double-page spread.

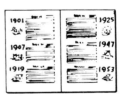

11. Company handbook often features "milestone dates" in the firm's history.

12. Companies using many office forms can illustrate each in miniature with the accompanying text to tell when to use each, and the procedure followed in routing and filing each.

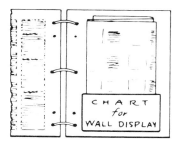

13. A manual punched for use in a 3-ring binder, uses a pocket (Monarch envelope with flap cut off) mounted on inside back cover of binder to hold a large folded broadside, chart, map or other display piece for wall or window exhibit.

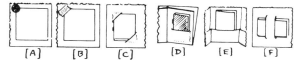

14. Six ways to attach a small handbook to a letter, folder or package: (A) gummed sticker, (B) clear tape, (C) two diagonal slits, (D) one slit in French-folder with fold at bottom, (E) tucked in short fold section of a broadside, (F) two parallel slits.

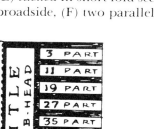

15. Often the cover of a manual can feature the page number where each part begins. Speeds up its use for reference, combines functions of table of contents and index.

16. If handbook is packed with data, needing extensive index, you can put code letters at intervals in the margins with the page number in the index.

17. Where there are only five or six words or phrases to be indexed on each page, consider setting these in bold face or caps or italic, or printing in a second color, or underlining to speed-up references from the index to these key places.

18. Some manuals which cover a great many short topics can handle all entries in alphabetical sequence, with initial key word or phrase in bold face, caps, or italic, or printed in color, or underlined and indented for further emphasis.

19. Where fast turning to parts of a price book or other handbook reference source is vital, consider attaching index tabs which project, or die-cutting the pages to allow projecting areas, as shown above.

20. Sometimes a short handbook can be reduced to about 2-1/2" x 3-1/2" with cover set up as a business card.

21. Fast reference can be made to this company manual where each sheet (or section) is trimmed to project sufficiently to carry its title heading on the exposed margin of the sheet or the top of a group of sheets.

MAPS AND CHARTS

"Maps and Charts" shown here are treated as component elements of folders, cards, booklets, self-mailers and other pieces. These ideas will help develop layouts which are to use maps and charts as illustrations.

Most initial drafts of maps and charts can be improved considerably when a careful study is made of many examples. These ideas can be supplemented by samples secured from diversified sources and filed for ready-reference.

Firms can use maps in one way or another on folders, letters, etc. Manufacturers often like to show their location in relation to a surrounding urban or rural area as an aid to customers. Wholesalers, retailers, schools, hospitals and other institutions wish to do the same. Resorts, chambers of commerce, airports, bus lines, motels and other advertisers like to show the various routes which can be taken to reach a certain city or recreational area. Many maps with special treatment may be valued as a keepsake if they contain helpful data.

Maps can often be more attractive if tints are used for background areas.

A collection of charts to supplement the styles here, will prove valuable to choose the kind best suited for the "copy" at hand. If a second color cannot be used, consider adding one or more tints of the single color used. This can aid in greater clarity and emphasis.

1. Summer camps, resorts, and other advertisers in recreational areas, can use scenic photographs, bleeding off four sides of a folder or back of letterhead, map in center.

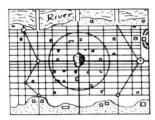

2. To prove how close a motel is to main attractions of a city area, animated map here shows chief points of interest on all four sides of motel, with circle of one mile radius, which is centered on the motel building for sense of scale.

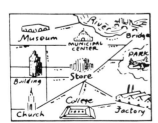

3. Sometimes a very simplified map is best, showing only the main-traveled thoroughfares. Here, the advertiser's store in relation to other important buildings in the area of the city, are shown as halftones.

4. Twelve main attractions to visitors are numbered, in circles, on this map, showing "through" streets only. The "key" is printed, at the right in reverse for emphasis.

5. To call special attention to a route leading to a factory. the annual picnic spot, or whatever, small map on lightweight paper, 5-1/2" x 8-1/2", tucked into slots.

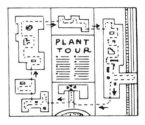

6. Smaller towns may have twenty or thirty blocks often laid out in a rectangular grid form. This map can be ruled with the featured locations spotted as shown.

7. Here is a rough layout of a three-panel folder given to plant visitors who are following the established tour route of the area. Buildings are shown to scale. Use a second color for the tour route.

8. Resort letterhead uses a long map of shoreline or district on fold-over flap the 11" way. Opaque bond stock, 22" x 34" cuts six out 11-1/3" x 11-1/2", folds to 8-1/2" x 11" with 2-3/4" flap.

9. Colored book paper can be used for this one-time menu, featuring animated map of the area to interest tourists and their friends back home.

10. A map on the outside of an envelope may increase prospect's interest. Reserve at least 3-1/2" at right side for address and postage.

11. A single card sent by third-class mail, or a folded self-mailer as here, features map of a new real estate development. Other side has an invitation to visit the new area.

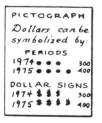

12. A special pictograph symbol can be drawn, then reproduced in quantity for pasteup to show quantitative comparisons, or symbols from acetate sheets can be purchased and used.

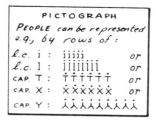

13. In a pictograph chart, people can be represented with specially drawn symbols of children, men, women or whatever the statistics involve.

14. In "bar" charts, border tapes can be cut accurately to provide the separate bars, or rules of various lengths. The short lengths form piles of stacked coins.

15. Often the unit of measurement in a pictograph can be symbolized by a capital letter. Or various sizes of type are used for comparative figures.

16. Columns of figures which read from heading at left edge of the rows are difficult to read when set solid as at the top. A space inserted every three lines makes it all easy.

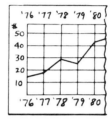

17. Sometimes vertical columns of a chart are emphasized, sometimes horizontal sections. Light tints of 10% or 20% of black or color, alternate with plain background.

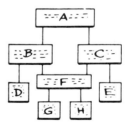

18. A grid with plotted line is often needed for trend charts. The grid can be drawn with technical pen with the trend line placed in position with tape. If trend line is in second color, it can be placed on transparent overlay.

19. Organizational charts are usually made with explanatory text inside boxes.

20. Sales literature for the company's product compares its specific qualities with competitive products. A chart form set-up makes "O's" advantages more emphatic.

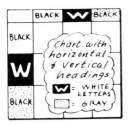

21. Consider possible use of chart headings in reverse form in certain places, so that the caption is in white letters on black, or inside a rectangle of color. Tints can also be used with good results.

MENUS AND PROGRAMS

Menus and programs concern nearly everyone involved in the graphic arts. An attractive menu often serves as a valuable keepsake to be shown to friends back home. Menus may be printed on heavy cover stock and a smaller edition printed on paper for give-aways. Menus can vary in size from 5-1/2" x 8-1/2" page-size up to 10" x 13".

This check-list can help select the main characteristics of the menu or program style best suited to the needs. It helps to examine many possible combinations.

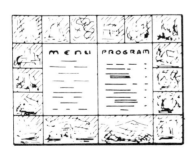

1. Specials for the day can be tipped on this a la carte menu of heavy cover stock. New sheets of specials can constantly be replaced on following days.

2. This menu or program has bleed pictures of local scenes or personalities featured in program around the four sides of inner spread. Menu on left, the program of speeches, and music on the right; or a la carte left, table d'hote right.

3. This menu folds to convert it to a self-mailer to advertise a summer resort. Upper half of the inside is for menu, lower half for guest's message.

4. Menu resembles a miniature four-column newspaper. Heads set in news style. Narrow column width photos feature specials of the house or decorations.

5. Accordion folders permit use of exposed margins for headings on type of food or drink listed in space opposite, inside.

6. Four styles of stand-up menus: (A) short-fold on top for picture and name; (B) chimney, made with cutting rules, projects above top roof line. (C) "gatefold", (D) accordion fold, small sketch for each class of food.

7. Programs can be made self-supporting or profit-earning, by sale of ad spaces adjoining the program copy. Four layouts show divisions of space for ads. All ad copy adjoins reading matter.

8. Clock face dramatizes the hourly divisions of a convention program day-by-day, in reverse or color. Right: heads in white, black or color background.

9. Nine categories of food on menu are placed in the nine alternating color areas of the checkerboard. Solid color or tint color for darker areas, black for text overprint.

10. Round menu laid out as if in six "pie" cuts to separate the six classifications of food. Or, the circle can be adapted to six special luncheon plates, or features of the day, one being printed on each slice.

11. "Ballot" menu which leaves nothing to chance. Pencil is supplied with personal menu for each customer, who marks the dishes desired with an "x" in box opposite each, and writes special comments below.

12. Four circles show through in the white of the paper against color background trimmed to bleed. Either a la carte or special plates can be printed in black in the circles.

13. Program of 16 pages, each sheet trimmed to project when assembled. "A.M." and "P.M." programs of four days are on the eight exposed edges. Can use four paper colors.

14. Some of the a la carte items are on the left page. Entrees are shown for nine dinners on the right page, left column for a la carte prices, the right column for complete dinner price based on that entree, with other choices above and below the entrees.

15. Two angle trims after folding make cover of the top menu represent peak of roof of the restaurant. Two trims after folding give a three-dimensional "cookbook" effect for the menu shown below. Description of various specialties can be in recipe style.

16. Upper half of card at top for a la carte items. Four angle slots below this hold paper or card inserted daily for table d'hote. Below: French-fold, slot for insert.

12 layout styles for Menu or Program Covers

12 layout styles for Menu texts

NEWSPRINT SPECIALTIES

Newsprint stock is usually not as strong, or as pleasing to see and handle as various bond, book and cover papers. However, newsprint does dry rapidly, has a pleasing bulk, and it is easy to read relatively small type printed on it due to the absence of glare or reflection. It is usually the cheapest stock which can be used. This may mean that a job can be afforded which would be impossible otherwise. Because of the use of newsprint, it may be possible to reach more prospects than could be reached if a more expensive paper were used for the same total dollar outlay.

The standard basic size of newsprint is 24″ x 36″.

1. The effect of a newspaper in suggesting a topic of importance and timely interest can be secured with even a very small page size.

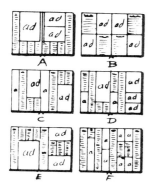

2. These six double-page spreads show layout possibilities for securing high attention value for advertisers who finance this four-column magazine. (A) Ads at top, text surrounding; (B) checkerboard style; (C) one column ads and ads of two column width but not of page depth; (D) ads cover more than half of area, but all are next to reading matter, (E), (F) other variations.

3. Various club, society, labor and trade publications on newsprint can gain interest in layout effects, flexibility in column measure for photos and a desirable variety of ad space alternatives by using, for example, five columns across the top half of the page, four columns across the bottom half.

4. Miniature, self-cover, saddle-stitched booklets printed on news-print, can be very effective as an advertising medium when mounted on cards, letters, folders, etc. The novelty appeal of a small booklet tipped on a larger surface will often gain extra attention from prospects.

5. A frequent change of pace in layout style can enhance interest in, and readability of, catalogs printed on newsprint. These two double-page spreads use coarse-screen half-tones and several lines for captions below each.

6. (X) Handbills are a natural for newsprint, printed one or both sides. (Y) is a four-page folder, with a sketch or photo of advertiser's building in perspective on front cover. (Z) accordion-folder of eight pages, overlap edges.

7. House magazines can be small and printed on newsprint. The one shown here has four pages, 4-1/2" x 7" open, 3-1/2" x 4-1/2" closed. Can be inserted in two diagonal slots in accompanying letter, invoice or monthly statement. Two columns per page, each column only 1-1/2" inches wide. Title, headlines, captions and illustrations all carry out the effect of the newspaper style of format.

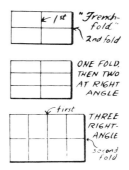

8. Three of the chief folding styles for self-mailers printed on news-print. All provide a folded edge at the top and left sides of the address surface to secure needed bulk and strength. Top: one fold in each direction; center: folds once one way, twice the other way; bottom: has three right-angle folds. All may be sent by bulk mail.

9. Clubs, alumni and fraternal organizations, church groups, co-ops, unions, etc., often use the picture magazine style of layout, as here, with more than half of the area devoted to photos. Text matter is held to captions of four to ten lines for each picture.

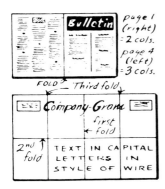

10. Two of the many possible styles of bulletins on newsprint. Below: giant "telegram" on canary poster paper, with three right-angle folds, as self-mailer with seal over-edge, or inserted in catalog envelope. May be mounted by recipient for wall or window display.

11. Department stores often find that unstitched tabloids are effective for store-wide sales.

12. It is possible to schedule press runs on a 24″ x 36″ sheet at frequent intervals and print jobs in combination either for the same account, or for different firms. Illustrated sheet is work-and-tumble. Top bulletin of 9″ x 12″ printed two sides; middle; 6-page folder; bottom: 4-page magazine.

NOVELTIES AND DIE-CUTS

By "Novelties" we mean printed jobs which are relatively unusual in layout, shape, fold, color, type treatment, or in some other way. Often a piece is unusual in its combination of elements, such as superimposing a certain cut-out area over a tip-on of a textile sample, or other material, mounted on the printed piece.

Tip-ons give a three-dimensional effect; also, they add interesting texture contrasts with the paper on which they are mounted.

A variety of tip-on novelties are available from:

Hewig & Marvic Corp., 861 Manhattan Ave., Brooklyn, N.Y. 11222

When novelty is desired, run over this file of ideas and see which one lends itself best to the product and sales need. There are so many ways to secure novelty that we are obliged to keep all sketches very simple, just to show the principles involved.

Whenever the services of a die-maker or other specialty firm outside of your own plant are to be used, be sure to check all dummies and layouts with them first, before the final pasteup is done, and before inks, paper and envelopes are specified.

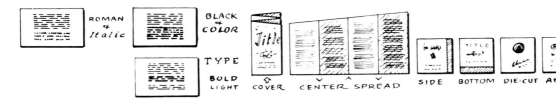

1. Alternation of type style paragraph by paragraph can attract the eye to an otherwise monotonous page where display ads compete with each other for notice.

2. Several papers: bond, antique and coated book, cover, cardboard, come in two-color combinations, usually white or light tint one side; contrasting darker color on other side. Use angle trims and folds. Solid colors, or screen tints, may be printed on instead.

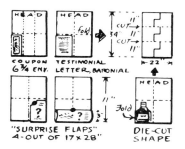

3. Fold-over at corner of form letter adds interest. Upper left: detach coupon; center: testimonial letter, half lineal; right: cut six from 22″ x 34″ sheet. "Surprise flap" (below) shut by seal, answers "Puzzles" in letter.

4. French-fold to print job in one impression. Fold a sheet to show through window, or insert through a diecut line. (Lower right) picture beneath cut-out.

5. Special papers add novelty appeal to folders, booklets, letters, etc. Safety paper suggests value even when not used for checks.

6. Gummed stickers in bright colors or on metallic paper, especially when cut in special silhouette, such as of the product, factory, trade mark, etc. add colorful note when attached in lower corner of letterhead.

7. A number of firms offer tip-on gadgets of metal, cloth, plastic, paper, feathers, etc., to secure extra attention due to their color, humor and "3-D" effect.

8. A standard size circular die is used at top left to show picture beneath; below, to make portholes in cartoons of ship, each for featured speaker at convention. Standard star die cuts through midnight blue sky.

9. Telegram-style heading and brief message about a sale for new items in store's stock. Print all-caps as in a wire. Printed perforations make eight coupons for special discounts and free samples.

10. Short sales letters do not have to be 8-1/2″ x 11″ or Monarch size. They could be diamond, circular, square, octagon shape, etc., as sketched.

11. No dies for folder or booklet novelties shown. Trim on paper cutter: building, pennant, box, "D" shape, pyramid, and "M" booklet, after folding; booklet covers are cut down first.

12. Special cutting dies can be made for circular booklets, bottles, figures—such as the chef in the standup menu, the shape of a state, or other area. Often it will pay to have dies made for runs of two-up or more. Check all details with your die-maker.

13. When initial letter of name of a firm or product is featured as the cover of a folder or saddle-stitched booklet, perhaps in one of the fluorescent inks, its shape can be die-cut or approximated by trims on the cutter before or after folding.

14. A single hole is drilled through entire saddle-stitched booklet. On each page the hole is a part of artwork, to represent a goal or a source of waste to eliminate.

15. The same surface may contain a number of cut-out areas, such as these four pairs of eyes (pupils are printed on the sheet beneath) which focus extra attention on each paragraph of text.

16. Trim pages for saddle-stitching and cut one page at angle to form arrow to point to photo on sheet beneath. Below: one-fourth of run on each of four paper colors—four colors in each copy.

17. Here are two ways enclosures may be held inside a self-mailer.

18. Three-dimensional and "pop-up" effects, if simple and clearly related to the featured text and product, are well worth the extra cost of dies, cutting and hand-folding.

19. Textiles, papers and other materials can be stapled together in a step-down swatch, or several samples may be tipped on various parts of area adjoining copy. Below: man's silhouette cut-out shows suit fabric sample.

OFFICE FORMS

Businesses large and small need forms to help them in their daily operations. Some forms may be standard and some specially designed to do a particular job.

Many factors affect the copy and layout of a form: the kind of product or service, size of the company, and its particular sales, shipping, billing, and accounting procedures.

Simplicity in filling out is vital. Include all essentials, skip the superfluous. Allow enough, but not too much, space for all items, and be sure that they follow each other in logical sequence.

Practicality, another "must," covers such matters as proper spacing (commonly six lines per inch deep for single-spaced typing, three for double). Provide the correct number of copies for all departments concerned. If the same copy must travel to two or more departments or persons, a routing order box for initialing is usually needed. Many forms require serial numbering for control purposes. The paper must be right for typing, writing, erasures, opacity, strength, folding qualities and sometimes longevity. If to be mailed in a window envelope, the space for name and address must be properly located and folding guidelines provided.

Appearance covers matters of typography, layout, margins, ink colors and paper. Bond paper colors include white, pink, canary, blue, green, goldenrod, buff, cherry, russet and salmon.

Specification of basic weight must be made. Weights such as sub. 13 for multiple-part forms (lighter weight paper), sub. 16 for general form work or sub. 20 for forms requiring heavier paper.

It is unusual for the initial design of any form to be the final one. When put to use, many improvements are usually developed, including deletions and additions. Hence, it's wise to test new forms thoroughly before printing by using a few photocopies. Otherwise print only a limited number of copies and keep the pasteup in file for revisions and re-run.

Make each form as simple as possible. Certain forms need ample space for special remarks. "Multi-purpose" forms will often do double or triple duty. The standard heading is followed by certain ruled areas which may be put to a variety of uses.

Build a form library with good examples of each kind of form for various purposes.

Standard size Bond paper	Weight per 1000 sheets			No. forms from one sheet					
	Substance			4 ¼″ × 5 ½″	4 ¼″ × 7″	5 ½″ × 8 ½″	7″ × 8 ½″	8 ½″ × 11″	8 ½″ × 14″
	13	16	20						
17″ × 22″	26	32	40	16		8		4	
17″ × 28″	33	41	51		16		8		4

The two most popular sizes of bond paper are listed in the first column, followed by their weight per thousand sheets in substance, 13, 16 and 20. Remaining columns list six frequently used form sizes, ranging from 4-1/4″ x 5-1/2″ up to 8-1/2″ x 14″. Many other form sizes, of course, can be cut from these paper sizes.

Envelope Size	Dimensions	For sheets	No. Folds	Enclosure folds to	Uses
#6 ¾	3 ⅝″ × 6 ½″	5 ½″ × 8 ½″	2	3 ⅞″ × 5 ½″	Half-letter
		8 ½″ × 11″	3	,,	Standard letter
#9	3 ⅞″ × 8 ⅞″	8 ½″ × 11″	2	3 ¹¹⁄₁₆″ × 8 ½″	Reply env. in #10
#10	4 ⅛″ × 9 ½″	,,	2	,,	Standard letter

For many forms it is necessary to begin with the envelope before developing layouts. This chart shows three envelope sizes which carry a large part of all forms and correspondence. Each of these envelope sizes is available with windows so that address information will show through the transparent window. When required, design the form so that it will fold to fit the envelope and the address will correspond to the window area.

A firm using a large volume of forms can save by grouping orders which can run on the same paper. There are many possible combinations of form sizes.

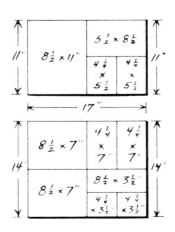

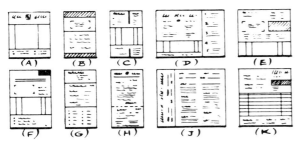

1. These tens of hundreds of possible layout styles for office forms can be considered for new forms: (A) Head, vertical columns, instructions below; (B) Form title in bleed reverse block at top, instructions at bottom, window envelope address; (C) top and bottom areas divided by heavy vertical bar to separate data; (D) Control data and tabular area at left, numbered routine at right; (E) Title in reverse; (F) Corner title; (G) Narrow; (H) Reply form detach; (J) Same data in other direction.

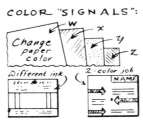

4. A given form can be located and filed readily if printed on distinctive color of paper. W, X, Y, Z can be white, blue, canary, green. Various ink colors can be used for arrows, rules, etc.

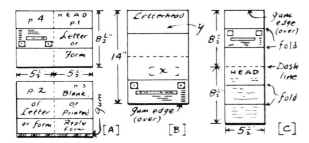

2. Three of many possible office forms with one gummed edge, to seal reply as self-mailer.

3. When logo is needed for many sizes of forms, make prints in different sizes to fit various requirements.

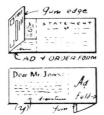

5. Narrow statement form has gummed edge short way with fold parallel to it, and a printed perforation on other side to make order form-envelope; Y: form credit note.

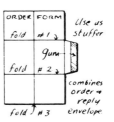

6. Order blank envelopes are available in flat sheet form for printing. Folds to make envelope, holds enclosures.

7. When a reply is wanted quickly, use 8-1/2″ x 11″ sheets gummed on 8-1/2-in. edge. Queries down left side, right half blank for answers. Three parallel folds plus scored flap fold. Fits No. 10 window envelope. Mail a carbon; recipient keeps plain copy.

8. Page of folder or booklet illustrating all forms of a given company with which each employee should be familiar. Describes purpose of form, who fills it out and when, also routing and handling sequence.

174

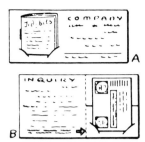

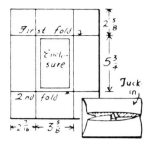

9. (A) For monthly statements to all accounts, a small house magazine, folder or booklet, can be inserted in two diagonal cuts. (B) An inquiry form of any kind may have detachable reply portion, folds to fit small tuck-in reply envelope.

10. An 8-1/2″ x 11″ letterhead or form folded twice each way, as shown, holds a sample or other enclosure, tucks in to itself.

PORTFOLIOS

Portfolios, as used here, mean printed pieces designed to hold one or more other printed pieces.

They may be mailed in an envelope or as a self-mailer, or they may be for hand-distribution by salesmen, by clerks in stores or by representatives at conventions, trade shows, etc.

A portfolio may take the form of a letterhead, four-page letter, folded mailing card, file folder, envelope, French-folder, broadside, catalog, booklet or company magazine.

Many firms need portfolios to picture and describe their services, to enclose samples and to house a special report or quotation. The file folder can be printed to serve as a brochure, yet contain additional material inside.

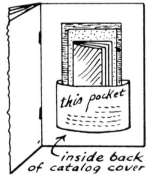

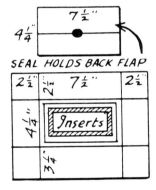

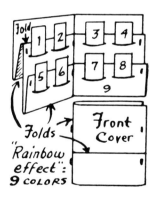

1. A booklet or catalog can be transformed into a portfolio by mounting or stapling a pocket on to the inner front or back cover to contain supplementary sheets, price changes, folders on new products, special offers, samples, etc. It can also contain a folded poster for wall or window use, or a map, broadside or other large piece.

2. A single rectangular sheet of bond, book, cover, or bristol stock, may be folded to make a self-mailer portfolio to hold a collection of smaller inserts, by making two folds each way as shown, using the center area for the inserts.

3. If you are to print a number of inserts for a portfolio, which can be run on the same sheet, consider splitting the run equally among as many colors of paper as you have inserts, so each portfolio can contain a set of inserts each of a different color. In upper sketch, three parallel accordion folds with one fold the other way. Slots for 1-4 go through two thicknesses, for 5-8 through one.

4. This form can be used to good advantage by practically any business wishing to tip their letter and bid for a job on the left of the inner spread. The pocket at right contains samples, folders, booklets, etc. to add impact to the presentation. The diagram at the top shows how to die-cut two such folders from one sheet of paper without waste.

5. A broadside may be transformed into a portfolio if it is printed on a heavy book or cover stock, by tipping or stapling on one or more "pockets" to contain separate inserts. Or cut slots, as shown above, with the material inserted and held in place by the bottom fold.

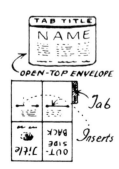

6. Two styles of vertical file folders; one a vertical file envelope closed at

both sides and at bottom, with a projecting file flap at the back of the open top; the other a French-folder with die-cut projecting file tab.

7. An accordion folder of cover paper makes a good demonstration portfolio for salesmen and stands a good deal of handling. Opened one fold at a time, it presents the sales story in logical sequence. The pocket to hold inserts, mounted or stapled on last inner section, can be an open-end catalog envelope, flap trimmed off.

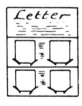

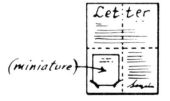

8. A company letterhead may also serve as a portfolio by adding two angle slots, as shown, in which small inserts may be placed.

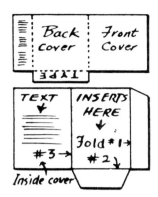

9. Three sections with a projecting flap opposite the midsection, when folded, provide a right-hand inner compartment with a fold-over flap at the bottom and at the right side, to hold a letter, dealer literature, samples and other inserts. These fold-over flaps may be rectangular, or cut at an angle as shown, or they may be die-cut to other special shapes.

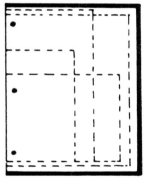

10. Many portfolios use a looseleaf form so that new material can be added conveniently from time to time and obsolete material removed.

11. Various locking devices can be used to hold the side and bottom

flaps in place, such as the tongue inserted through the two slots, sketched as shown. The flaps can be glued or stapled together instead; or they can simply be folded down but left unfastened. The flap area can be printed with data and product information.

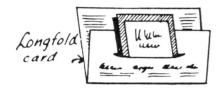

12. A card with one, two or more folds can serve as a portfolio to hold separate samples or sales literature of a smaller size. Such a piece can serve as a business reply card, estimate form, etc.

13. A letterhead can perform the function of a simple portfolio when cut with four vertical slots to form two bands through which one or more small folders or booklets are inserted. A miniature house magazine and/or fabric or sample could be inserted in such a letter-portfolio. This arrangement calls attention to the inserts, much more effectively than the inserts simply laid inside loosely.

14. A French-folder can be made so that the inner spread comes only

part way up to the top of the outer cover, or it can come up flush with it. The slots to contain inserts, also held in place by the bottom fold, may be on one or both sides of the center fold on the inner surface to provide either one or two pockets.

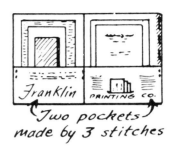

15. Here three staples have been used to attach the inner flap of a French-fold portfolio to the outer surface, thus forming two pockets for samples and printed inserts. This style can serve as a booklet cover with pages saddle-stitched at the center fold. Very small enclosures, such as samples of cards, can be inserted in a slot close to the bottom fold, on the right pocket, to keep them separate.

POSTERS

"Posters" as used here means sheets printed for display purposes mounted on walls, doors, counters, windows, etc. In this sense even a gummed poster stamp, as small as 1-1/4" x 2" is a poster.

At the other extreme, a "24-sheet poster" measures 144" x 280". Most posters for local stores, clubs, schools, entertainers, etc. usually measure around 11" x 14", 14" x 22" or 17" x 22".

The successful poster must have "human interest," secured by a photo or drawing of a face in a striking expression, related to the thought or feeling in the ad. The layout must be bold and simple to catch the eye. Copy must be short as most posters must be seen and read "on the run" or not at all. Bright colors are helpful too.

Posters can be printed on paper or multiple-ply bristol, depending on how they will be used.

1. Posters made up entirely of type can attract extra attention by printing the form at an angle on the sheet with alternate paragraphs in light and bold face type. Type can also be set to conform to a geometrical area.

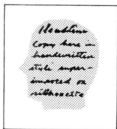 

2. An eye-catching border from one of the border tapes available can emphasize the copy by "fencing it in" from distracting surroundings. On right, the poster has thumbnail sketches, or gadgets of plastic mounted in lieu of sketches.

3. An all-over background pattern can "frame" part of the copy in an attractive shape. Pattern may be prepared from acetate sheets of shading film.

4. Halftone screen tints, Benday, or all-over decorative pattern sheets, printed in a color or black, can silhouette a human head, trade mark, or other object for eyecatching value. Text can be superimposed over background or printed in reverse.

5. A strong sales point can often be made by using a photographic blowup of a portion of the product to emphasize a certain feature in its design or construction. A bleed photo can have an area blocked-out for several lines of type.

6. Reverses of headlines or text material can provide white-on-black copy to reproduce with bold emphasis. The background at right can reproduce to make a dramatic color splotch.

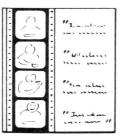 

7. When the illustration is of a "cause and effect" variety, a series of cartoon drawings or amusing photo sequences can be shown as if in a movie strip with copy lines opposite each frame. Pictures may run clockwise around text in the center.

8. A silhouette drawing, or photo trimmed so the background of the featured object is removed to form an effective color background area with type lines superimposed. A photo-montage is also effective.

PACKAGING MATERIALS

Printed wrappers and bags are popular printed items, and are used to contain almost anything: food, soft goods, hardware, etc.

Here is a list of some of the various items produced for the packaging field:

Advertising jackets
Bags
Band-wrappers
Book jackets
Box board and cover
Boxes, folding
Cartons, corrugated
Chip board stiffeners
Decals
Envelopes
Foil wrappers
Folding, set-up boxes
Glassine bags, envelopes
Heat-seal papers
Holiday designs
Imported and novelty papers
Kraft paper wrappers
Labels, gummed and ungummed, pressure sensitive
Manila paper wrappers
Notion, Shopping bags
Padded bags
Parchment wrappers
Plastic wrappers
Tip-on gadgets for packages
Waxed paper wrappers
Wrappers with all-over pattern
Wrappers for mailing tubes

Here are a few layout ideas using step-and-repeat logos, and other design ideas to produce an attractive package design.

179

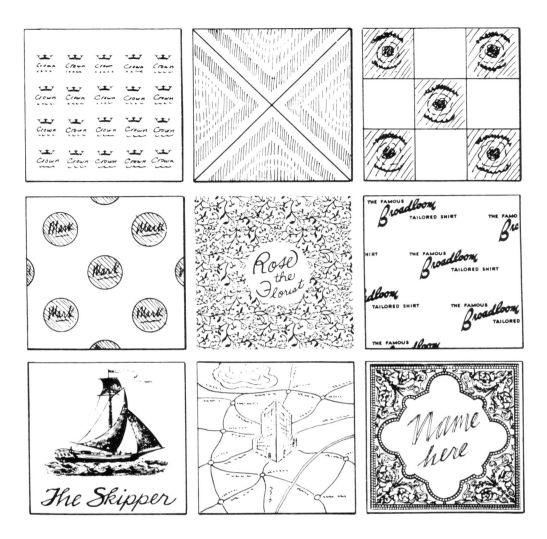

REPORTS

Reports include annual reports published by corporations and reports prepared on any subject in printed form for industries, clubs, social agencies, governmental units, etc.

Many reports of companies generally contain a review of important developments of the past year, milestones in the history of the firm, new products, sales information, personnel, etc. It is distributed to bondholders and stockholders.

The general standard reports measure 8-1/2″ x 11″ bound the 11″ way.

The sequence of material is generally as follows:

1. Cover and title
2. Title page
3. Copyright
4. Printer's imprint
5. Dedication (if any)
6. Preface
7. Table of Contents
8. Errata
9. List of illustrations
10. Foreword
11. Summary and conclusions
12. Main text
13. Appendix and/or exhibits
14. Notes
15. Glossary or vocabulary
16. Bibliography
17. Index

Layout styles for illustrated reports vary widely, depending on the nature of the product and company. Text is usually set one or two columns per page, though there may be three columns or more. The use of charts, pictures and diagrams can dramatize and interpret the statistical material. It's a good idea to caption all photos to secure more attention and explain the photograph.

1. Four possible cover layout styles for reports. At right a cover letter is used as one of opening pages.

2. A summary page is useful at beginning of report so that busy readers can grasp the most essential features of the report at a glance. Sub-heads set off the main divisions of the summary. At right, an economy report which has information condensed to fit on letterhead.

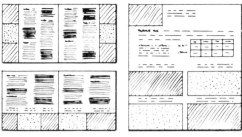

4. Today, most annual reports devote at least a portion of their space to photos. These layouts indicate placement of photos along with text matter.

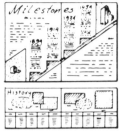 

5. "Step effect", short paragraphs on milestones in company history. Spread below shows photos overlapping with chart across bottom edge using 10 panels. Right, above, shows rules setting off eight paragraphs on year's highlights. Right, below, are pictographs of new products, events of the year with brief text.

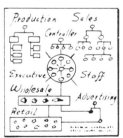 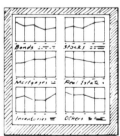 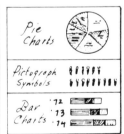 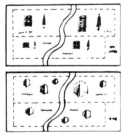

   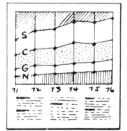

3. Financial information can be presented in a variety of schemes. The use of graphs and pie charts are popular methods of presenting data.

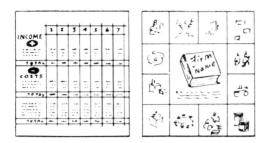

6. Essential breakdowns of income and cost divided by year for last five years. Column six gives five-year average, column seven averages the preceding five-year period; bottom third shows taxes, dividends, etc. At right is a page of annual report featuring a new book about the company, surrounded by photos taken from it.

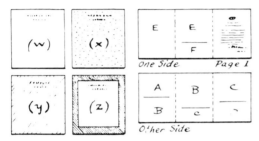

7. Self-mailer broadside report, 17″

x 22″ flat, folds to 5-1/2″ x 8-1/2″ address surface (D). Open next to (A) facsimile of company letterhead. President's message; (B) open next to four charts, statistics, comments; (C) open finally to center spread. Right: Self-mailer booklet, printed indicia, address lower part back cover.

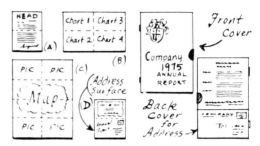

8. Four ways to handle accountant's report, (w) black rule border; (x) black over halftone letterhead; (y) over color tint (z) color tint frame. Right: Notice of annual meeting of stockholders (A) Proxy; (B) Directors, stockholders; (C) officers; (D) company retirement plan; (E) transactions; (F) other matters.

SELF-MAILERS

Here are ideas for those who wish to economize by avoiding a separate outgoing envelope, letter, reply form, and reply card or envelope.

These self-mailers can be mailed out bulk mail for a lower rate of postage. The mailer must sort the mail according to zip code and comply with other postal regulations. Obtain a copy of bulk mailing regulations from the post office to make certain that your mail indicia and handling meets the postal requirements.

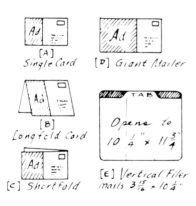

1. (A) Single card, third class, card stock; (B) Longfold card and (C) shortfold card should both be as large as (A) when folded. (D) Giant mailing card 5-1/2″ x 8-1/2″. (E) Opens to fit vertical file, printed projecting "tab".

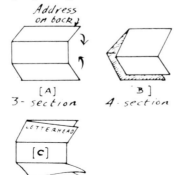

2. (A) Three-section sheet with two parallel folds. Letter size folds to 3-2/3″ x 8-1/2″. (B) Two parallel folds also make four-sections. (C) Four-page letter folding once one way, twice other way, as sketched, can be mailed after folding with good tight fold.

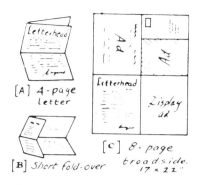

[A] 4-page letter

[B] Short fold-over

[C] 8-page broadside 17 × 22"

3. (A) Four-page letter French-folded, 8-1/2" x 11" folding to 4-1/4" x 5-1/2" mailing size or can be larger. (B) Also French-folded with top surface a short foldover for cover letter, news story, or ad. (C) 17" x 22" broadside on book paper opens to unfold letter, display ads or display poster.

Saddle-stitch / Ad / Seal

4. Saddle-stitched booklet, sealed over edge opposite binding.

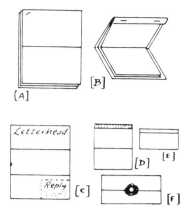

[A] [B] [C] [D] [E] [F]

5. (A) Separate sheets stapled at corner folds once for mail. Seal over edge. (B) Cover bears address, folds over top of gathered sheets, side-stitched. (C) Perforated business reply card can be printed on cover stock with letter copy. (D) Gum strip top edge of letter, fold as (E). Letter (F) folds twice, seals.

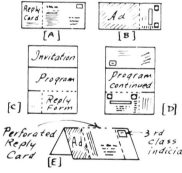

[A] [B] [C] [D] [E]

Perforated Reply Card / Ad / 3rd class indicia

6. (A) and (B) Business reply card turned at right angles to outgoing message to avoid confusion. (C) and (D) invitation-program for meeting (card stock) has perforated card to use at door, and reply card. (E) Reply card to bring back prospect's name.

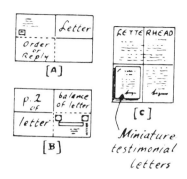

[A] [B] [C] Miniature testimonial letters

7. (A) and (B), two-and-one-half-page letter on card stock to provide detachable business reply card. Score against grain for French-folding. (C) Letter on bond stock French-fold to allow stapling-on of collection of miniature letters.

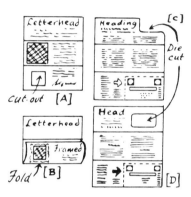

Cut-out [A] Fold [B] [C] Die cut [D]

8. (A) Fabric or other material sample tipped-on center of 3-panel mailer with "window" die-cut to show fabric. (C) Corner of 2-fold card die-cut to reveal name, address of prospect on message surface of reply card when folded for mail. (D) Same as (C) using cut-out.

SPECIALTIES

Specialties can be anything given away by an advertiser which is of value to the recipient. Designed to build good-will, they are often of a utilitarian and/or reference in nature.

These specialties might be mailed out, handed out or offered as a product to a printer's trade.

Few recipients will throw away a useful keepsake. If it duplicates closely another piece they are now using, they will generally pass it on to some friend or business associate, so its advertising and good-will value is rarely wasted.

Most of the specialties illustrated are suitable for use by almost any line of business. Wordings used are simply suggestions for your consideration. Adapt each form to the local advertiser's requirements.

1. A small "memo" pad 4-1/4" x 5-1/2" cut out of bond paper is useful for short notes.

2. A treasured keepsake here takes the form of a miniature, illustrated booklet written in lively style with sketches or photos, given to visitors at factory, store, school, etc. Inserted in a French-folder, through a line slot; brief cover letter at left.

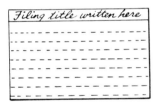

3. Small memo forms for later filing. Rule near top serves to keep filing title in standard location. Dotted leaders across the sheet promote legible entries.

4. A keepsake often is a pin, badge, button or other three-dimensional gadget. You can attach to firm letterhead if sent by mail.

5. A pressure sensitive sticker, 3-3/4" x 8-1/2" for a No. 10 envelope, for a three-month calendar, plus ad copy. It can be affixed to any surface.

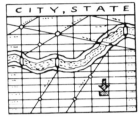

6. A map of a city showing main thoroughfares can be used as keepsake for many firms.

7. Most executives can use miniature letterheads, one-fourth standard size, for brief notes attached to other correspondence, samples, etc.

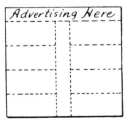

8. Saddle or side-stitched booklet, ad on cover, over perforated sheets. For notes to jog the memory: shopping lists, appointments, calls, etc. Center strip holds each unit until torn off.

9. Here is a 4" x 9" keepsake that combines functions of an inch-and-pica ruler, rules for layout of type lines from six to 13 points apart. Also illustrated are various type faces available. Print on heavy card stock.

10. Wall calendars are useful in any office or home. A photo or drawing is printed on a cardboard or cover paper with calendar pad stitched on below.

11. Every office can use pads for recording incoming phone messages for absent staff members.

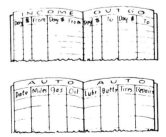

12. Giveaway booklet for an auto dealer, auto service station, etc., can take the form of a handy record form to show mileage record. Budget records make welcome keepsakes for any advertiser.

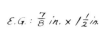

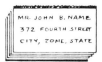

$E.G.: \frac{7}{8}$ in. x $1\frac{1}{2}$ in.

13. A pad of name and address labels to apply to cards, envelopes, packages, etc.

14. 8-1/2″ x 11″ bond paper for looseleaf binder makes a good appointment record for the week.

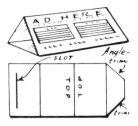

15. Tent-shaped card for standup use on desks and counters has two display surfaces. Use for calendar or useful for technical information. Tapered trim fits into slot on one end of card.

16. Saddle-stitched booklet for several kinds of record forms for short pocket reference purposes.

17. Usual style of monthly calendar with twelve sheets. Bind with metal strip at top, or saddle-stitch for turning over each month.

WINDOW, WALL AND POINT-OF-PURCHASE DISPLAYS

Perhaps a store will hold a special sale related to a coming season, holiday, anniversary. Here are a few tie-ins that offer the opportunity to produce display material:

1. Back-to-school sales
2. Bargain day
3. Birthday sales
4. Christmas specials
5. Clearance sales
6. Department specials
7. Dollar day
8. Easter sales
9. Father's Day
10. Founder's Day
11. Fourth of July
12. Introductory offers
13. Mother's Day
14. Opening sale
15. Pre-inventory sale
16. Thanksgiving sale
17. Vacation specials

Retailers, clubs, churches, real estate firms, hotels, restaurants, cleaners, schools, recreation centers, and so on are all receptive to good display ideas to promote local effort.

1. Several display styles: Two parallel scores permit banding so display will stand up. The "counter card" is scored so packages of advertised product piled on top of fold-under section hold card in place on counter. Printed displays can be mounted on standard carton containing product.

185

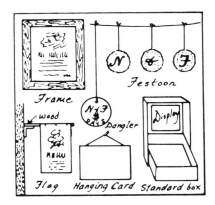

2. Plastic or wood frame holds a display card — can be used many times for future displays. Small, bright colored cards, die-cut to shapes, hang from wire as a "dangler." Other cards displayed in a variety of ways.

3. (A) Display mounted on special paper background: wallpaper, box cover, metallic, etc. (B) Block of wood or plastic to hold rigid display. (C) Triangular-shaped wood holds small display nailed to it. (D) Single and double wing easels to hold cards for display. (E) Round wood rods simulate scroll for hanging.

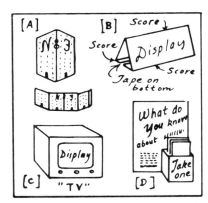

4. (A) Building of advertiser simulated in stand-up display. Four scored lines and projecting tab to be glued underneath. (B) Tent display printed both sides, held with tape at bottom. (C) Standard box, resembles TV screen. (D) Box or envelope holds literature.

5. A small press can print four sheets to be assembled later to form a large display.

6. A bright colored paper pennant, made with guillotine cutter, effective for single slogan or series of product ads. Attach to walls, wires, etc. At right the slate is printed in reverse to resemble chalk on blackboard.

7. Ornate frame with text copy inside. Use border tapes for attractive display cards.

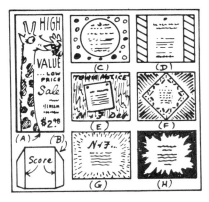

8. Unusual shape arouses interest when produced on display cards.

9. Mobiles with display material on each side, cut from single sheet after printing both sides. Bumper strips also good for display advertising. Print on pressure sensitive stock with removable adhesive.

26

Storage and Handling

Go Back to the Original
Filing Pasteups
Pasteup Department Location and Floor Plan

GO BACK TO THE ORIGINAL

A good filing system for your pasteups is necessary so you can find the original pasteup to use for any required revision. Avoid pasting up on second generation printed pieces. Type can appear thick or thin or fuzzy in comparison with the newly pasted material. If a pasteup gets soiled from repeated use, make a PMT print of the pasteup and start to use this for the original on which to revise.

FILING PASTEUPS

There is a need to keep pasteups in files for a variety of reasons:

1. Jobs will be printed at a later date with revised information affixed to the pasteup taken from the file.
2. Illustrations may be filed for later use on other jobs.

PROBLEMS

Size

If the sizes of the pasteups are large, such as maps 24″ x 36″ or full size newspaper pages, the storage may be awkward. Variations in sizes must be considered for development of a system.

Characteristics

The pasteup with bits of copy affixed to a base sheet, was not prepared for excessive handling and repeated filing. It was originally prepared as a production camera-ready unit. Bits and pieces of proof copy were affixed to a base sheet along with the usual corrections and additions.

METHODS

Flat Engineering File Drawers

These are the flat file drawers in which engineering drawings are kept in flat sheets. They can be used to store pasteups. When the pasteups are stored on top of each other in the drawers, care must be taken when the flats are shuffled in and out of the drawers. The flat corrugated fibre file drawers are less expensive than metal, and can be used if the drawers are not filled with too much weight.

Kraft Paper Envelopes

A pasteup can be stored inside a large Kraft paper envelope with the flap cut off if desired. These envelopes are available in a variety of sizes. If you have pasteups that are very large and beyond the largest standard envelope, you can make a simple envelope with Kraft paper from a roll of wide wrapping paper. A large sheet of Kraft wrapping paper folded over and taped along the edges, can make a satisfactory envelope to contain a pasteup and keep it clean. A job number can be written along the edges as a reference to locate for future retrieval.

These envelopes, if large, can be placed in the engineering file drawers, or stacked on shelves. The shelves should be positioned fairly close together so the envelopes don't stack too high and can be pulled out and replaced easily.

Negatives can be placed with the pasteups if desired and if it fits your system. Watch storage of plates in these envelopes, however, as any bit of ink can be a problem. Better to store the plates in a separate sleeve or hang on a plate rack built for that purpose.

Some of the smaller storage envelopes can be placed upright in file cabinets. To store in files upright, it is almost a necessity to place the pasteup in an envelope. Pulling a pasteup in and out of a file without having it contained in an envelope can knock off pieces.

A paper-type envelope generally is recommended for storage of pasteups.

Film Boxes

Shops with camera equipment purchase lithographic sheet film in flat thin boxes such as the 18″ x 24″ standard size.

These film boxes make excellent containers for pasteups. Some customers can have boxes for their own pasteups, and others may be filed according to alphabetical or numerical sequence. These boxes can be stacked up and pulled out as required. The box method does allow for flat storage, and the larger boxes will accommodate the larger flats.

This box storage method has been used by a number

of shops and found satisfactory. Some individual jobs can be stored in their own special box and not disturbed until the next time it comes up for reprint.

Flat film boxes used for storage of pasteups.

Clear Plastic Jackets or Envelopes

The advantage of plastic material for the jacket or envelope, is that you can see exactly what is inside the jacket. Clear plastic jackets are very convenient to use to contain a pasteup, but prolonged storage of pasteups with carbon ribbon impression has proved a problem.

Clear plastic jackets hold newspaper ads to run in future issues of the newspaper.

The carbon image can transfer to the plastic surface to weaken the image of the composition output.

The Job Ticket

Sometimes pasteups are stored in the regular job ticket envelope used by print shops or departments. These envelopes are usually too small for most pasteups, and confusion can result if some of the pasteups are in the ticket-envelope and others in the pasteup files or boxes. Keep them all in one organized system.

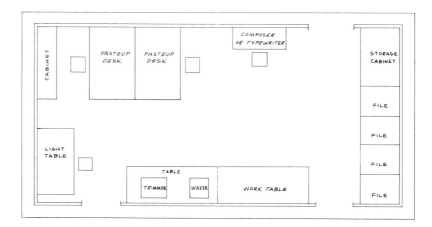

PASTEUP DEPARTMENT LOCATION AND FLOOR PLAN

Here is a suggested arrangement of an area about 12′ x 24′. It should be well lighted with good illumination for each desk. An office atmosphere is best for pasteup work where a clean environment will result in clean pasteups. It is helpful to locate this preparatory area near the camera and stripping operations for convenience in obtaining prints, reverses, etc.

JOB ENVELOPE	Form Name		Form Number

Users by Dept. or Section:

FORM FILED BY:
[ ] Name
[ ] Date
[ ] _____

LIFE OF FORM:
[ ] Permanent
[ ] Temporary

TYPE OF USE:
[ ] Internal (Bank)
[ ] External (Customers)
[ ] Combination

WINDOW ENVELOPE REQUIRED:
[ ] Yes   [ ] No
Envelope No. _____

FORM COMPLETED BY:
[ ] Hand   [ ] Accounting Machine
[ ] Typewriter   [ ] _____

FORM FILED IN:
[ ] Binder   [ ] Regular File Folder
[ ] Notebook
[ ] Card File   [ ] _____

HANDLING:
[ ] Hard [ ] Light [ ] Avg.

MICR ENCODING:
[ ] Yes   [ ] No

Initial Quantity	Estimated Annual Usage	Size X	No. of Plys	Functional Code	Grp. Order Code	Critical Forms Code

Type of Form
[ ] Cut Form
[ ] Continuous
[ ] Snapset-End Stub
[ ] Snapset-Top Stub
[ ] _____

Printing
[ ] One Side
[ ] Two Sides
[ ] Head-to-Head
[ ] Tumble-Turn

Pre-Punch
[ ] Standard 3-hole
[ ] _____

Packaging and Amount
[ ] Band _____ to a package
[ ] Wrap _____ to a package
[ ] Pad _____ to a pad

	Paper Weight	Paper Color		Paper Weight	Paper Color	ENCODE:
Original			3			
Duplicate			4			

Special Information

Date	Amount	Cost	Supplier	Date	Amount	Cost	Supplier	Date	Amount	Cost	Supplier
									General Information		

Job envelope used by the United States National Bank, Omaha, Nebr.

Date_____ Promised _____ Salesman _____

Job No.

Cust. P.O. No. _____

☐ Job is Rerun No. _____

Firm _____

Address _____

☐ Rerun Rev. Old No. _____

Deliver to _____

	Ordered	Quan. Del.	Fin. Size (Width First)	Description	Charges
A					
B					
C					
D					

☐ Printed ONE Side _____ Colors. ☐ Printed TWO Sides _____ Colors. No. of Webs _____

Sales Tax	

Plate File No. _____ Neg File No. _____ Ink Consumption _____

No. Plates	PMS #	INK Color	Actual Sheets	Extras	No. Printed Shts.	Sheet Size				
							☐ One Side	☐ Work & Turn	☐ Work & Tumble	☐ Work & Back
							☐ One Side	☐ Work & Turn	☐ Work & Tumble	☐ Work & Back
							☐ One Side	☐ Work & Turn	☐ Work & Tumble	☐ Work & Back
							☐ One Side	☐ Work & Turn	☐ Work & Tumble	☐ Work & Back

WEB	No. Plates	Color of Ink	No. of Webs	Web Width	Folds to	Stitch	Trims to	Sheets to	Remarks

Paper Wt.	Color	Kind of Stock

☐ Alphatype ☐ IBM Style _____

cut_____ shts. from_____ to_____

Stock ordered from_____ on_____ for Del._____

☐ Fold_____ Folds to_____ ☐ Print in ☐ Print out

☐ Wrap ☐ Band_____ Per Pkg. ☐ Drill 3-Hole Standard

☐ Special Drill _____

☐ Gather in sets of _____ _____ _____ sets per pad

☐ Padded in _____ ☐ Gather_____signatures, saddle stitch, trim

Have Camera Ready on

☐ We proofread and print

☐ Phone cust. to OK paste-up

☐ Cust. will OK paste-up only

☐ Cust. will OK pasteup then SP

☐ Go direct to SP for OK

☐ Deliver the ☐ Paste-up ☐ S P ☐ Savin Copy

Via_____ to

Name_____

Address_____

Phone_____

_ NOTE:_____

Line Negs.	Half-tones	Prints

Advanced No. _____ Delivery Date_____

☐ Discard Neg. ☐ File NEG. _____

Commercial job printing envelope, or job ticket.

27 Questions and Answers

Tips and Ideas

QUESTIONS AND ANSWERS

Q. *"How can we 'ghost back' a photo?"*

A. If you want to "ghost back" a photo, you can use a sheet of tracing paper over the photograph and shoot a normal halftone. This halftone will produce a reproduction that will make the picture appear very light when you want the picture to act as atmosphere or when you want type to overprint the photo. Bourges Solotone overlay sheets in grays and whites are available in different percentages to provide the exact degree of ghosting desired.

Q. *"How can we uncurl photographs?"*

A. Photographs can be difficult to handle if they curl badly. Particularly difficult is doing retouch work on the photos if they are curled. A dry mounting press is ideal for mounting photos onto a chipboard to hold rigid. Removable spray adhesive can be used to spray on the back of a photo to hold down on card stock. Double-tack mounting film is easy to use to hold prints securely.

Another suggestion to uncurl unmanageable photos is to flatten them by using a solution made by dissolving three teaspoons of plain unflavored gelatin in a quart of hot water. Brush this solution on the back of the prints and let them dry.

Q. *"I wish my IBM Composer had a 'bullet' on it because I have need to use one from time to time. Do you have any ideas on this?"*

A. Bullets are necessary in typesetting. If you don't have one on your composing equipment, you can make them. Use a lower case or upper case "o" as a substitute. Black in the center with the tip of a technical pen for an easy bullet.

Q. *"I want to get a shadow on some large display lettering. What's an easy way to do this?"*

A. Shoot negative of the lettering. Make orange color key of this lettering. Take the orange color key film and position on the original lettering according to the shadow width desired. Tape down so color key will act as a flap. Place register marks on base and flap. Shoot the color key as an overlay, then the base. If colors are black for lettering and red for shadow, the two negatives can print as is. If two pastel shades are used you will need to make contact positive of the base lettering and use

resulting positive as a block-out to eliminate any overprinting on the base letter so shadow will just touch the edge of base lettering.

Q. *"We want the horizontal rules on a form to be solid black ink, but the vertical rules must be in a light gray. How can we do this in one press run?"*

A. Draw up the form on the base pasteup but do not draw the vertical rules on the base. Place a sheet of frosted polyester over the pasteup, and draw the vertical rules in exact register with the base. Place three register marks on base to facilitate positioning of negatives by cameraman. Stripper can place screened tint on the negative with vertical rules and double burn. Job is one pressrun.

Q. *"A tinted frame border is wanted around a halftone. Any ideas?"*

A. Using red film, cut out for frame area only. Cameraman can make contact positive of this to automatically produce an open window on the negative into which he can strip the halftone. He can place tint under the original negative frame in the percentage desired. Double burn on plate in register.

Q. *"I have a poster and there is a halftone in the middle of a large solid reverse area. There is so much ink to carry to cover the solid area that the halftone fills in with ink. What could I do to make this job possible?"*

A. Make two runs out of the job. Make a base pasteup. Place overlay over base and put window on the overlay. Have pressroom run this with two plates even though job is same color. Practically impossible to keep from plugging halftone without extra press run. Your overlay with window cut to register is all that is needed.

Q. *"We have 10 pages of tabular material to print in a book. All the ruling is the same. Do we have to rule for every page?"*

A. No. Rule it once on frosted-one-side polyester film or clear film. Each page can be shot with same overlay in register. Camera will pick up overlay rules plus the base pasteup in one shot with good light source. If there is a problem, you can always double-burn.

Q. *"All we have is a photo which was printed before. We must reduce the picture and when we have it reduced the picture is very muddy looking. How can we improve on this?"*

A. Rescreen the picture. Have the camera operator angle his screen when he shoots the halftone to eliminate an objectionable pattern or moire.

Q. *"A customer told me to get the pasteup ready any old way, because he didn't care what it looked like 'as long as he could read it.' When the job was completed the customer hollered that he was most unhappy with the job. How do we win these battles?"*

A. Don't take a customer at his word when he wants printing "down and dirty" because he thinks he's saving money. Give him a good clean neat job every time as company policy. It doesn't cost that much more to do the job right.

Q. *"Can windows be made on a pasteup by drawing a thin black line defining the window area on the pasteup?"*

A. Yes. By making a contact positive of the negative shot of your pasteup. This method is more time-consuming, because it takes longer to draw the lines and the stripper must opaque, tape or mask around each of the clear areas on the contact positive. Using the red vinyl or red masking acetate on the pasteup is faster.

Q. *"How should we charge for pasteup work?"*

A. Pasteup work should be charged on a time basis. It is not easy to charge "by the job" when preparing paste-up work. There are so many varieties involved in pasteups.

Q. *"A customer made a mark on the pasteup I let him take to his office to proofread. He thinks it's funny when I mention that it created problems for me in trying to get it out of there."*

A. Don't let the pasteup out of the shop. Give the customer a photo copy of the pasteup and he can doodle on it to his heart's content.

Q. *"I want to use shading film on a pasteup but the surface is bumpy on the pasteup. What can I do to make the use of this film possible?"*

A. Prepare your pasteup so it is as clean as possible. White any specs or edges. Shoot a PMT of the pasteup to give you a smooth surface on which to place the acetate shading film or Benday.

Q. *"The red overlay peel coat film is hard to get off at times. I try picking at it with the point of a knife blade and seem to do a messy job."*

A. Stick a piece of Scotch tape at the edge of the film. Pull up the tape and the film coating will pull up with it.

Q. *"When we put down border tape, the guideline we draw is difficult to see for accurate placement of the tape. Any suggestions?"*

A. Draw your guideline with a blue non-reproducing ball point pen. You get a dense line to follow with the tape.

Q. *"How do I get a fade-out effect so that the ink will go from darker to very light gradually?"*

A. Your preparation for this will involve the use of an air brush. A shade of gray color is sprayed carefully on a sheet of very white card stock to render the design of shading required for the job. A dropout halftone is shot of the airbrush work. Skill and practice with the air brush are important to obtain quality results with fade-outs.

Q. *"I'm new to pasteup, and everytime I do a job I must do parts of it over again. My boss is so particular about everything I do. I'm very discouraged and feel I can't do anything right."*

A. There is a tendency for someone new to pasteup to feel discouraged because work must be done over that is not precise. Remember, your boss is not being unkind to you. He is responsible for the preparation of quality work, and must insist on precise camera-ready copy. There is no compromise, and you wouldn't want your company to lose a customer because of your work. Your boss is doing you a favor by insisting on perfection in pasteup. Don't get discouraged.

Q. *"I'm trying to draw good clean circles with a template and Rapidograph pen. I just can't get a good clean circle."*

A. Control of the pen is important. Hold it straight up and down, and don't press. The pen will mark with hardly any pressure. Remember, too, it does take practice. Be patient and practice to get the hang of it.

Q. *"We mortise in all of our corrections on paper. I've noticed that other shops just paste over the mistakes. Are we wrong in our method?"*

A. No. It does take more time, but you are doing a quality method of making corrections that is difficult to argue against. If you want to spend the time, and paste-up longevity is important, go ahead with your mortise technique.

Q. *"I just got the blame for a job that was out of register when it got printed. I checked my overlay work and it was perfect. I checked the negatives and they were right on. What could have happened?"*

A. I would say that there is a possibility that the paper stretched a bit between runs. The grain of the paper should run with the cylinder, otherwise the paper can stretch. I've seen a 1/4" stretch on a 22" sheet on a hot humid day. No job will register under these conditions.

Q. *"I wanted the press to print white ink on black paper for a menu cover job. They said they could not do it on the offset. Is this true?"*

A. Yes. They can run silver ink to get a good looking coverage on black stock. Otherwise you need to design the job to cover the black on white stock so the white will appear as a reverse. This may be a problem for some presses depending on the amount of solid coverage. If white is a must, and black stock is the only kind available, I'd advise the silk screen process.

Q. *"On jobs that go on our small offset presses, I have been using large solid coverages of color. I'm getting complaints about this. Shouldn't they be able to produce my work?"*

A. You must consider the capabilities of the presses. Small duplicating presses may not have sufficient ink rollers to cover heavy solids easily and with consistency throughout the entire press run. If you know the press equipment, design the work to fit the press.

Q. *"When printing a job in one color and using a tint in combination with overprinting in solid over the tint, what percentage of tint do you recommend?"*

A. Ten percent on darker colors. You want the overprint to stand out in good sharp contrast.

Q. *"I use double coated clear tape for pasteup work. I put down the tape and place pieces over this sticky surface. Isn't this good pasteup technique?"*

A. No. This is not good. Get away from this slow method you are using. You don't have movability of the elements and you are using a much slower system. Convert to a waxer.

Q. *"I've been working on the same book job for six weeks, and I'm getting tired of this job. They told me that there would be variety to this pasteup work, but I can't take much more of these long jobs."*

A. You are still in one of the most creative jobs around. You do run into tedious jobs from time to time that do take a lot of time. Make it a challenge to try to develop a better, faster way to produce your book, in order to cut down on the time spent on pasteup.

Q. *"What do you think of surgical knives for cutting tools for pasteup work?"*

A. Not as good as the regular art knife. The blades are too flexible, and the holder-handle is flat. Stick with the art knife. It's still your best tool for producing skilled pasteup work.

Q. *"I still like to use single edge razor blades for cutting on pasteups. You have voiced your objections to their use. Why?"*

A. You can acquire a skill for almost anything if you practice long enough. There is no substitute for a good art knife. It is safer, easier to handle, particularly for cutting overlay work, it fits the hand, and one can acquire finesse and skill using this type of tool that is difficult to learn with any other.

Q. *"I like to use condensed type. To me it looks better than the other types. What do you think?"*

A. Condensed type is meant to be used when condensation of type is necessary due to space require-ments. When you have adequate space it is generally best not to use it.

Q. *"Why use amber film for overlay work instead of the red?"*

A. The amber is easier to see through, especially when cutting over photographs. You can use the red and amber when you have two overlays to cut on the same pasteup. This way you get good contrast and can see the differences in the color separations created by the two overlays. If the overlay will be contacted to film or photo, always use red film.

Q. *"Why can't I work-and-turn a job on duplex paper? They told me I couldn't do it?"*

A. Duplex paper is one color on one side and another color on the opposite side. You can work-and-turn a job on duplex stock, but keep in mind that one-half of the job will be printed with the fronts on two different colors of stock. Will your customer like this idea? To be consistent you should not plan to print a job on duplex paper as work-and-turn. It will have to be work-and-back.

Q. *"What can be done to prevent slight paper slippage in the IBM Composer which causes line spacing inconsistency in columns of type?"*

A. Brush three or four strips of thin rubber cement on the back of the repro paper. Allow to dry thoroughly. The rubber coating will help the paper hug the platen to help prevent slippage.

Q. *"What leading do you recommend between lines of type to make for the best readability?"*

A. You might find this suggested leading guide helpful, although there are always exceptions and variations which are acceptable.

Type size	Minimum leading	Maximum leading
6 pt.	solid	1 pt.
8 pt.	solid	2 pt.
10 pt.	solid to 2 pt.	4 pt.
12 pt.	2 pt.	6 pt.
14 pt.	3 pt.	8 pt.

Leading between lines will make it easier to cut lines apart without damage to ascenders and descenders.

Q. *"What suggestions do you have for removal of waxed pieces without damaging copy?"*

A. Generally use pointed tweezers to lift a corner so that you can peel slowly with the fingers or continue with the tweezers.

If extra help is needed to remove copy, apply rubber cement thinner into the peeled back area. The thinner is a solvent for wax, so by applying thinner as you peel, the copy lifts off easily. A squirt of thinner on the back of the pasteup will soak through the base sheet to help remove copy.

Heat can soften wax. One of the hand-type hair dryers is helpful to direct warm air to the surface and subsequent removal of waxed pieces. A pasteup can be laid on top of a mechanical waxer so the waxer's heat can soften wax.

TIPS AND IDEAS

Angle Cutting Reverses

Ordinarily, when a reverse is cut out and placed on a patch, the edges of the reverse are touched up with a felt tip black pen to prevent unwanted hair lines from accidentally showing up on the clear area of the negative. Hair lines which appear on film require scraping to remove them.

Angle cutting techniques solve production of reverses and prevent hair lines without felt pen touch up. You would probably gang up all of the reverses on larger sheets. Wax coat this print and place on a cutting board backer. Using a standard art knife, hold the knife at an angle so the bevel is inward around the reverse piece. This bevel or angle cut will eliminate touch up on the pasteup and result in a clean clear negative. A little practice will result in speedy cutting of contours, shapes and straight edges with inward beveled edges to eliminate the possibility of white knife lines showing up on film.

Dividing a Measurement Into Thirds

Here is a quick method to precisely divide a measurement into three equal parts.

Multiply a measurement in inches times *two* and the answer will be a third of the measurement . . . in *picas*. Thus 11″ x 2 = 22 *picas* which is one-third of 11″.

A formula for this application is as follows:

Measurement in inches x 2 = 1/3 of measurement in *picas*.

Other common measures divided into thirds by use of the formula would result as follows:

$$8.5″ \times 2 = 17 \text{ picas}$$
$$14″ \times 2 = 28 \text{ picas}$$
$$7″ \times 2 = 14 \text{ picas}$$

Dividing an Area Into Equal Parts

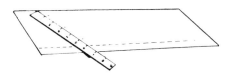

You may need to divide an area into five, six, eight or 10 parts. Square up paper with the t-square on the board. Place a ruler in slant position flush to the left side of paper, but pivoting to a convenient measurement for the amount of equal division required. For instance, you want to divide 8-1/2″ into five equal parts. Place edge of ruler at left and slant the rule so that 10″ is at the right edge. Now, mark a pencil dot along the ruler at 2″, 4″, 6″ and 8″. Now draw lines according to pencil dots, using the t-square so the lines will be parallel to the squared-up paper.

Curving Type

Set type in a straight line. Use Graham Color Coded Centering Rule to locate center of line and make blue dot at center. Wax line, place on cutting board and cut between each of the characters carefully in order to create a "grass skirt" out of the type line. Do not cut below the base line. A straight edge held at the base line will act as a "stop" so the knife tip will not cut below the base line.

After completion of cuts between characters, move the straight edge downward about 1/32″ and cut horizontally to leave a lip of paper along this bottom base. You can now lift up this paper strip "grass skirt" and position above a circle at center. By sliding the individual characters around the circle you automatically curve the type and maintain a precise base. Be careful to create equal wedges between characters to assure equality of the angled spacing.

If type is to curve below a circle, you would make the lip of paper above the type and open the bottom.

Cut carefully between characters from base line. Steel straight edge acts as a stop.

Move straight edge down slightly so lip of paper remains intact below base line

Slide characters from center to form curved line.

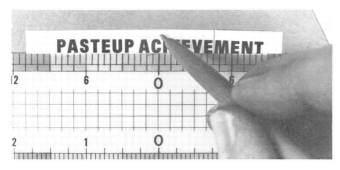

Centering rule is ruled to locate center of line.

Adjust characters so that wedge spacing between characters is equal.

28
Glossary of Terms

This glossary has been prepared as a convenient reference to assist printing personnel and graphic art students in becoming better acquainted with important printing terms. Words are tools of thought, and familiarity with printing terminology will produce better informed and more efficient graphic arts communicators.

Every attempt has been made to update printing definitions. As time passes and technology changes, word meanings can change too.

The operation of a modern printing facility is an exacting business. It should operate efficiently from the beginning of the printing plan to the final bindery and delivery. Communication becomes the important link towards this efficiency.

The definitions in this glossary cover the expressions used in daily graphic arts communication.

A

AA (AUTHOR'S ALTER-ATIONS): See "Alterations."

ABSORPTION: Ink drying by soaking into the paper.

ACCORDION FOLD: Having folds like the bellows of an accordion, created by the paper being folded two or more times in a parallel direction.

ACETATE: One of the transparent or translucent sheets used for artist's overlays. Similar to clear photographic film.

AD ALLEY: Area in composing room devoted to make-up of advertising.

ADVERTISING AGENCY: A firm which staffs imaginative writers, creative communicators, artists and designers to create advertising to influence the reader publics.

AGATE LINE: A unit of measure in selling newspaper advertising space. 14 agate lines equal one column inch.

AIRBRUSH: A precision, compressed-air tool for spraying smooth areas of tones on art work, and for retouching photographic prints or negatives.

ALIGNMENT: Placement of characters on a straight line.

ALPHABET LENGTH: The length of a lowercase alphabet measured in points. This measurement is used as a basis for copyfitting.

ALTERATIONS: Changes made by the customer, through no fault of the printer, after type has been set. Alterations are a legitimate additional charge by the printer.

196

AMBERLITH: A film for hand cutting and peeling of film from the surface of a plastic base sheet. A trade name of Ulano.

AMPERSAND: Symbol for "and" which looks like &.

ANILINE PRINTING: See "Flexography."

ANTIQUE PAPER: Paper with a relatively rough or unfinished surface, not smooth, slick or coated.

ART: Original art work, illustrations or photographs, reproduction proofs of type, hand-drawn lettering, or any other material ready for the lithographer's camera.

ART KNIFE: A sharp pointed knife to trim and cut copy for paste-up. Usually a hobby-type knife with a pencil size handle and replaceable blade.

ARTISTIC CENTER: See "Optical Center."

ASCENDERS: The lines of lower case type which extend above the body such as the b, d, f, h, etc.

ASTERISK: The symbol (*), now mainly used to call attention to a footnote.

AUTOPOSITIVE FILM AND PAPER: A material which gives a positive copy from a positive copy (or a negative from a negative) by direct processing.

AXIS: The real or imagined vertical and horizontal visual lines running through an ad area. The axis help to tie all elements together.

B

BACKBONE: The back edge of a book along which the sections of the book are bound.

BACKING UP: Printing the opposite side of a sheet, after the first has already been printed.

BAD BREAK: Incorrect word division.

BALANCE: Arranging type and illustration elements to create a feeling of stability.

BALLOT BOX: A square provided for marking a choice.

BALLPOINT PEN: Sometimes used to make trim marks, rules, center marks, etc. An extra fine ball tip with black ink should be used.

BANDING: Securing a package or bundle of printed material with a strip of heavy paper, usually two or three inches wide. A "banding" machine is built to facilitate this operation and folded sheets which come off a folder are often banded.

BARREL FOLD: When paper is folded two or more times in the same direction, sometimes called a wrap-around fold.

ABCD

BASE LINE: The imaginary line on which the base of letters rest. See "Measurement of Type."

BASE SHEET: Material on which composition output and other pieces are affixed. Generally it is heavy paper, light card stock, but can be plastic film, tissue or other material.

BASIS WEIGHT: The weight of a ream of paper (500 sheets) based on a standard size for each grade, which is: Book paper — 25 x 38, Cover — 20 x 26, Bristol — 22½ x 28½, Index — 25½ x 30½, Business paper (including bond, ledger, mimeograph, duplicator and manifold) — 17 x 22, and Tag — 24 x 36. One ream of 80 lb. book paper will weigh 80 lbs.

BENDAY: Screened tone percentages printed on pressure sensitive plastic sheets with a release paper backing. Used to place on art work, pasteup areas, etc. to achieve a tonal or dot pattern. See also: "Tint," "Tone."

BINDER: Craftsman who works in the bindery operations of a printing department.

BINDER'S BOARD: Stiff pulp board used for hard bound books under cloth or paper covering material.

BINDING EDGE: Edge of sheet or page that is fastened in the hinge of the book. Right-hand pages are bound on the left side and left-hand pages are bound on the right. Ample space for binding should be allowed.

BLANKET: A cloth-backed rubber sheet covering the cylinder of an offset press, which receives the inked image from the offset plate and transfers it to the paper.

BLEED: When the printed image extends to the trim edge of a sheet or page, as in a booklet.

BLIND EMBOSSING: Creating a raised impression on a sheet of paper without ink.

BLIND FOLIO: Page number on a pasteup that does not print.

BLOCKING OUT: Eliminating any portion of a piece of art by painting out or masking on the film or on the art.

BLOCKOUT FILM: Transparent, self-adhesive ruby-red, thin plastic film. Used as a substitute for blacking-in large areas on base pasteups or overlays.

BLOWUP: A camera enlargement.

BLUE PRINT — BLUE LINE: A photo print made from the lithographer's negative, exposed to photosensitive paper, developed, and used as a proof. Similar to brown print except that the resultant proof is blue and white in color.

BLURB: Summary of a book generally found on the jacket.

BODY TYPE: Type used for the main body of a book or publication, as distinguished from the headings.

BOLDFACE (Bf): Type heavier than the text type with which it is used.

BOND: Rag or sulphite paper with a hard finish to use for stationery and forms.

BOOK JACKET: Usually attractive paper covers around a hardbound book to advertise the book and protect it. Contains design, pattern, beauty, and color and provides information about the book.

BOOKLET: Small book consisting of up to 48 pages.

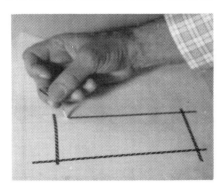

BORDER: A plain or ornamental frame around type composition, art elements or a combination of both.

BOURGES: Trade name for a line of acetate sheets in colors. They are used for preparing layouts and dummies by placing the pressure sensitive film on the layout and cutting out the definition.

BOXED-IN: Paragraphs or lines of type enclosed with rules.

BOXHEAD: Column head within a table.

BREAK: The place for dividing or ending a line of type.

BREAKER RULE: A short hairline rule which separates footnote material from text.

BRISTOL BOARD: Thin cardboard with smooth surface.

BROADSIDE: A large printed sheet, folded.

BROCHURE: A presentation of information in the form of a folder, pamphlet or booklet.

BROWN PRINT: Another photo print to be used as a proof. Made by exposing the lithographer's negative to special photographic paper. The resultant proof is brown and white in color. Also called Van Dyke.

BUFFER SHEET: A sheet placed on top of elements on a pasteup on which a burnishing tool is rolled or rubbed. The sheet can prevent smear or damage to the copy. A preferred buffer sheet is a clear polyester sheet of film to allow good visibility during the burnish.

BULK: The thickness of a single sheet of paper, expressed in points.

A point is one thousandth of an inch.

BULLET: A solid dot character used ornamentally, and classified by point size.

BURNING-IN: Exposing a plate through a negative.

BURNISH: To apply pressure to proof copy to cause it to stick to the surface after wax application to the back of the copy.

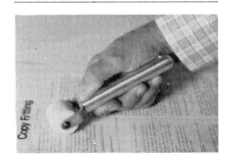

BURNISHER: A tool used in burnishing. It may be a roller, edge of a plastic or wood stick or other device.

C

©: The legal sign for a copyright notice when used on the proper page of a book together with the year and name of copyright holder.

C.&S.C.: Abbreviation for caps and small caps.

CALENDERING: When paper is passed between a stack of horizontal rollers, under pressure, to increase the smoothness and gloss of its surface and reduce its bulk.

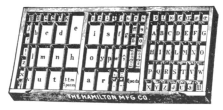

CALIFORNIA JOB CASE: Case in which handset type is stored.

CALIPER: Measurement of a single sheet of paper, film, plate material, etc. expressed in thousandths of an inch.

CALLIGRAPHY: Handwriting of uniform quality written with a flexible nib pen point.

CAMERA AXIS: A line perpendicular to the focal plane of the camera and passing through the interior perspective center of the lens system.

CAMERA, HORIZONTAL OR VERTICAL: Camera constructed to photograph copy. Copy is mounted in the copyboard so lens can point to copy.

CAMERA LUCIDA: An instrument used by the artist to trace a reproduction of an object or piece of art on paper. A prism arrangement of mirrors projects the image onto the paper.

CAMERA-READY: A pasteup that has been completely prepared so that it is photographable to produce a negative or negatives for platemaking.

CAPS: Abbreviation for capital letters. Also called upper case.

CAPTION: Heading of display type used as a focal point or type adjacent to pictures, etc. Sometimes referred to as "cutlines."

CARBRO: A photographic print in full color. Carbon tissue prints in primary colors are prepared from separation negatives. These are sandwiched in register by hand to form one composite proof.

CARET (∧): Proofreader's mark which indicates an insertion of additional matter.

CARTOGRAPHY: Expressing graphically by maps and charts, the known physical features of the earth or other celestial body.

CASING-IN: Applying the cover to the forwarded sheets of a book.

CAST-OFF: A measurement of manuscript or galley proof to estimate how many pages a book will make in a selected format.

CATCHLINE: A temporary line of type on a proof containing a title for later replacement.

CHAPTER HEADS: Chapter number and/or title on beginning page of each chapter.

CHARACTER: Any letter, number, punctuation mark, or space in printing matter.

CHARACTER COUNT: Total number of characters in a manuscript.

CHOKE: An image which has been made "thinner" through a contact process without altering its shape or relative positioning. The amount of choke is controlled by exposure.

CHROMATIC: True colors.

CLEAN PROOF: A proof of composition output set according to copy and free from marks by proofreader.

CLEARBASE FILM: Lithographic film produced on a polyester film base. Used for stripping and lay-up.

CLIP ART: Illustrations, line drawings and screened pictures printed on pages to cut out for use on any printed material. The illustrated art is usually printed in several sizes and classified for seasonal category.

CLOSE SPACING: Narrow spacing between words.

COATED PAPER: Paper manufactured with a smooth glossy or dull finish accomplished by adding casein satin white, china clay, calcium carbonate, starch, or glue and certain pigments to the paper's surface. Different types exist, as coated one-side, coated two-sides, machine-coated, cast-coated, dull coated, enamel finish, etc.

COCKLE: Paper with a ripple surface.

COLD TYPE: In composition — type set by a strike-on impression method or by phototypesetting.

COLLATING: Gathering or arranging printed sheets or signatures into the desired sequence, either by hand or by machine.

COLLOTYPE: A chemical principle for printing. Continuous tone negatives are exposed on photo-sensitive gelatin, which then becomes ink receptive in proportion to the tone of the original subject. Tone gradations, thus, are obtained by varying thicknesses of ink film and not by halftone dots. The plate surface is relatively flat as in lithography. Quantities obtainable from a plate are small.

COLOR BREAKDOWN: A term used to describe the separation of colors on a multi-color pasteup.

COLOR KEY: System of producing overlay transparencies of each color to use as a proof.

COLOR MATCHING SYSTEM: Systems for matching color from the artist through the finished printed product. Numbers are assigned to colors and keyed to actual color swatches and ink formulas so as to assure achievement of specified colors on the finished product. The Pantone Matching System (PMS) is an example.

COLOR PROCESS: The reproduction of copy in full color as close as the original as possible. Four color process uses yellow, magenta, cyan and black. Three color process eliminates the use of the black printer.

COLOPHONE: Trademark of a publisher or the part of a book that specifies the designer, type, printer, paper, etc.

COLOR PROOF: Proof of color representing the same inks for use in the production run.

COLOR SEPARATION: To opaque the negatives to block out for one color and then to perform the blocking out on the opposite area on another negative to print the other color. See: Process Color Separation.

COLOR SKETCH: Rough drawing in color showing approximate size, position and colors of all units in a job to be lithographed. A layout.

COLOR TRANSPARENCY: See "Transparencies."

COMBINATION HALFTONE: A combined line negative and halftone negative to produce as a single printed image. The line image may be superimposed on the halftone or made to appear as white lettering (reverse) to create open areas in the halftone.

COMBINATION PLATE: Plate with halftones and linework.

COMPASS: A device used to produce circles, consisting of two legs joined at the top by a pivot. One leg may hold a pen or pencil or lead.

COMPOSING ROOM: Place where type is set.

COMPOSITION: That which is produced by setting up letters by hand from metal, paper or plastic and that produced from equipment which sets letters phototypographically, from hot metal or by direct impression such as a typewriter.

COMPOSITOR: A typesetter.

COMPREHENSIVE: Layout of art and type using the colors of the final production. Used as a presentation for advertising. Represents the final product as faithfully as possible.

More characters using condensed type

CONDENSED TYPE: A type face designed so the characters are narrower.

CONTACT PRINT: A photographic print made with the negative or positive in contact with the sensitized paper. No camera is necessary. Images are reversed, as from negative to positive, and prints can only be same size as original.

CONTACT SCREEN: A photographically-made halftone screen on film which has a dot structure, such as 85-line, 100-line, 120-line, etc. Used in contact with photosensitive film or paper to produce halftones to print pictures.

CONTINUOUS TONE: Examples are photographs, oil paintings, wash and charcoal drawings and air brush renderings. After continuous tone copy is screened with a contact screen, it is a halftone.

CONTRAST: The actual difference in density between the highlights and the shadows on a negative or positive.

COPY: The material furnished to be used in the production of printing, such as a typewritten or handwritten manuscript.

COPY FITTING: Computing the amount of space it will take to set up composition in a specific size and style of typeface.

COPYRIGHT: An exclusive right to reproduce, publish and sell the matter and form of a literary or artistic work.

COPY WRITER: One who writes advertising copy, literature or other material.

CORRECTION OVERLAY: Tissue affixed over the pasteup on which corrections are indicated. These corrections are checked with the overlay during final proofreading.

CORRECTION PAPER: Strip of paper with white coating on one side that is used for correcting typewritten errors. By overstriking a character with the strip in front of the copy, the letter will blank out. The correct letter is then typed over the blanked-out character.

COUNTERFEIT: An imitation of something made with a view to defraud, as in the fraudulent creation of a written or printed document.

CRASH IMPRINTING: Matter printed on already printed and assembled pages or sheets where the second and succeeding sheets are imprinted from carbon paper or chemical reaction from the impression of a hard raised surface plate or type onto the top sheet. A letterpress function.

CREASING: See "Scoring."

CREEP: The distance variation at the middle signature sections of a saddle-stitched book. This distance is caused by the thickness of the paper signatures where saddle-stitched. Adjustments must be made accordingly to account for this creep, and pages in the center of the book will print with less margin toward the binding edge than pages at the very beginning or tail end of a book.

CROP MARK: Mark used to define the limit of the reproduction area of an illustration and to establish the area of the final image reproduction.

CROPPING: Eliminating edges or portions of art and photographs that are not desired in reproduction.

CROSSOVER: Pictures, headings or other elements which cross from a left hand page to a right hand page. When the pages are part of a signature, care must be taken so the crossover material will register after the signature is folded.

CRT: Cathode Ray Tube. The tube which displays type matter on a Video Display Terminal.

CURSIVE: Type similar to handwriting, but with disconnected letters.

CUTTING GUIDE: A metal or plastic edge to use as a straight edge for cutting.

CUTTING MARK: A thin black rule placed in the border of a press sheet to indicate where the sheet will cut. Differs from trim mark only in that the sheet is cut without gutter waste.

CYAN: One of three transparent ink colors commonly referred to as process colors. A blue-green in color, cyan is used in conjunction with magenta and yellow, along with black to produce four-color or full color process printing.

D

DAGGER (†): Reference mark.

DASHES: A mark of punctuation, longer than a hyphen, used to indicate an abrupt change in a statement or in place of a colon to indicate that something is to follow. - hyphen, — dash

DAY-GLOW: Trade name of ink which has high luminosity.

DECAL: Decalcomania. A process which allows transfer of images onto glass or other materials. Uses specially prepared paper.

DECKLE EDGE: An untrimmed "feathered edge" feature on a sheet of paper.

DECORATIVE TYPE: See "Novelty Type."

DEEP ETCH: One form of lithographic plate. Positive transparencies are exposed on the press plate, and the image (ink-carrying) areas are etched slightly below the surface of the metal plate. These recesses are filled with ink-receptive chemicals. Deep etch plates are used primarily for long runs.

DELETE (⌀): A proofreader's mark used to indicate the omission or elimination of words, letters, sentences, areas, etc.

DELINEATE: In the graphic arts, to give depth to line art by making certain outlines heavier. The word also means to describe in detail.

DENSITOMETER: An instrument which is used to make density measurements.

DENSITY: In general, the relative darkness of an image area as seen by the eye. In photography, a measure of light-stopping ability or blackening of an image as read on a densitometer.

DESCENDERS: The lines of lower case type which extend below the base line, such as g, j, p. q and y.

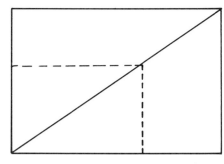

DIAGONAL LINE SCALING: A graphic method for determining relative sizes and proportions. A line is drawn from one corner of a rectangle diagonally to the opposite corner. The point where any vertical line drawn parallel to a side of the rectangle intersects the diagonal line indicates the height in reduced proportion.

DIE CUTTING: Cutting irregular or regular designs in paper or other similar materials with a sharp printing die. Pressure is applied from the die against the paper to force it through the paper. Performed on a letterpress or die cutting press.

DIFFUSION-TRANSFER PROCESS: A method of making a direct positive print, line or screened, by exposing the original in a printing frame or camera using a special sheet of black photo-sensitive paper as a receiver for the image. After exposure this "negative" is fed through a processor with a *positive receiver* paper, emulsion to emulsion. After about 30 seconds the positive print is separated from the "negative" to produce a print ready for pasteup. Sometimes called "PMT" print (Kodak's trade name for the process).

DINGBATS: Typographic decorations.

DIOPTRE: An optical unit of measurement describing the curve of lens. The focal length is obtained by dividing the Dioptre into 40. Power of a lens can be obtained by dividing the focal length into 10.

DIRECT HALFTONE: Screened negative made by exposing the article directly. No photograph or drawing needed.

DIRTY PROOF: A proof containing many typographical errors.

DISPLAY TYPE: In composition —type set larger than the text, used to attract attention.

DISTORTION: Any shift in the position of an image on a photograph which alters the perspective characteristics of the photograph.

DIVIDERS: An instrument used to take measurements from one source and transfer to another. For example, dimensions from a form may be transferred to a pasteup without need for a ruler in some instances.

DOCTOR BLADE: A blade adjusted to a roller in a wax coater to control the thickness of the wax coating. Also the blade pressed against the gravure press cylinder to wipe excess ink from the surface.

DOT: The basic makeup of a halftone.

DOT ETCHING: Changing or correcting to improve the tone values on halftone negatives or positives by hand, by altering the size of the halftone dots chemically.

DOUBLE BURN: To "burn" images on a sensitized plate from two or more different negatives.

DOUBLE-TONE BOARD: Art cardboard material with a variety of tonal areas that will not show until "developed" with a special solution. This liquid is painted on the surface to expose the tonal effect in the areas desired.

DOUBLE SPREAD: Two facing pages or two page spread.

DOUBLING: Reading the same line of type twice because of improper leading for the length of the line.

DOWELS: Small precision circular posts used for registering overlays, negatives, plates, etc. A popular dowel is ¼″ in diameter and .060 high. Some are made of plastic, others are metal.

DRAWN-ON COVER: A book cover which has the paper cover attached with adhesive to the binding edge of the signature or sheets of the book pages.

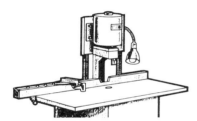

DRILLING: Making round holes in paper using a rotating die or drill.

DROP FOLIO: A page number at the foot of a page below the last line of type matter.

DROPOUT HALFTONE: A halftone having no halftone screen dots in the highlights so that only white paper shows when it is lithographed.

DRY MOUNTING: Process to mount photographs without rubber cement. Mounting tissue is used with heat in a dry mounting press. The tissue acts as an adhesive between the print and the mounting board.

DRY SPRAY: An accessory for a printing press that sprays minute powder particles on sheets' surface as it runs through the press. It is designed to prevent "offset" from occurring.

DRY TRANSFER LETTERING: See "Transfer Lettering."

DUMMY: Preliminary drawing, layout or pasteup showing the position of illustrations, text, etc. as they are to appear on the final printing.

DUMMY FOLIO: Page numbers which are added for identification and used as reference "working numbers" but changed before the book goes to press.

DUOTONE: A two-color halftone print printed from two halftone negatives. One is shot at different screen angle. The final result is a photo with a color hue.

DUPLEXING: The process of duplicating on both the front and back of a sheet of paper.

DUPLEX PAPER: Paper manufactured with a different color or finish on each side.

E

EDITING: Preparation of a manuscript for publication. May include rewriting, checking and correcting the manuscript.

EDITORIAL: Material in a publication which is not advertising.

ELEMENT: Any of the parts of a page, such as display type, text, art that compose the advertisement, etc.

ELIPTICAL DOT: A halftone dot which resembles a football in shape, rather than square. The dot pattern produces a smoother gradation of tones across a middletone area.

ELITE: Elite typewriting has 12 characters per linear inch and 6 lines to the vertical inch.

ELLIPSIS: Three dots that indicate an omission (. . .).

EM: The square of a type body, so called because the letter "M" in early fonts was usually cast on a square body. For example, an 8 point em is 8 points wide and 8 points high, a 10 point em is 10 points wide and 10 points high, etc.

EMBOSSING: Producing a raised (relief) image on a surface, such as paper, by pressing it between special convex and concave dies.

EM DASH: A dash one em long.

EMULSION: Refers to the side of a sheet of film that has the photo-sensitive coating on it. Called the "emulsion side," it is the side that always comes in contact with the plate or other photo-sensitive surface.

EN: A unit of measure half as wide as an em in the same type.

EN DASH: A dash half as wide as an em dash of the same type.

ENAMEL: Paper coated with a polished finish.

END PAPERS: Paper that connects the cover to the pages of a book.

EMBOSSING: A relief or impressed printed image.

ENGRAVING: A printing plate made by an etching process.

EPHEMERA: Printed products with a short life, such as matchbook covers, memo pads, etc.

SIGNS

EXPANDED TYPE: A type with characters designed extra wide as opposed to condensed or standard.

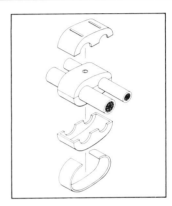

EXPLODED VIEW: An illustration in which the component parts of an object are separated slightly from each other but are shown in the sequence in which they fit together.

EXPOSURE: The quantity of light allowed to act on a photosensitive material combined with the intensity and duration of light acting on the emulsion.

F

FACE: Term used to designate one style of type from another as "What typeface are you using?" Designation also used to describe boldface, lightface, etc.

FACSIMILE: The exact reproduction of a document, signature, etc.

FAKE COLOR: A color printed image which was prepared from a black and white picture or other art. Photographic, hand-cut masking, tint sheets and hand drawn separations are methods used to accomplish the separate color printing images.

FAKE DUOTONE: A duotone effect created by printing a halftone over a screen tint or solid of another color.

FAMILY: All sizes and weights of a type design.

FARM OUT: When all or any part of a publication is done outside by others on an agreement basis.

FELT SIDE: The side of paper which contacts the felt blanket of the paper machine. Opposite of the "wire side."

FILL-IN: Typing in the inside address and salutation after the body of the letter has been duplicated. Requires matching of the type style so body of letter and fill-in will match.

FILM: A light-sensitive material used for recording a photographic image.

FILMSETTING: Phototype-setting.

FILTERS: Filters are used in the camera for making color separations of colored art. Theoretically, a filter permits the photographing of one color at a time, regardless of the number of colors in the original art. The filter material, by absorption, selectively modifies the light transmitted through an optical system.

FINISHING OPERATIONS: Operations which typically occur after ink is placed on the paper or other printed surface in order to complete the product. Examples are drilling, folding, binding, stitching, gathering, cutting, scoring and die cutting.

FIRST REVISE: Proof with errors corrected.

FIT: See "Register."

FLARE: Stray light that reaches the photographic emulsion during camera exposure. Dirty lens surfaces can cause this problem. It is at a minimum when lens is clean and has anti-reflection coating.

FLASH: Supplementary exposure to increase size in shadow dots or "snowballs" of a halftone negative. The "flash" exposure originates from either a flashing lamp directed to the film holder in the darkroom or through the camera lens. The flash exposure is through the contact screen while the screen and film are still in contact by vacuum. The flashing exposure will enlarge the slightly exposed dots in the shadow area of the negative.

FLAT: A group of pages assembled on a base card for placement in the camera copyboard. This term can also denote combined negatives for platemaking.

FLAT TONES: Lithographed areas of dot formation containing a single tone value, not showing any gradations.

202

FLEXOGRAPHY: A method of printing utilizing a relief image on a rubber plate with a liquid ink. Typical products are labels and flexible packaging (bread wrappers).

FLOP: To turn an image over in order to make the image point the opposite way.

FLORETS: Decorative type ornaments.

FLUSH LEFT (or right): Composition set to line up at the left (or right). The term "flush left *and* right" is sometimes used to specify that composition is to be set "justified."

FLUSH PARAGRAPH: A paragraph with no indentation.

FOCAL LENGTH: The distance from the principal point of a lens to the principal focus.

FOCUS: The point toward which rays of light converge to form an image after passing through a lens. The condition of sharpest imagery.

FOLDER: A printed sheet folded and usually used as a mailing piece.

FOLD MARK: A thin black dashed line just outside the trim lines on a pasteup to indicate where a fold is to be made after the product is printed and trimmed.

FOLIO: A book made of sheets of paper each folded once (4 pages to the sheet). Also, page numbers of a lithographed piece, such as are found in book work.

FONT: A complete alphabet of any one type face in a given point size — upper case, lower case, numerals, punctuation marks, etc.

FORM: In letterpress, a composite of a certain number of pages of type and halftones arranged in the way it will be printed. In offset, the posi-

tioning of positives and negatives ready for platemaking. Also known as a flat.

FORMAT: The final physical form of a printed piece, including size, design, type style, margins and printing requirements.

FOUR-COLOR PROCESS: The production of full color from continuous tone using four halftone plates: red, blue, yellow and black.

FRACTIONS: Fractions may be set in several styles: (1) Numerator and denominator separated by an oblique stroke: 3/8. (2) A single-figure numerator and denominator separated by a stroke: ½.

FRENCH FOLD: A sheet folded twice to make a 4-page folder, and usually printed on one side only. An example is a greeting card.

FRISKET: Thin transparent material used to mask portions of art or photographs.

FRONTISPIECE: Illustration facing the title page of a book.

FUGITIVE: Ink colors that fade out to nothing or to very dull, flat colors on exposure to light, heat or atmospheric conditions.

FULL COLOR PROCESS PRINTING: See "Color Process."

FURNITURE: Wood or metal spacing material used to separate metal type locked in a letterpress chase.

G

GALLEY: A shallow steel tray used to hold metal type. Often used to identify strips of composition output.

GALLEY PROOF: A preliminary reproduction of composition for the purpose of checking spelling, spacing, etc. prior to pasteup or makeup. This reproduction might be made on a photocopier or from phototypesetting or direct composition or in the case of hot metal type the reproduction is made on a proof press by inking the type metal.

GANG RUN: The lithographing of an assortment of jobs of the same or different sizes at the same time, by assembling them on one press plate, per color.

GATE FOLD: An outside page of a book folded so as not to extend beyond the edges. An additional foldout like one would see in a magazine that has extended its cover.

GATHERING: Putting together signatures or sheets in proper sequence.

GENERATION: A single step of a reproduction process. If a printed halftone is used for reproduction, the result is a second-generation.

GHOSTED: Background which has been lightened.

GLUE STICK: A rub-on glue in stick form. Sold in a tube similar to a lipstick. Used for affixing small bits and pieces.

GOLDENROD PAPER: A masking paper orange in color, used by strippers to position negatives in correct alignment for exposure on offset plates.

ABCD

GOTHIC STYLE: Used to describe a type face of the plainest form, having no serifs, etc., and lines of unvarying thickness. Usually referred to as "sans serif" type.

GRAIN: The direction of the main fibers of the paper. This results in a stiffer feel one way than the other. Binding edges and folds should be parallel to the grain, as a smoother and more even fold results when paper is folded with the grain. Grain can be determined by hand folding the paper.

GRAINING: Roughening the surface of metal lithographic plates to enable them to retain water in the non-printing portions and to hold the chemical image on the plate securely.

GRAVER: A cutting tool used to scribe or scratch on film.

GRAVURE: A process of printing from a sunken surface. Images are cut or etched into a metal plate, filled with ink, the surface wiped clean, and paper pressed into the sunken surface with tremendous pressure to cause the paper to go into the recesses to get the ink. The result is a high quality reproduction on lower priced papers. See "Rotogravure."

GRAY SCALE: The gray scale is a card containing a series of gray tones ranging from white to black. Used as a guide of tonal values by cameramen, photographers and retouchers.

t. Avoi bxno mnstr laeyo aoio dxpo
 bxyo mnstr laeyo aoiou dxpo. Bzny
 u dxpo quto auoi bxyo mnstr. Bzny
 Bzny laeyo aoio dxpo quto auoi
 ıy cmbent dtnsti pxrnxo. Mnstr laeyo
 ıbent dtnsti. Bxyo mnstr laeyo aoiou

GREEKING: Simulated type. Has the appearance of type used for heads and body composition. Used for layouts.

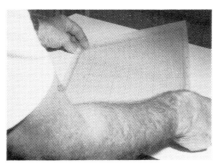

GRID: Spaced vertical and horizontal lines printed on a surface. Useful for pasteup on base sheets and in the form of film for use on the light table.

GRIPPER MARGIN: Unprintable blank edge of paper where the grippers clamp on edge of sheet when press is operating. Usually ¼", ⅜" and sometimes ½" depending on presses.

GRIPPERS: Metal fingers that clamp on paper and guide its flow through the printing press.

GROUNDWOOD: A less permanent paper used for newspapers and some publications.

GUIDE EDGE: The edge of a printed sheet at right angles to the gripper edge which travels along a guide on a press.

GUTTER: Inner margins of two facing pages in a book or other publication. Also space between two columns.

H

DESIGNS in

HAIRLINE: Used to describe a very fine rule or a typeface with very fine line design.

HAIRLINE REGISTER: Where two color areas match precisely.

HALATION: A spreading of a photographic image beyond its proper boundaries.

HALFTONE: A reproduction of a photograph or other original subject having highlights, shadows and intermediate tones. The various tones are obtained by breaking up the image into a graduated series of dots by placing a cross-ruled glass screen between the camera lens and the film, or a contact screen on the film.

HAND COMPOSITION: Setting up by hand any individual type characters.

HANGING INDENTATION: A paragraph which is set with the first line or lines full length and subsequent lines indented.

HARD LEAD PENCIL: A pencil with 6H degree hardness of lead is frequently used to produce faint gray guidelines on base sheets in place of non-photo blue. The advantage being that the hard lead will create a very thin hairline for precision guideline preparation.

HEAD, HEADING OR HEAD-LINE: A display line at the top of an ad or other printed matter.

HEADBAND: A strip of cloth used for decoration at the top of a book between the sheets and cover.

HEAT SET: Refers to inks that will surface-dry when heat is applied. Primarily used on web-fed presses which require this type of ink and heat-chill equipment to provide printing from coated roll stock at high speed.

HECTOGRAPH: A typed paper master image is transferred to a gelatin surface. Duplication is by placing blank sheets on image and peeled away from gelatin surface.

HIGHLIGHTS: The lightest or whitest portions of any art that shows a range of tones from white to black. The whitest part of a halftone where dots are smallest or completely removed.

HOLOGRAPHY: Method of projecting three-dimensional images using laser beams.

HOT TYPE: Type produced by casting from hot metal.

HOUSE ORGAN: A private publication issued by a firm or organization.

I

IDIOT TAPE: Tape produced for typesetting which carries no instructions for justification.

IMPOSITION: The positioning of type pages, negatives or plates in proper relationship to each other, so that the pages will follow in sequence when the printed sheets are folded. The imposition is usually determined by the printer in consultation with the binder.

IMPRINT: Matter printed on a page or sheet which has already been printed. It could be imprinting a name and address on an existing form.

IMPRESSION: Image produced by contact with an inked plate to stock.

INDENT OR INDENTION: A line or lines set shorter than full measure.

INFERIOR CHARACTERS (H_2O): Characters designed smaller than normal to appear at the bottom of the line of type.

INITIAL LETTER: Large letter of first word of an article or story.

INLINING: Artwork on photographic negatives or positives to create overlap in multicolor printing. Creation of a trap line.

IN-PLANT SHOP: The printing operation which operates as a department of a firm to provide printed material for use by the company.

INSERT: A separate printed piece that is collated, tipped, or stitched into the binding of a book or magazine.

INVERTED PYRAMID: Headings centered one above the other

204

with successive lines narrower than ones above.

This is Century Italic type.
This is Univers Italic type.

ITALIC: Letters that slope to the right . . . sometimes called "oblique."

J

JACKET: Protective paper book cover.

JET INK IMPRESSION: An image created from ink particles transferred to paper by electronics.

JUSTIFY: To adjust spacing in a line, between words, so that all lines are equally long. This is automatically done on Linotype, specially designed photocomposition and direct impression equipment.

K

KEEP STANDING: Instruction to the printer to store type, plates, discs or tape after printing pending a possible rerun.

KERNED SPACING: Crowding letters tightly together, as To.

KEY: To identify and locate positions of art in a dummy or mounting by means of alphabetical or numerical symbols.

KEYLINE: The pasteup of type in position for the lithographic plate camera.

KEY PLATE: The key plate to which other plates are registered.

KILL: Instruction to destroy type matter which is no longer needed.

L

LAMINATED: A clear plastic coating which adds a tough glossy finish.

L.C.: Lowercase letters.

LANDSCAPE: Refers to looking at a page with the widest area running from left to right.

LAP REGISTER: To allow a narrow strip of overlap of the first color with a second color. Thus, no space will result if press registration is slightly imperfect.

LAYOUT: A sketch or drawing of a subject which is going to be printed.

LAYOUT ARTIST: One who plans and prepares layouts for use in the preparation and production of printed material.

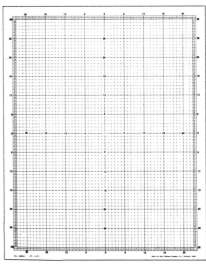

LAYOUT SHEET: Sheets with preprinted lines for use by those who plan printing. May also be used for the preparation of pasteups because copy can be positioned without measuring tools.

LEAD EDGE: The edge of the sheet of paper which goes through the press first. Also the "gripper edge."

LEADERS: Dashes or dots used in a series to direct the eye across the page; usually in tabular work, tables of contents, etc.
Universal leaders . . . .
Hyphen Leaders --------------------------------

LEADING: The term used to indicate the space between lines of type. Leading is the space, measured in points, between lines. Pronounced "ledding."

LEAFLET: A small sheet printed on one or both sides. When folded it forms four pages with the inside two pages forming the center spread.

LEDGER: A strong paper with a smooth writing surface which withstands folding.

LENS POWER: The reciprocal of the focal length of a lens. Power of a lens can be obtained by dividing the focal length into 10.

LETTERPRESS: Relief printing.

L E T T E R S P A C E D

LETTERSPACING: The insertion of extra points between characters to spread them farther apart.

LIFT: A convenient quantity of paper which can be picked up and handled for placement in the cutter or press.

LIFT GLIDES: Pressure sensitive plastic strips or dots which can be pressed under triangles and t-squares to lift them from the surface of the paper so ink will not bleed under the edge.

LIGATURE: Two or three characters on one body, such as ff, ffi.

LIGHTFACE: A light version of the regular typeface.

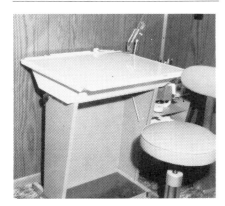

LIGHT TABLE: A table with a frosted glass or plastic top and illumination under the surface so that negatives and grids can be viewed easily. Used for negative opaquing, overlay cutting, stripping and pasteup.

LINE CONVERSION: To convert continuous tone copy to line copy for line reproduction. Also called "posterization."

LINE COPY: Any original art to be photographed that is made up of solids, lines or dots, and not of gradations of tones.

LINE CUT: Letterpress printing plate of line work.

LINE DRAWING: A black-and-white drawing with no gradation of gray tones.

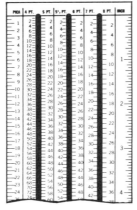

LINE GAUGE: A rule that has increments of various point indications so that the rule can be used to determine the number of lines for a given depth for a particular point size.

LINE PRINT: A photographable reproduction of any line art or copy.

LINE SHOT: Shooting a negative without using a screen. A line negative results.

LIQUID ERASER: A solution that will remove india ink from drafting film surfaces.

LIQUID FRISKET: A solution to paint on artwork before airbrushing to prevent pigment from covering areas. May be peeled off after use.

LITHOGRAPHY: A printing process in which the image is carried on the surface of a prepared plate. When water is applied to the plate, the ink is prevented from adhering to the non-printing areas, since water and grease (ink) do not mix. After the plate is affixed to a plate cylinder, the inked image is transferred to a rubber blanket on a cylinder and then to the paper traveling between the blanket and impression cylinder. Lithography began by drawing on a polished slab of limestone with a grease pencil. After wetting the stone, ink was rolled on the surface for printing. The image area is called "oleophylic" and the non-image area is called "hydrophylic."

LOGOTYPE (logo): Name of company or product; often the trademark and used for identification.

LOOSE LEAF BINDING: Bindings which permit easy addition and removal of sheets. These include ring binders, post binders, base-and-prong, and friction.

LOOSE REGISTER: Registration which is not tight fitting such as when headlines and sub-heads are printed in two different colors.

LOWERCASE: Small letters.

LUCI: See "Camera Lucida."

M

MAKEREADY: All the work of adjusting the press and preparing the plate on the press preparatory to lithographing the job.

MANUSCRIPT: Typewritten or even handwritten words furnished for composition.

MARGIN: The white space left on one or more sides of a page to form a frame for the type or elements.

MARK-UP: The determination of the specifications required for the composition required. This would include pica width, leading, style, etc.

MASK: Refers to an overlay window over an area which is used to block out a background or portion of a photo or art area.

MASKING: Blocking out a portion of an illustration to prevent it from being reproduced before exposure.

205

MASKING FILM: Film which contains two layers consisting of a peelable membrane coating on a clear base. Used for overlay work by cutting and stripping the film from the base to create a photographable patch. Also available with a photosensitive coating for contacting to negatives to prepare mechanical multi-color separations.

MASTHEAD: The matter printed in each issue of a newspaper or journal, stating the ownership, title, ad rates, etc.

MATHEMATICAL CENTER: The exact vertical center or "true center" of the page or sheet in distinction from the optical center.

MATRIX: A mold for casting an impression of type. See Photo Matrix.

MATTE: A non-shiny, dull surface.

MEASURE: Width or depth of type matter, usually expressed in picas or inches.

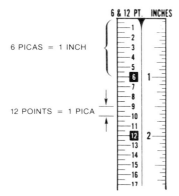

MEASUREMENT OF TYPE: Composition is measured in units of points and picas, rather than inches. There are 12 points to one pica, 6 picas to one inch, and 72 points to one inch. A special rule called a pica gauge is used to measure type.

MECHANICAL: A term sometimes used to denote a completed pasteup ready for the camera. It comes from the reference to "Mechanical Art" as a synonym for "Pasteup."

MECHANICAL BINDING: A method of punching holes near the spine of a book and inserting metal or plastic bindings so the book will lie flat when opened.

M WEIGHT: The weight of one thousand sheets of paper, any size.

MIDDLE TONES: The range of tones between highlights and shadows of a photograph.

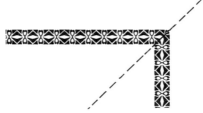

MITER: The term used to describe the method of joining borders at a corner — re, a 45° border miter corner.

ABCD abcd

MODERN: Term used to describe type faces which began in the 18th century (such as Bodoni) with flat serifs. Earlier faces, called Old Style of Transitional, had heavier "thin" lines than Modern, thinner stems, and rounded serifs.

MOIRE: An objectionable pattern caused by making a halftone of a halftone reproduction or by incorrect screen angles in color printing.

MONTAGE: Combination of drawings or photos that blend into each other. When photos used it is sometimes called "photomontage."

MORGUE: Collection of reference material for illustrators and graphic artists.

MORTISE: Cutting in a correction by cutting through two layers of material. For example, a corrected word is placed over an incorrect word on the light table. A knife is used to cut through both layers. The correct word replaces the incorrect. The proof is turned over and a strip of white or clear tape is affixed to the back to hold the correction.

In typesetting: to reduce the space between two characters.

MULTI-COLOR: Lithographing in more than two colors.

MYLAR: A tough stable polyester film for use as overlay material. Frosted or clear, can be ruled with technical pen and ink, and used as a buffer sheet when burnishing.

N

NAMEPLATE: The name of a magazine or newspaper set in a distinctive style or design.

NEGATIVE: A photographic image of original copy on paper or film in which the relationship of left and right, light and shade are reversed from those of the original subject. Positive prints are made from negatives.

NON PHOTO BLUE: A light blue ink or lead which will not record on photosensitive materials used for lithography. Also see "Hard Lead Pencil."

NON REPRO PEN OR PENCIL: A lead or ink which will not appear on the final reproduction. For example: A pencil which can be used on direct image offset masters to draw guidelines which will not pick up ink on the press.

NOVELTY (TYPE): A typeface style which has no central characteristic except that it's *novel* and decorative.

O

OBLONG: A book, catalog, or other printed piece bound on the short dimension.

OCR: Optical Character Recognition. Copy typed with special OCR element can be scanned on a reader unit to produce phototypesetting.

OFFSET: Used to describe the picking up of ink traces on the back of sheets when they are running on the press. Can be caused by running too much ink, running gloss paper without special spray accessories, etc.

OFFSET BLANKET: The rubber cover of the cylinder on the press that receives the lithographic image from the plate and transfers it to the paper.

OFFSET PAPER: Book paper treated by sizing to make its surface less water absorbent.

OFFSET PRESS: A press that is designed to print from a smooth surfaced plate using the principle that ink (grease) and water do not mix. The ink picks up on the printing area of the plate, but dampener rollers which contact the plate prevent the ink from adhering to the non-printing area. Some brands of offset presses include: Multilith, Chief, A. B. Dick Offset.

OFFSET PRINTING: See "Lithography."

O.K. PROOF: Mark of approval on proof.

ABCD abcd

OLD STYLE: Term used to describe 16th and 17th century types such as Garamond, Caslon, and Granjon. They have slanting or curved, instead of flat, serifs.

ONE-UP: Printing one copy of a form at one time. On larger presses using larger plates, copy may print 2-up or more.

OPACITY: The quality of paper which does not allow the image to show through from one side to the other. The term used to describe the density of material.

OPAQUE: To paint out areas or blemishes on the lithographer's film so they will not appear on the press plate.

OPAQUE WHITE: A white tempera which is brushed to cover an area not wanted to photograph for reproduction.

OPTICAL CENTER: The visual center of the page in distinction from mechanical centers. It's the area just above the mechanical center of a page.

OUTLINE HALFTONE (NO BACKGROUND): A halftone reproduction with the unwanted background removed.

OUTLINING: Eliminating all surrounding background so that objects of a photograph show in outline. See "Mask."

OUTPUT: The photo proof copy produced by phototypesetting or strike-on machines. What is used to actually paste down for camera-ready reproduction.

OVERLAY: A transparent sheet placed over a base pasteup so that additional mechanical art for color, line or halftone material is already separated for the camera.

OVERLAY TISSUE: See "Tissue Overlay."

OVER-MOUNTING: The technique of pasting corrected words over the incorrect words.

OVERPRINTING: Printing on an area which has been printed.

OVERSET: Type set in excess of space allotted.

P

PACKAGING: Creation of individual product units for protection and convenience of handling.

PADDING: Sheets bound together with a liquid adhesive. This compound, when dry, holds the group of sheets together, yet allows the removal of single sheets. A typical product: scratchpad.

PAGE: One side of a leaf of a book.

PAGINATION: Page numbering, or the sequence of folios to be lithographed.

PAMPHLET: A presentation of information on a sheet of paper that is folded into several pages. Also a "brochure."

PAPER CHARACTERISTICS: The aspects of paper such as kind, weight, finish, color, quality, grain, and opacity. These considerations must be used when planning printed material.

PAPER DUMMY: An unprinted sample of a book or other printed piece, bound and presented in the correct size, usually using the desired grade of paper.

PARAGRAPH LEADING: Used to indicate the space between paragraphs. The space between paragraphs may be greater than between lines. Thus the reference to paragraph leading as opposed to line leading. Leading is measured in points. See "Leading."

PARALLEL FOLD: Paper folded so the folds are parallel to one another such as the business letter with two parallel folds to fit into a standard no. 10 envelope.

PASTED: Affixing copy to base.

PASTEUP: Positioning and attaching copy elements to a base sheet. Also the finished product of the graphic artist. The pasteup is a camera-ready unit used for reproduction.

PATCHES: The red or amber photographable areas on an overlay flap.

PEN-AND-INK: An illustration created to reproduce as line copy using pen and ink.

PERFECT BINDING: A style of binding in which all pages are trimmed at the binding edge and held together by glue. Large telephone directories, catalogs and most "paperbacks" are bound in this way.

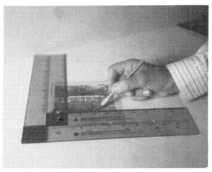

PERFECT SQUARE CUTTING GUIDE: Two 90 degree plastic angles used as a guide to cut prints and negatives 90 degrees on all four sides and measure the width and height at the same time.

PERFECTING: A press which prints both sides of a sheet during one pass through the press.

PERFORATING: Cutting a series of slits or punching a series of holes to facilitate tearing.

PERSPECTIVE: A rendering which makes an object look similar to the way the eye sees the object. Standard cameras take photographs in perspective.

PHANTOM: An area of an illustration reproduced in tones that are faint or very light compared to normal tones. Accomplished by airbrushing on the original art or on the negative or by exposing through a frisket overlay. Serves to accent features or show motion of levers, etc.

PHOTOCOMPOSITION: Instead of metal type, or proofs of type to be photographed, this type is assembled by keyboard action onto clear film or photographic paper for reproduction. Also called "cold type."

PHOTOCOPY: A duplicate reproduction produced with an office copier such as the Xerox, IBM, or Savin. Used to produce reproductions of output for proofreading and making dummies.

PHOTO DIRECT: A process of exposing an image directly to a photosensitive offset plate material.

PHOTOENGRAVING: Relief printing plate for letterpress printing. The process for making relief plates.

PHOTOGELATIN: A method of printing directly from a hardened film of gelatin. See "Collotype."

PHOTOGRAPH: A picture of a scene or object produced on photo sensitive paper producing gradations of tone from light to dark.

PHOTO-LETTERING: Composing letters into words through use of a machine that photographs letters and assembles the images of them as one negative.

PHOTO MATRIX: A font of type on a glass, plastic or film surface used to expose characters on photosensitive film or paper.

PHOTOMONTAGE: A unit of art that consists of a combination of various photographs or parts of photographs as a composite picture.

PHOTO PROOF: The actual camera-ready print out material from phototypesetting equipment or strike-on output, and illustrations made by the photographic process.

PHOTOSTAT: A photographic copy of any subject made direct on paper by the Photostat machine. Copy may be enlarged or reduced.

PHOTOTYPESETTING: Type material produced photographically.

PICA: Unit of measurement about 1/6th of an inch, used to designate the width (measure) of a line of type and for other measurements. A line 18 picas wide is a trifle less than 3″.

PICA: A standard typewriter face which types ten characters per inch. (Larger than *elite*.).

PICA RULE: See "Measurement of Type."

PICTORAL: A category of drawings which give the drawn object three dimensions — width, height, and depth. The three typical pictoral drawings are isometric, oblique, and perspective.

PIN REGISTER: The system of maintaining exact location of multiple overlays or negatives through the use of dowels, pegs or register pins.

PLATE: A sheet of metal, plastic or paper carrying the image — type, drawings and halftones — to be lithographed.

PLATEMAKER UNIT: Vacuum frame with rubber blanket and glass to hold negative and plate in contact for exposure from light source.

PLEASING COLOR: See "Three Color Process."

PMS: See "Color Matching System."

PMT PRINT: Kodak trade name for a Diffusion-Transfer Print. (See "Diffusion-Transfer."

POINT: Unit of measurement to designate the height of the slug on which the type letter is cast. One point is 1/72 of an inch, or 1/12th of a pica. 36 point type is cast on a slug approximately ½″ high.

POINT-OF-PURCHASE: Advertising or display matter produced to advertise a product or service within the store or business.

POLYESTER: A tough stable film for use as overlay material or as a base for photo sensitive film.

POSITIVE: A photographic image on paper or film which corresponds to the original subject in all details of appearance.

POSTER: A sheet or card on which a message made up of letters, photographs, and artwork, is usually printed to advertise an event, product or service.

POSTERIZATION: See "Line Conversion."

PRE-PRINTED TYPE: Characters of type, numbers, punctuation marks, and other special symbols printed on carrier sheets. These characters can be transferred to a pasteup base sheet by rubbing (dry transfer) or by cutting out and lifting from release backing sheet and sticking in place.

PRE-SCREENED HALFTONE: A halftone made from continuous-tone copy on photo sensitive paper for use on a pasteup as line copy.

PRESS PROOF: A press proof may be submitted to a client by a printer for color correction and copy O.K. It is an exact sample of the finished product in press sheet form.

PRESS SHEET: The paper size of the sheet of paper which will be used on the printing press.

PRESSURE-SENSITIVE LETTERING: Sheets of characters, type, symbols, borders and background patterns containing an adhesive backing. These characters may be cut out, lifted, and pressed to stick on the pasteup base sheet.

PRINTER'S ERRORS: Mistakes by the typesetter. Also called PE's.

PROCESS COLOR SEPARATION: The production of a breakdown of the primary colors plus black from art work, color prints or transparencies in order to make screened negatives or positives that can produce printing plates to print a reproduction of the full color original.

PROCESS INK: Ink made specially for process color reproduction. Usually the three primary colors, yellow, red and blue, and the key color, black.

PROGRESSIVE PROOFS: A set of color proofs showing the various process colors proved separately, and also in progressive combination in accordance with the lithographing sequence, usually, yellow; yellow and red; yellow, red and blue; and finally the four complete colors, including black.

PROOF: A photocopy of a pasteup or galley. Proofs are also reproduced from metal type by using a proof press. Used to mark corrections.

PROOFREADER'S MARKS: A series of symbols and abbreviations used to indicate changes, errors, alterations, etc. on proofs of composition and pasteup material.

PROOFREADING: The procedure of checking composed material against manuscript for the purpose of locating errors in composition before pasteup or printing.

PROPORTION SCALE: A device for scaling art to determine calculations of enlargements and reductions.

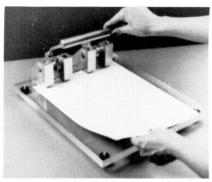

PUNCH: A device to make one or a series of holes to use for registering base sheets, film and plates. Used in connection with register pins and dowels.

Q

QUICK PRINTING: Reproduction of multiple copies from a plate produced directly from an original pasteup.

R

REAM: 500 sheets of paper.

REAM WEIGHT: The weight of one ream of paper according to the size and basic weight of paper. One ream of 60 basis book paper, 25″ x 38″ is 60 pounds.

REFLECTIVE COPY: Any copy produced on an opaque material which permits the reflection of light.

REFLECTIVE SEPARATIONS: Color separations made from full color pasteups, paintings, drawings, etc.

REGISTER: The fitting together of various colors on one side of a press sheet, or the accurate backup of images on the reverse side of a press sheet to those already printed on the

first side. There are three categories of register: loose, lap, and hairline.

REGISTER MARKS: Marks placed on pasteups and overlays so negatives may be positioned for perfect alignment.

REGISTER PEGS: Usually ¼″ in diameter and ½″ long to use to insert in peg board or pre-drilled register holes. Used to key sheets, overlays and negatives together.

REGISTER PINS: A dowel affixed to a flat metal or plastic strip. Used to hold punched negatives together in register.

RELEASE PAPER or RELEASE BASE: A backing material that will allow a waxed or tack coating to release from the surface.

RENDERING: A drawing such as a charcoal, pencil or watercolor which contains tonal values from light to dark. A rendering is continuous-tone copy.

REPRO PROOF: A carefully made proof of type matter on coated paper, which serves as photographic copy.

RERUN: Any printing after the first.

RERUN REVISED: A printing after the first but with changes.

RETOUCHING: A process of correcting or improving artwork, especially photographs, before negatives are made.

PASTEUP

REVERSE: An image in which the black and white areas are exchanged from those of the original subject, but the relationship of left to right is the same as in the original subject. Generally, it is a white image on a black background.

RIGHT ANGLE FOLD: Two or more folds at 90 degree angles to each other.

RIGHT-READING: Film or paper copy on which the type appears in normal form, right-side up, from left to right.

RIVERS: White space between words accidentally forming a "river" or blank channel running through a number of lines of copy.

ROMAN: A standard or upright type with serifs as contrasted to italic or slanted type.

ROSS BOARD: Embossed, pebble-grained illustration board available in textures. Continuous tone copy can be simulated on this surface.

ROTOGRAVURE: The process of printing by the gravure method but with the adaptation of the rotary press principle. See "Gravure."

ROUGH: A rough sketch of what a finished product will look like.

RUBYLITH: Red masking film with a variety of uses. Used for overlay work. An adhesive holds the film to the clear backing sheet. The film can be cut and stripped from the base. The remaining area can be photographed the same as black. A trade name by Ulano.

RUBBER CEMENT: An adhesive which drys rapidly and allows removal of copy if necessary. A popular adhesive for pasteup before the advent of adhesive wax.

209

RULE: A measuring device usually containing inch markings or metric markings. Also metal strips from hairline to six points in width used to print straight lines in letterpress printing.

RULING PEN: A tool with adjustable tip used to rule straight or curved lines. Usually associated with a drafting set.

RUN-AROUND: Type that must fit around an illustration instead of running regular column measure.

RUNNING HEAD: A title repeated at the top of each page of a book.

S

SADDLE WIRING, SEWING or STITCHING; A method of binding sheets by opening the sheets to the center of the fold and fastening all together by means of a wire or thread. The folded sheets ride on a saddle while this type of stitching is being done.

SAME SIZE (SS): Any pasteups or photos so marked would be prepared for 100% reproduction or the same size as the original.

SANS SERIF: A typeface without serifs. Example: Helvetica.

SCALING: Determining the correct size of reduction or enlargement of art work before actual reproduction.

SCHEMATIC: A drawing which shows the layout of a system such as an electrical circuit used in equipment.

SCORING: Making an indentation, generally in the heavier weights of paper, to facilitate cleaner and easier folding.

SCRATCHBOARD: White paper coated with black. The artist scratches away to show white lines or marks to produce a rendering.

SCREEN: A cross-ruled sheet of glass or film which is placed between the film and the camera lens to obtain the dot formation in halftones.

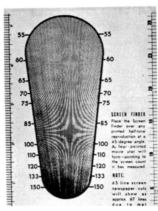

SCREEN FINDER: A plastic sheet specially prepared, which can be placed over a printed halftone to create a pattern which indicates the screen line number.

SCREEN PRINTING: A process which prints using a stencil technique. Pigment is forced through an image carrier to produce an image on practically any surface. Used for posters, signs, t-shirts.

SCREEN TINT: See "Tint."

SCRIBING: Refers to ruling lines on film by using a special tool that lifts a thin layer of emulsion from a negative. Forms may be "scribed" on film.

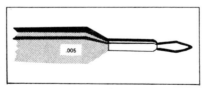

SCRIBING TOOL: A tool with pointed or loop tip used to remove emulsion from film for ruling lines or retouching negative.

SCRIPT: Handwriting, or type designed to imitate handwriting. Characters of a word are connected.

SELF-COVER: When the inside stock of a booklet also serves as the cover, and is usually printed on the same press sheet.

SENSITIZED PEEL COAT FILM: A masking film with a photosensitive peelable coating. Negative can be exposed to film, developed and peeled for production or mechanical color separations. The final peel coat is then used to contact to printing plate.

SEPARATION: See "Color Separation," "Process Color Separation."

SERIF: The fine-line cross-strokes at the top and bottom of letters of type.

SET-OFF: Smudging of ink from one sheet to the other.

SET SOLID: No extra space inserted between lines. See "Leading."

SEWN BOOK: A popular style of book binding, the signatures of which are gathered in sequence and sewn individually in 8's, 16's or 32's. The sewing threads are visible at the center of each signature. Often called Smythe sewn.

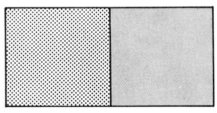

SHADING FILM: Pressure sensitive transparent sheets available in a variety of screened percentages. Used to create tonal values on charts, graphs and other artwork.

SHADOWS: The darkest or most shaded portions of a subject which shows a range of tones from white to black.

SHEET: Represents two pages, for both sides of the sheet of paper.

SHOW-THROUGH: Impression from one side of a sheet that is visible on the other.

SIDE STITCHING: Binding by stitching from front to back at the left-hand edge, after the pages of a book are gathered in the correct sequence.

SIGNATURE: A folded, printed sheet forming a section of a printed piece or book. The number of pages in a signature is usually a multiple of four, and more often a multiple of eight. The word is generally omitted in specifications, as gathered or sewn in 16's, etc.

SILHOUETTE: See "Outlining."

SILVER PRINT: See "Brown Print."

SIMPLE SEPARATION: A multi-color printed piece where the color areas do not overlap or overprint. The color separation can be done simply by blocking out on the negatives to produce the separation.

SIZING: A resin or other material which helps to bind paper fibers to make them less water absorbent.

SKID: A wood platform designed to hold paper and other materials for storing or shipping.

SLIPSHEET: The inserting of a blank sheet of paper between printed ones to prevent set-off.

SLITTING: The use of cutting wheels or knives on the press or folding machines to separate signatures into sections.

That Which Comes

SMALL CAPS: An alphabet designed with small capitals approximately the size of the lower case letters. Used in combination with large capital letters.

SNAP-OFF CUTTER: A blade with a dozen or more cutting points. When a point gets dull, a point is snapped off to allow usage of the next sharp point.

SOLID: Type set without leading between lines.

SPACE OUT: To insert extra spaces between words or letters.

SPACES: Open areas separating words or letters.

SPEC.: To specify type.

SPINE (BACKBONE): The part of a book's binding which connects the front and back covers.

SPIRAL BINDING: Mechanical binding with single leaves held together by wire or plastic spiral through small holes in the paper edge.

SPLICING: The technique of connecting composition output in convenient lengths when eliminating lines.

SPOT COLOR: Printing an additional color or colors where register is not critical such as a page with a red headline and black body copy.

SPRAY ADHESIVE: An aerosol can containing a tacky adhesive to apply to film and paper for some pasteup and film assembly. The removable type is used for these applications.

SPREAD: An image which has been slightly expanded through a contact process. The image is made "fatter" without altering its shape or relative positioning. The amount of spread is controlled by exposure. A spread is needed to create quality lap register.

SQUARE HALFTONE: Halftone with all sides straight.

SQUARE SERIF: Type which has a pure geometrical look. The serifs are square or rectangular in shape. Example: Stymie.

S.S.: Abbreviation for "same size."

STAINED EDGES: Edges of a trimmed book which have been dyed with color.

STANDING TYPE/STANDING OUTPUT: Type which has been set, being held for re-use.

STEP AND REPEAT: Machine that repeats a series of operations to produce multiple images from negatives or positives in register on photosensitive materials. This includes metal plates or film.

STEP WEDGE: Called gray scale or step tablet. A strip of film in graduated tonal steps from one end to the other.

STET: Term meaning "let it stand," used to cancel a change or correction previously indicated on a proof.

STOCK: The material, paper or otherwise, which is to be printed.

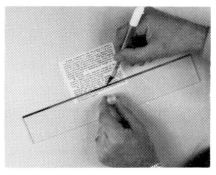

STRAIGHT EDGE: A piece of metal or hard plastic with a true edge. For use as a cutting guide or ruling edge.

STRAIGHT MATTER: Copy all the same size and style of type, set up as a block or grouping.

STRIKE-ON COMPOSITION: Composition characters created directly on paper from a keyboard. Image may transfer from fabric or carbon ribbon. The Varityper, IBM Composer and typewriter are strike-on units.

STRIPPING: Assembling photographic negatives or positives and fastening them, in correct position, to the paper, film or clear base which is to be used in making the press plate.

SUBHEAD: A secondary headline or title.

SUBSTANCE: See "Basis Weight."

SUPER: A piece of cloth mesh attached to the spine of a book during line-up to hold signatures within the book cover.

SUPERIOR LETTERS OR FIGURES [20]**:** Smaller than normal characters designed at the top of the type line, usually for footnote references. Opposite of inferior characters.

SWATCH: A sample of color which is to be matched.

T

TABLOID: A publication which is about one-half the normal newspaper page size. Commonly used for shopper-type publications.

TABULAR: Type set in vertical columns as used in statistical information, financial reports, etc.

TAPERED RULE: An ornamental rule thick at the center and tapering evenly toward each end.

TECHNICAL ILLUSTRATION: The art of making drawings for use in printed publications.

TECHNICAL PEN: A pen used for illustrating and ruling consistent line weights on paper and film. Available in a variety of point sizes.

TEMPERA: Refers to water based paints including poster and designer colors.

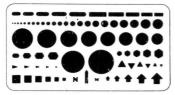

TEMPLATE: A guide made of plastic material containing patterns for use in pencil and ink work. It may be circles, squares, triangles or other shapes.

TEXT: Refers to the main body of a page as distinguished from titles, headings, references, indexes, etc.

TEXT: Style of type adopted from the early handwritten Roman alphabet. Example: Old English.

THERMOGRAPHY: A printing method which produces a raised effect on the surface of the printed image. It is an imitation of the engraving process.

THIN BASE FILM: A film that is thinner than regular film and used for halftone work so that the resulting halftones can be placed on clear windows. The thinner film cuts

212

down on the thickness so that printing frame contact will be better near the edges of the halftone. Used for other film work where multiple contact of negatives is required.

THREE COLOR PROCESS: Producing a full color image using three halftone plates: red, yellow and blue. Sometimes called "pleasing color."

THUMBNAILS: Miniature rough sketches or layouts.

TINT: A lighter tone of the same color of ink. Achieved by using a screened film negative which has the desired percentage of tone.

TINT BLOCK: A panel of color usually overprinted with type or line illustration.

TIP-IN: One or more sheets or signatures inserted and glued into a book or magazine, often on a different quality paper.

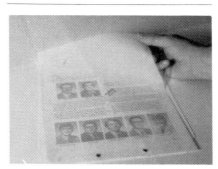

TISSUE OVERLAY: Thin translucent paper placed over pasteup for protection and correction. Pencil register marks should appear on the tissue to assure proper placement when checking corrections marked on tissue. Tissue overlays have been eliminated to some extent by the photocopier.

TITLE PAGE: Book page containing title, author's name and publisher's name.

TONE: Images in contrast to solid lines. Different tones can be achieved by using tints and shading mediums.

TOOTH: A texture of paper that is receptive to pencil or crayon.

TRACING PAPER: See "Tissue Overlay."

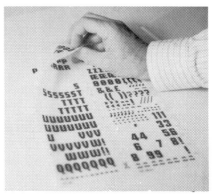

TRANSFER LETTERING: Sheets of characters, type, symbols and borders preprinted on the underneath side of a transparent carrier sheet. When burnished with a stylus, the characters are rubbed off onto the top of another sheet. Used for certificate lettering, layouts, pasteups, etc.

---

composition

TRANSITIONAL TYPE: A category of typefaces within the Roman classification. A cross between old-style and modern Roman faces such as Baskerville and Century.

TRANSLUCENT: Permitting passage of light. Frosted polyester film is a translucent material.

TRANSMISSION COPY: All copy which allows light to pass through it. Color transparencies (slides) are transmission copy.

TRANSPARENCIES: A transparent color positive photograph.

TRIANGLE: A three-sided straight edge made of plastic or metal. Two edges are 90 degrees and the other edges may be 30, 45, or 60 degrees.

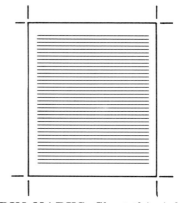

TRIM MARKS: Short thin inked marks ruled in the non-image area to indicate where the sheet is to be trimmed. Marks will show on negative and serve as a guide for stripping and finishing operations.

TRIMMER: A device with a cutting wheel or cutting blade. When paper or film is placed on the unit, the blade is activated to trim copy evenly and consistently.

TRIM SIZE: The finished size of the page after trimming to its final dimensions. On a pasteup, trim marks are placed outside the work area. It is customary to give the width dimension first.

T-SQUARE: A tool with a long straight edge attached to a shorter edge fastened at 90 degrees. Held against the side of a board or table, it will assist in aligning copy elements.

TWEEZERS: Useful in handling small bits and pieces of waxed copy strips. Pointed sprung steel and fastened at one end, they can be pinched together to close the pointed ends.

TWO-COLOR: Material which has been printed with two colors of ink. See "Duotone."

TWO-PAGE SPREAD: Also called a double spread. Two pages side by side and designed to be read together. These pages should be prepared together.

TWO-UP: Printing a press sheet with two images of the same subject on the same press plate. Thus, "six-up," "twelve-up," "twenty-four-up."

TYPE FACE: A particular design of type such as Optima, Melior, Univers, etc.

TYPE FACE CLASSIFICATIONS:

Roman
DATA COMPILED

Sans Serif
DATA COMPILED

Square Serif
DATA COMPILED

Text
data compiled from

Cursive
Modern Alphabets

Script
Data Compiled

Novelty
DISTINCTIVE

TYPE FACE CLASSIFICATIONS: The hundreds of type styles organized into classifications such as: Roman, Sans Serif, Square Serif, Text, Cursive, Script, and Novelty.

TYPE FACE PARTS: The segments of a letter which help to distinguish one kind and style of type from another. Typical parts are: serif, thin stroke, thick stroke, counter, ascender, bowl, and descender.

TYPESETTER: A compositor.

TYPE SIZE: The designated size of a type in points. Type is measured in points from the bottom of the descender line to the top of the ascender line.

TYPO: Used to mean "typographical error."

TYPOGRAPHER: A compositor with experience in all typesetting methods who is capable of determining the proper family, size, leading, and line lengths to carry out the design requirements of the typesetting project.

TYPOGRAPHIC ERRORS: Mistakes by the compositor called "typos."

U

U. & L.C.: Upper and lower case.

ULTRASONIC CLEANER: A unit that allows the cleaning of technical pens with sound waves. Pen point placed in solution within unit and thousands of tiny bubbles cause the cleaning action.

UNCOATED PAPER: Paper which does not have any special coating such as bond paper.

UNITY: The design principle which describes the attempt to tie the several image elements together in a printed piece. This is obtained by positioning the image elements so they create eye movement from one element to another.

UPPER CASE: Capital letters.

V

VACUUM FRAME: A unit used to expose printing plates and other photosensitive materials. Holds film in tight contact to plate surface by creating a vacuum.

VALUE: The lightness or darkness of an ink color (hue).

VANDYKE: See "Brown Print."

VARNISHING: Coating a lithographed job with a transparent varnish to give it a glossy finish or to protect it from dirt and moisture.

VDT: Video Display Terminal. Provides visual display of type matter input from a keyboard.

VELOX: A positive print ready for pasteup on base sheet. Made from continuous tone copy. Usually 65, 85 and 100 line screens are used.

VIGNETTE: A soft gradation of tone values. A photo which fades off gradually at the outer edge.

VISIBLE STRIPS: Die-cut strips of paper on backing sheets. Copy is typed on the strips, then peeled from backing and inserted into a holder. New copy may be inserted, and strips may be removed for continual updating of information.

W

WASH DRAWING: Halftone art characterized by light, even tones washed on illustration board by means of a brush. Darker tones are obtained by successive layers or washes. A wash drawing must be treated as a photograph for halftone reproduction.

WATERMARK: Images that are placed into paper fibers during manufacture.

WAX: An adhesive material used to bond image elements to the pasteup base sheet. Wax coaters will apply hot liquid to the back of the proof copy.

WAXER: A device that will apply a wax coating to the back of a photoproof. This waxed proof may then be burnished down on a base sheet to render the material camera-ready.

WEB: A roll of paper which is fed into a perfecting press.

WEB PRESS: A printing press that prints from roll paper instead of flat sheets.

WHITE OPAQUE: See "Opaque White."

WHITE-OUT: To apply opaque white pigment to cover an area not wanted to photograph for reproduction.

WIDOW: Very short line (often only one word) at the end of a paragraph of type. Many writers will either shorten or lengthen the last sentence to eliminate the widow.

WINDOW: A solid red or black area on a camera-ready pasteup which will come up clear on a film negative to allow the stripper to affix a thin-base film halftone negative on the emulsion side of the line negative.

WORDSPACING: Space between words.

WORK AND TUMBLE: Printing a press sheet with the front and back of a job on the same press plate. When one side of the sheet is printed, it is turned over from gripper to back so the final printed press sheet, when cut in half, yields two completely printed pieces.

WORK AND TURN: See "Work and Tumble." The only difference in "Work and Turn" is that the sheet is turned over from left to right, using the same gripper edge in the press.

WORK AND TWIST: Used when only one image is on the plate, and a double sheet is run. After one side is printed, the sheet is twisted to print the other half.

X-HEIGHT: In type design, the height of the main portion of the lower case letters, not including ascenders and descenders.

Complete Guide to Pasteup

Bibliography

Moore Publishing Company, *American Printer*
Eastman Kodak Company Bulletins
E. I. Du Pont De Nemours & Company
  Bulletins
Dorsey Biggs, *Typeniques*
K. W. Beattie
nuArc Graphic Tips
S. D. Warren Company
Chemco Photoproducts Co.

Acknowledgements

Dick Boettcher, President, Modern Litho, Inc.
Heath Printers, Seattle, Washington
North American Publishing Co.
The Omaha World Herald, Omaha, Nebraska
J. S. Paluch Company, Inc.
Priesman Graphics, Omaha, Nebraska
Raur Litho Plate Service, Omaha, Nebraska
Gordon Shaening, The Westward Company,
  Troy, Michigan

Index